Stateless Literature of the Gulf

Stateless Literature of the Gulf

Culture, Politics and the *Bidun* in Kuwait

Tareq Alrabei

I.B. TAURIS
LONDON • NEW YORK • OXFORD • NEW DELHI • SYDNEY

I.B. TAURIS
Bloomsbury Publishing Plc
50 Bedford Square, London, WC1B 3DP, UK
1385 Broadway, New York, NY 10018, USA
29 Earlsfort Terrace, Dublin 2, Ireland

First published in Great Britain 2022
This paperback edition published 2023

This book was made possible by NPRP grant # NPRP9-225-5-024 from the Qatar National Research Fund (a member of Qatar Foundation). The book was completed during the author's Post-Doctoral Fellowship at the Doha Institute for Graduate Studies, Doha, Qatar during the period October 2016 – July 2017. The contents herein are solely the responsibility of the author.

For legal purposes the Acknowledgements on p. vi constitute an extension of this copyright page.

Series design by Adriana Brioso

A catalogue record for this book is available from the British Library.

A catalog record for this book is available from the Library of Congress.

ISBN: HB: 978-1-7883-1457-2
PB: 978-0-7556-4488-9
ePDF: 978-0-7556-3531-3
ePUB: 978-0-7556-3530-6

Typeset by Integra Software Solutions Pvt. Ltd.

Contents

Acknowledgements vi
Note on transliteration and translation vii
Arabic transliteration table viii

Introduction 1
1 The '*Bidun*' 17
2 A literary community's struggle for presence 37
3 Cameleers of the national spirit: *Bidun* poets and Kuwaiti literary history 61
4 The desert apocalypse: The last bedouin, the first *Bidun* 81
5 Representations of the *'Ashish* 113
6 'Crossing borders': '*Sons of Kuwait*' in the diaspora 145
Conclusion 159

Notes 162
Bibliography 167
Index 188

Acknowledgements

I have been very fortunate to have been assisted by many of the writers whose works I've analysed in this book. In the initial stages, the poet Dikhīl Khalīfa opened his personal library to me and went to far lengths to provide me with copies of out-of-print editions of many Bidun writers. My gratitude extends to Muhammad al-Nabhān, Karim al-Hazza', Jassim al-Shimmiri, the late Nasir al-Ẓafiri and Sulayman al-Flayyiḥ's sons Bassām and Usama.

My gratitude is extended to my colleagues who have consistently been generous in offering their valuable critical insights: Alexandria Milton, Maha Abdel Megeed, Abdulrahman al-Farhan, Nora Parr and Talal al-Rashoud. In particular, Faisal Hamada's suggestions have been useful in polishing some of the arguments in the book. I am also indebted to those who have offered a helping hand in providing necessary sources related to my work: Ola Husni Mansur, Abbas Haddad, Shurouq Muẓaffar, Abdulla al-Falah and Claire Beaugrand. It is important to mention that the help of my friends and colleagues does not necessarily equate an endorsement of the arguments developed in the book.

The Doha Institute for Graduate Studies offered me the opportunity to develop my PhD thesis into a manuscript as a postdoctoral researcher in 2017. I have benefitted greatly from my time there under the guidance of Ayman El-Desouky and the administrative support of Eid Mohammad, Raed Habayeb and Miriam Shaath.

I also wish to thank the editor of I.B. Tauris series Library of Written Culture and Identity Rory Gormley and his assistant Yasmin Garcha for their patience and continuance support in seeing this book come to fruition. I am also indebted to Atef Alshaer for initially recommending the book series.

Finally, this book would not have been possible without the constant support of my family. I am indebted to every one of them. In particular, the support of my brother Khaled has been fundamental. A very special thanks and appreciation is due to my wife, Bashayer, for her admirable endurance in keeping up with a household under the pressures of academic publishing.

Note on transliteration and translation

This book uses a simplified system of transliteration based on the *International Journal of Middle Eastern Studies*. Names of famous places (al-Hasa) or common first names (Abdulaziz), as well as nouns naturalized into English (saluki), have not been transliterated using diacritics.

All translations are mine, unless otherwise indicated.

Arabic transliteration table

Consonants

ء	ʾ
ا	a
ب	b
ت	t
ث	th
ج	j
ح	ḥ
خ	kh
د	d
ذ	dh
ر	r
ز	z
س	s
ش	sh
ص	ṣ
ض	ḍ
ط	ṭ
ظ	ẓ
ع	ʿ
غ	gh
ف	f
ق	q
ك	k
ل	l
م	m
ن	n
ه	h
و	w
ي	y

Short Vowels: a, u, i
Long Vowels: a, u, i (not ā, ū, ī)
Doubled: يّ iyy, وّ uww
Diphthongs: و aw, ي ay

Introduction

This book aims to introduce the contemporary literary phenomenon of *Bidun*, or stateless, writers in the Gulf, Kuwait primarily, and in the diaspora. Historically denied all forms of official legal documentation, the works of *Bidun* writers, in their struggles with the machinations of the nation state, political, cultural and historical, offer a unique literary and cultural phenomenon. The phenomenon has regional and global significance in the way it has produced new radical possibilities for intrinsic articulations of belonging, presence and self-positionality, through complex modes of affiliation beyond the official acts of absencing, labelling and objectifying representations.

Since 1979, the date of the publication of the first work by a *Bidun* poet Sulayman al-Flayyiḥ, *Bidun* writers have been relatively prolific publishing poetry collections, which constitute the majority of these works, and to a lesser extent short stories and novels. *Bidun* writers residing in Kuwait and abroad have been highly visible and influential within national, regional and, more recently, international cultural contexts. Given the historical and ongoing influence of *Bidun* writers, the literary phenomenon, which this book calls '*Bidun* literature', has not received much attention within academic scholarship. Some *Bidun* writers have been singled out in works of literary criticism but have not yet been approached in a comprehensive manner as part of a wider literary phenomenon which we can call *Bidun* literature.

While there has been limited academic scholarship on *Bidun* literature, scholarly interest on the *Bidun* issue has received much attention in recent years. The *Bidun* issue has been studied, both directly and indirectly, mainly from the different academic disciplines in the social sciences, including international relations (Beaugrand 2010), anthropology (Longva

1997, 2000, 2006), political science and urban studies (al-Wuqayyan 2006; al-Aradi 2008; al-Wuqayyan 2009; al-Nakib 2010, 2014), social geography (al-Moosa 1976), history (al-Hajeri 2014), sociology (al-Fahad 1989) and law (al-Anezi 1989, 1994). The majority of the non-academic literature on the *Bidun* is composed of descriptive reports and briefings related to human rights issues (Human Rights Watch 1992, 1995; Bencomo 2000; al-Najjar 2003; Refugees International 2007; Human Rights Watch 2011; Shiblak 2011; The Home Office 2014). There has also been a recent increased interest in the *Bidun* as disenfranchised individuals susceptible to joining international terrorist organizations. One example is the case of Muhammad Emwazi, aka Jihadi John, the ISIS member whose family lived as *Biduns* in Kuwait before migrating to the UK in 1994.[1]

Knowledge produced on the *Bidun*, so far, has been dominated by a descriptive approach and limited to the considerations of the different disciplines in the social sciences and human rights discourse as will be discussed in more detail in Chapter 1. Of the studies referenced above, none refer to the literary and cultural output of the community. One exception is Faris al-Wuqayyan's study titled '*'Adimu al-Jinsiyya fi al-Kuwait: al-'azma wa-l-tada'iyat*' (The Stateless in Kuwait: The Crisis and Consequences) (2009). In the study, the literary voice of the *Bidun* is conceived in terms of reflecting a stateless condition or an experience; another form of ethnographic 'documentation' that would reveal the community's conditions.

Approaches to '*Bidun* literature': Anthropological and activistic readings

Current approaches, though minimal and incomprehensive, to *Bidun* literature have been dominated by anthropological and activistic readings of the body of works. Such readings, albeit driven by 'sympathetic' or 'committed' impulses, function by eliciting *Bidun* literature to speak in a particular way to further an activistic position relating to legal rights of the community or to correspond to a totalizing anthropological condition. When the literary voice is elicited, it is inevitable to fall into the trap of dismissing the text's capacity to go beyond narratives of victimization and passivity. Such an approach to *Bidun* literature is a corollary of an ontological conception of statelessness as a condition where literary voice cannot be comprehended beyond the expression of a condition of lack.

A study of *Bidun* literature, like any other marginalized literature, is not free of tension between an anthropological and a more aesthetic reading of literary texts. The dangers of an anthropological approach to '*Bidun* Literature' are best exemplified in the aforementioned study by al-Wuqayyan. After a detailed overview of the history of the *Bidun* issue, al-Wuqayyan turns to *Bidun* literature to find a corroboration of the historical experiences of the community. *Bidun* literature, he writes, is mainly concerned with the 'prevalence of a melancholic tone and a tragic use of language that almost always revolves around the loss of rights and the dispossession of identity' (al-Wuqayyan 2009). Yet al-Wuqayyan's conclusion is presented as a causal generalization that is not necessarily informed by any reading of the literature. The voices of *Bidun* writers are elicited in this case to speak in a particular way to fit an anthropological conclusion.

In her work on the 'figure of the refugee', Liisa Malkki comments that '[a]lmost like an essentialized anthropological "tribe" … [r]efugees thus become not just a mixed category of people sharing a certain legal status; they become "a culture," "an identity," "a social world," or "a community"' (Malkki 1995:551). Malkki's comment speaks to those dangers of an anthropological dealing with the *Bidun* community. In purely anthropological readings, the *Bidun* are reduced, through a necessary assumption derived from their literary production, to an archetypal victim always responding in a repetitive manner to a totalizing condition of statelessness. Instead, what is at stake in approaching literary works is just the opposite. It is a way to understand how such extrinsic universalizing depictions are challenged through individualized narratives and articulations.

The other, more prevalent, approach to *Bidun* literature is the activistic approach. While also driven by 'sympathetic' impulses, activistic readings approach literary works of *Bidun* writers as legitimizing documents to advocate the *Biduns*' rights for citizenship and to demonstrate their contribution to the nation (al-Ḥarbi 2009; al-Wuqayyan 2009; al-Faysal 2011; al-Wushayḥi 2011). In the activistic mode of reading, what is often overlooked is the texts' capacity to transgress the very notions of national belonging in its official guise and the writers' other worldly concerns.

The most compelling example of this activistic approach is the publication compiled by Fatma al-Mattar under the title of *Judhoor* (Roots) (2012). The compilation includes more than fifty poems, short stories and one-act plays in both Arabic and English by young unpublished *Bidun* writers. As described in the cover page, the publication 'includes contributions submitted to the *Bidun* Creativity Contest and Judhoor Contest to demonstrate the talents of creative Kuwaiti-*Biduns*'. Prizes were allocated for the winners in the contest: a first prize of 500 KD (approx. 1000£), a second of 300 KD (approx. 600£) and a third of 200 KD (approx. 400£). Copies of Judhoor were sold for 1 KD (approx. 2£) and its proceeds were directed to *Bidun* families in need (Anhar 2012).

The texts are coupled with images documenting the 2012 *Bidun* protests and the government's suppression of it. Interestingly, the nature of the contest, in addition to the monetary incentive, focused on a specific expression of *Bidun* literature, specifically a direct expression of what it means to be *Bidun* in light of recent political events. Similar to an academic conference's 'call for papers' where one is required to relate to the conference title, the literary works compiled in *Judhoor* were made to speak in a certain way that relates to the activistic nature of the publication. Passing by some of the titles of the contributions, one can identify its overarching themes, namely, the depictions of the injustices practised on the community ('*Bidun* and Racism', 'The Suffering of a *Bidun*', 'the *Bidun* Are Undeserving', '*Bidun* until the Day of Judgement', 'A Child, and I've Become an Old Man', 'A *Bidun* Child's Thoughts', 'The Story of a *Bidun*', 'The *Bidun* Poem', 'A Citizen without a Homeland', 'If the World Only Knew I Was *Bidun*'), a prevalent rhetoric of blame to the homeland, ('Between My Friend the Homeland and I', 'A Homeland Gone with the Wind', 'A Stranger in My Homeland', 'To My Torturer') and a general pronouncement of loyalty to the homeland ('We Adore It', 'I love Kuwait', 'Why Migrate?'). More importantly, as many of these titles suggest, there seems to be a direct uninterrogated self-identification with the label *Bidun*. Rather, one of the main impulses behind the literary activity of many *Bidun* writers is this quest for intrinsic metaphor as a mode of resisting imposed labels as will be discussed throughout the book. While clearly advocating *Bidun* rights, *Judhoor* restricts literary expression to further an activistic position.

A literary approach

The other, less prevalent, approach to *Bidun* literature involves, simply put, an attentive act of listening to the aesthetic aspects in the texts through a critical close reading of the literary works. While attentive listening to the works may overlap with anthropological and activistic conclusions, it nevertheless attempts to understand *Bidun* literature from an analysis of the literary texts and its critical contexts and cultural connections. These readings demand first and foremost a perceptive engagement with the text and an acknowledgement of its capacity to allow possible reconsiderations of fundamental questions relating to official notions of belonging. It also allows for the possibility to approach the phenomenon from within its own articulations outside of the ready-made impositions.

So far, instances of attentive listening that closely read literary texts have been incomprehensive and are limited to newspaper and online articles. This approach has been mostly championed by writers trained in literary criticism or who are active within the cultural circles. Yet these attempts lack in terms of scope and analytical rigor. Because of their own brevity, these attempts will be reviewed in brief.

In January 2012, Najma Idris, a lecturer of Arabic literature in Kuwait University published an extensive newspaper article titled '*Bidun* literature'. In this article, Idris offers samples of works by *Bidun* writers including Sulayman al-Flayyiḥ, Nasir al-Ẓafiri, Ali al-Masudi and Mona Kareem as they relate to questions of identity and statelessness. She defines *Bidun* writers as 'those … who have found themselves victims of an administrative, political, and humanitarian impasse' (Idris 2012). The term *Bidun* literature is then used without further discussion. However, what is of importance in the article is that it reads literary texts of *Bidun* writers as a point of departure in analysing the questions of history, identity and belonging.

Another online article is by the literary critic Suʿad al-ʿInizi titled 'The Representations of the Exiled *Bidun* in Thought, Literature and Art'. The rather ambitious title provides a brief overview of the different cultural representations of the condition of statelessness. Nevertheless, the section on *Bidun* literature highlights the multiplicity of the depictions of the stateless condition. Al-ʿInizi maintains that the 'creative efforts that emerge out of the impositions of the *Bidun* issue … do not establish a clear *Bidun* identity, but are scattered instances' (al-ʿInizi 2013). Again, what is key in the preceding conclusion is that it is informed by the works of *Bidun* writers and does not necessarily offer grand conclusions. However, the critique of this particular approach is that the condition of statelessness is approached analytically solely from the prism of exile (i.e. the Exiled *Bidun*). In her discussion of 'the refugee condition', Liisa Malkki criticizes the way in which literary studies aestheticize exile as an individualized experience while dismissing other conditions of displacement as monolithic masses (Malkki 1995). She writes '[e]xile connotes a readily aestheticizable realm, whereas the label "refugees" connotes a bureaucratic and international humanitarian realm' (Malkki 1995:513). Echoing Malkki's critique, *Bidun* writers occupy their own unique fractured space that needs to be considered.

In August 2011, al-Kut TV's *Salam Ya Kuwait* aired an episode titled '*Bidun* Literature', interviewing the *Bidun* writers Karim al-Hazzaʿ and Dikhil Khalifa, who worked as an assistant producer in the TV channel. It was an unprecedented effort by the media and *Bidun* authors to approach *Bidun* literature as an undisputed literary collectivity. In the episode, *Bidun* literature was presented as a literature with a unique identity rising from a shared history of exclusion and present living conditions. The participants presented *Bidun* literature as a subcategory existing within Kuwaiti literature. However, it is distinct in its themes, poetic impulses and focus. Speaking as members of the *Bidun* literary community, Khalifa and al-Hazzaʿ naturally demonstrate knowledge of the corpus and an awareness of the intricacies of both the communal and singular historical experiences of *Bidun* writers. More importantly, specific literary works were highlighted and analysed to arrive at conclusions relating to the particularity of *Bidun* literature. One example would be Khalifa's insistence on presenting literature as form of resistance or 'a message to say that no matter how many obstacles you put in our way, we [the *Bidun*] will find ways to overcome them' (Al-Hazzaʿ and Khalifa 2011).

These dominant approaches highlight one of the main issues at stake in approaching a highly politicized 'stateless literature': the tendency to highlight the former term over the latter. Although certainly informed by the political and anthropological view of statelessness, an approach to *Bidun* literature must equally consider the aesthetic and literary capacity of *Bidun* works to transcend that condition. This book is primarily motivated by this insight, and more specifically, the following question: how can the aesthetic impulse behind this unique body of literature be approached in a literary critical manner? In other words, this book aspires to avoid reading '*Bidun* literature' as 'literature on the *Bidun*'.

Chapter Outline

The book attempts in its first chapter to establish the contextual groundwork for the study by asking the following questions: Who are the *Bidun*? What are the discursive practices that have produced the *Bidun* as a sociopolitical category? The chapter brings to light the shortcomings of the dominant modes of knowledge production, driven mainly by the considerations of area studies and the social sciences, in which the *Bidun* have been approached. The chapter then argues for the need to go beyond the descriptive representations of the *Bidun* by engaging critically with the cultural and literary production of *Bidun* writers.

The second chapter attempts to make a case for *Bidun* literature as a literary collectivity while highlighting the dangers and the ensuing debates surrounding the study of *Bidun* writers. The chapter provides the necessary contextual background concerning the materialities of cultural production in which *Bidun* writers actively negotiate their presence within the exclusionary forces of state-sanctioned cultural institutions by creating their own affiliative cultural networks and spaces of representation.

Chapter 3 examines the ways in which *Bidun* (stateless) poets negotiate and contest their placement within dominant narratives of national literary history in Kuwait. The chapter offers an analytical overview of the dominant modalities in which national literary history in Kuwait has been conceived as it relates to questions of national beginnings, periodization and the placement of stateless poets. Read against the existing modalities, the chapter analyses the *Bidun* poet Saʿdiyya Mufarriḥ's *The Cameleers of Clouds and Estrangement* (2007) as a revisionist account of national literary history that opposes the exclusion of *Bidun* writers. This is achieved by an emphasis on the inclusivity of literary and cultural belonging over the exclusivity of limiting notions of official national belonging.

Chapter 4 explores how *Bidun* writers utilize the desert space poetically as a pre-national site of historicizing modern statelessness and contesting notions of uprootedness. The central poet whose works are analysed in the chapter is Sulayman al-Flayyiḥ (1951–2013). The chapter begins with an analysis of the reception of al-Flayyiḥ within the national literary circle. In the poet's reception, the desert space is imagined and represented as an ahistoric site of timelessness, purity, innocence and authenticity. The chapter then examines how both al-Flayyiḥ's autobiographical reflections and poems contest ahistoric representations of the desert. The desert space as presented by al-Flayyiḥ is a site to reclaim a sense of uncontested origin and belonging and a site where pre-national conceptions of territoriality, sovereignty and belonging are legitimated. The second part of the chapter explores al-Flayyiḥ's affiliation with the *Ṣa'alik* poets in the Arabic literary tradition as an act of self-postionality that situates the poet within a wider Arabic literary tradition.

Chapter 5 explores the representations of the spatial metaphor of the *'Ashish*, the shanty towns where many of the *Bidun* once resided, as a unique space of *Bidun* experience and exclusion, especially in novels featuring *Bidun* characters. The chapter analyses five novels that characterize the *Bidun* community. The analysis of these novels distinguishes between two modes of representing the *'Ashish*: the ontological and the relational. In novels depicting the *'Ashish* in ontological terms, including Buthayna al- 'Isa's *Unheard Collision* (2004), Fawziyya al-Salim's *Staircases of Day* (2011) and Ismail Fahad's *In the Presence of Phoenix and the Loyal Friend* (2013), the *Bidun* characters' voice is often restricted to mere expressions of a stateless condition and narratives of victimization. On the other hand, al-Ẓafiri's novel *Scorched Heat* (2013) contests the reductive representations of the *Bidun* characters prevalent in the Kuwaiti novel. Al-Ẓafiri's novels emphasize the relational aspects of the *'Ashish*, or '*Bidun* experience' both spatially and temporally. The space of the *'Ashish* is always represented in relation to national, exilic and diasporic spaces. Temporally, the history of the *'Ashish* is understood in relation to national historiography and wider narratives of displacement in a postcolonial context.

The final chapter is concerned with notion of 'crossing borders' for *Bidun* writers in the diaspora. The case of the Canadian-Kuwaiti-*Bidun* poet Muhammad al-Nabhan is central to the chapter. The chapter traces his travels in-between many borders from Kuwait to Canada as an asylum seeker and in his many attempts at forging digital and analogue literary networks that transcend those borders. While these attempts express an incessant desire to find affiliative spaces above and beyond official state categories, they nevertheless continuously negotiate their presence within the material considerations of officiality manifest in bureaucracy, the omnipresence of papers, border controls and geopolitical realities.

Scope and sources

Proposing a '*Bidun* literary community', as will be discussed in Chapter 2, does not necessarily constrict the community to an isolated and bounded poetic terrain. Rather, it naturally is situated within wider fluid, multileveled terrains and textualities; overlapping with wider topographies, namely, national literature, regional (i.e. Gulf literature), modern Arabic literature, and broader thematic categories of exilic, diasporic, migrant and minority literatures. While encompassing such categories, *Bidun* literature as Muhsin al-Ramli put it

> has not been studied as it should be, even though it is much harsher than exile, alienation or migrant literatures, which have been studied thoroughly and still are … it is even wider and more complex because issues of exile, migration and alienation are only parts of statelessness.
>
> (al-Nabhan 2005:7)

Bidun writers share a wider space of marginality with other marginalized communities in the Arab world. The *Bidun*-Palestinian cultural connection is substantial and extensive and is well-worth a separate comparative study. This connection was a result of shared experiences of statelessness, albeit with different historical trajectories, and marginalization. Interactions between Palestinian and *Bidun* writers in Kuwait were most prevalent within local journalism, where many Palestinians and *Bidun*s worked to earn a living. During the 1980s for example, the *Bidun* poet, Sulayman al-Flayyiḥ who worked alongside the Palestinian caricaturist Naji al-Ali in *al-Siyasa* newspaper, recalls how the latter was infuriated after another Palestinian colleague bent down to kiss the hands of an affluent Kuwaiti patron. As a result '[Naji al-Ali] turned to me and said: listen to me you Bedouin man, in this country everyone has a boss (*ʿam*). What do you say: I become your boss (*ʿam*) and you become mine?' (al-Flayyiḥ 2009a). Later in his memoirs al-Flayyiḥ expatiates on his relationship with al-Ali writing, 'I felt that I belong in my poetry and political stance to Palestine because of my relationship with Naji al-Ali' (al-Flayyiḥ 2009a).

The *Bidun*-Palestinian cultural connection is also evident in the works of many *Bidun* writers. Saʿdiyya Mufarriḥ writes in the introduction of her anthology of Palestinian poets titled *Memory's Pains*:

> [T]he task [of editing the anthology] … wasn't difficult. I know the chosen poets quite well. I have grown up, in the poetic sense, under the shadow of their writings … many of them have helped in shaping my Arab national consciousness in an early age.
>
> (Mufarriḥ 2010b)

Similarly, in her poetry collection titled *Merely a Mirror Laying* (1999), Mufarriḥ dedicates five poems to the Palestinian poets Fadwa Tuqan, Muhmud Darwish, Ibrahim Nasrallah, Murid Barghouthi and a final poem 'to her alone', (Palestine). Muhammad al-Nabhan, in his poem titled *The Palestinian in My Blood*, describes the Palestinian as 'my neighbor, classmate, Arabic teacher, factory manager, family doctor, my poet, the calligrapher, the *Kanafani*, Cafeteria worker, the merchant, the driver, the painter, the journalist … who taught me once how to seek my homeland from afar' (Al-Rubayiʿ 2018). In addition, this shared space of marginality is expressed in the ubiquitous presence of Palestinian characters in novels concerning the *Bidun* such as Ismail Fahad's *In the Presence of the Phoenix and the Loyal Friend* (2013) and Nasir al-Ẓafiri's *Scorched Heat* (2013), which will be analysed in Chapter 5.

On the figurative level, *Bidun*, as a state of unrecognized existence, can be an all-inclusive category for all marginalized individuals, particularly within the Arab world as the Lebanese writer Shawqi Buzaiʿ suggests. In a TV interview, Buzai comments: '[I]f the *Bidun* have taken their name from not being recognized as full citizens, then I believe we are all *Bidun* in this Arab World' (Demaghtech 2012b). Similarly, Muhammad al-Nabhan comments that one of the main impulses behind the establishment of the literary e-zine

Ufouq.com while in Canada in 2000 was to offer '*Bidun*s of the Arab world' a space to express their voices.

Taher Ben Jalloun, the Moroccan Francophone novelist, identifies with the metaphorical aspect of *Bidun* in his novel *The Hotel of the Poor* (2000), where he writes:

> I am of the type of people who endure pain silently. I called myself '*Bidun*' as a result of a memory of an uneasy travel experience in the autumn of 1975 to Kuwait. There, I discovered, 15 kilometres from the capital a camp where the Kuwaiti government would keep distanced illegal immigrants who are without '(*Bidun*)' citizenship. These are men who have destroyed their identity papers to avoid expulsion. They call them *Bidun*, creatures from no-space. They are shadows of men who work in daylight and disappear at night in caves or worn-out tents.
>
> (Jalloun 2000:5)

While recognizing the metaphorical associations of term *Bidun*, the primary literature (*Bidun* Literature) that is of particular interest to this book is literature published by writers who are currently *Bidun* or who were *Bidun* at one point in their life regardless of their current citizenship status or current place of residence. Born *Bidun*, many writers have been compelled to leave Kuwait's borders in pursuit of a better life elsewhere. Some important examples include Nasir al-Ẓafiri and Muhammad al-Nabhan who have gained Canadian citizenship, Sulayman al-Flayyiḥ who has become a Saudi citizen. The body of literature is composed of published novels, poetry collections, short stories and articles in literary journals and newspapers (both analogue and digital). All works considered in this book are written in *Fuṣḥa* Arabic.

Given the wide range of works and genres already published in *Fuṣḥa*, including the domain of *Shaʿbi* poetry requires its own methodological approach. While acknowledging the political and aesthetic valence of *Shaʿbi* poetry, a study of *Shaʿbi* poetry is fraught with a different set of challenges. The first challenge relates to the difficulty of accessing sources and poems. These sources include *Safaḥat al-Adab al-Shaʿbi* (local newspaper sections concerned with *Shaʿbi* poetry) in newspaper archives in Kuwait and the Gulf, contributions to online cultural forums, participations in TV programmes concerned with *Adab al-Shaʿbi*. A number of poems remain within the realm of oral transmission, which requires another, more anthropological, approach. Secondly, analysing works written in *Sha 'bi* requires mapping out the generally unfamiliar cultural scene of *Sha 'bi* poetry in Arabia, which is beyond the scope of this book.

The historical range of works that will be analysed will be between 1979 and 2018. This initial pool encompasses a variety and wide range of *Bidun* writers, texts and genres. The selected texts do not by any means intend to be fully representative of the wide range of themes, literary styles, genres and articulations of belonging prevalent in the works of *Bidun* writers. Rather, the selected texts are treated as case studies illustrative of the different manifestations of belonging in the works of *Bidun* writers.

The book relies heavily on previously untranslated sources. The first category of sources is the collection of the literary works published, all in Arabic, by *Bidun* writers between 1979 and 2018. Access to such material proved to be a challenge in the initial phase of the research as most of the works, especially between 1979 and 2010, have had limited circulation and are out of print. While recent publications are available in bookshops, many of the older literary works consulted in this study have been copied from private libraries with the help of poets such as Dikhil Khalifa and Abdulla Falah or, with respect to works of writers residing outside of Kuwait, have been sent to me by the authors. Other literary works have been accessed through the al-Babtain Central Library for Arabic Poetry in Kuwait, which has been instrumental to the research.

The second category of sources is local and Arabic literary scholarship that relate to the general analysis of the works of *Bidun* writers. Chapter 4 on literary history brings to light the debates within the local scene relating to Kuwaiti literary history. In the treatment of the *Ṣa 'alik* tradition in Chapter 5, the book utilizes a range of Arabic scholarship on the issue. In addition to the aforementioned al-Babtain Central Library for Arabic Poetry, the SOAS main library and the library of the Kuwaiti Writers' Association have been useful in accessing such sources. In addition, the Kuwaiti Writers' Association's monthly periodical *Majallat al-Bayan* has been an important source, especially in the discussion of the reception of the *Bidun* poet Sulayman al-Flayyiḥ in Chapter 5.

The third category of untranslated sources is internet material whether it be online archives of newspapers, contributions in online cultural forums, publications in cultural e-zines and debates in social media and interviews with *Bidun* writers on YouTube. Internet sources have provided vital material especially in discussing the materialities of cultural production in which *Bidun* writers operate, tracking the ongoing debates surrounding the general phenomenon of *Bidun* literature and providing contextual notes on different *Bidun* writers, which are threaded throughout the chapters of the book. One of the major challenges in accessing internet sources is the ephemerality of online sources. One example of the vulnerability of such sources is the total disappearance, sometime in 2013, of the archive of the cultural e-zine *Ufouq.com* established by Muhammad al-Nabhan in 2000. To avoid broken links in the bibliography, I have since 2013, created an online blog (http://Bidunliterature.blogspot.com) as backup for most of the internet sources that have been used in the book. These alternative links are included in the Bibliography.

In addition to the untranslated sources, the research involved conducting interviews with the following *Bidun* writers: Dikhil Khalifa in Kuwait, Muhammad al-Nabhan in Bahrain, Jassim al-Shimmiri in Kuwait and Mona Kareem via Skype from the United States. Unfortunately, Sulayman al-Flayyiḥ, who is the central poet of interest in Chapter 5, passed away in August 2013. Thus, I have relied on his autobiographical reflections published in a series published in *al-Jarida* newspaper titled *Memoirs of the Northern Bird*. The primary purpose of these interviews was to investigate paratextual insights related to questions of publication, circulation and reception of their respective works. The information obtained in these interviews has been mainly utilized in Chapter 2 discussing the materialities of cultural production. Other writers, such as Saʿdiyya Mufarriḥ and Nasir al-Ẓafiri, have had a significant number of published interviews that address the issues of interest mentioned above. Mufarriḥ, for example, published a book titled *Seen (2011)*, which is a compilation of her interviews published in online forums and newspapers.

It is also important to stress that this book explores a contemporary phenomenon. Since beginning my research on the topic as postgraduate student at the School of Oriental and African Studies (SOAS) in 2011, I have been constantly trying to catch up with the ongoing political events, new publications by *Bidun* writers and the debates surrounding the general phenomenon of *Bidun* literature in different media outlets. Throughout the process of writing the book, the *Bidun* issue has seen a drastic shift in terms of the community's social, political and cultural visibility. In February 2011 many in the *Bidun* community started a series of public protests against the government's lack of initiative in dealing with the issue. These protests, which were partly driven by energies released in the events of the 'Arab Spring', shifted the political discourses on the representation of the *Bidun* and generated an increased interest in the issue on both the national and international levels.

Concomitant with the rise of national and international interest was an increased sensitivity, within the national context, towards any public political debate regarding the *Bidun*. The increased sensitivity towards the issue can be read within a general trend of consolidation of political power within the executive branch in the post-'Arab Spring' political ambience. The government introduced stringent measures to contain the political upheaval. A number of *Bidun* activists have been arrested and prosecuted for their involvement in public talks and protests.

The increased visibility of the *Bidun* was reflected in cultural production within the national cultural context. Prior to 2011, there were two novels featuring *Bidun* characters: *Upturned Sky* (1995) by the *Bidun* novelist Nasir al-Ẓafiri and *A Collision Never Heard* (2004) by the Kuwaiti novelist Buthayna Al-ʿIsa. Since then, and concomitant with the increased attention on the form of the novel in Arabic literature, there has been a surge in the depiction of *Bidun* characters in novels. These novels include Fawziyya al-Salim's *Staircases of Day* (2011), Saud al-Sanʿusi's *The Bamboo Stalk* (2012), Ismail Fahad's *In the Presence of the Phoenix and the Loyal Friend* (2013), Nasir al-Ẓafiri's *Al-Sahd* (2013) and *Kaliska* (2015), Basma al-ʿInizi's *A Black Shoe on the Pavement* (2013), Abdullah al-Buṣayyiṣ's *Stray Memories* (2014) and Hanadi al-Shemmiri's novella *A House Made of Tin* (2015). Short story collections featuring *Bidun* characters include Abdullah al-ʿUtaybi's *ʾIkʿaybar* (2011) and Muna al-Shimmiri's *The Rain Falls, the Princess Dies* (2012). Thus, the focus of the chapters in the book had to attend to such shifts. Chapter 5 considers this surge of interest by analysing novels featuring *Bidun* characters.

* * *

Finally, whenever I have been asked about my research topic, particularly within contexts familiar with the *Bidun* issue, the discussion almost immediately turns into a discussion on the politics of citizenship and the validity of the

Bidun's claim for citizenship rights. The discussion seldom reaches the second word of the book title: 'Literature'. Within a wider academic context, where knowledge on the issue is minimal, the challenge of arriving at the second word of the title is greater. In my experiences in presenting my work in an academic setting, the emphasis on the descriptive sociological and political element of my work is often regarded more valuable than any literary insight offered. Feedback, almost always, tends to veer towards an elaboration on the issue itself rather than the impact of the literature. These experiences have pressed me to constantly refocus the presentation and framing of the book to emphasize the critical and literary insight while negotiating it with descriptive aspect. The structure of this book re-enacts my research experiences as it begins with Chapter 1, dedicated wholly to the *Bidun* issue. Yet later in the chapter, and throughout the book, the focus shifts towards the critical and analytical aspects of the literary production of *Bidun* writers and how a literary approach offers novel insights into intrinsic articulations of the community.

1

The *'Bidun'*

'There is nothing stable about the *Bidun* issue' (Human Rights Watch 2011:3). This instability is manifest in the very nature of the term *Bidun*. Since the advent of the modern Kuwaiti state in 1962, the *Bidun*'s legal denomination has been changed six times in response to the state's legal necessities at different times. To begin with, Salih al-Faḍala, the current chairman of the Central Committee for Illegal Residents, claims that *Bidun* is a 'false term' (Ḥadath al-Yawm 2011). As he puts it, 'nobody is *Bidun;* everyone must have a place to where he belongs. Their true officially recognized name in the state of Kuwait is "illegal residents"' (Ḥadath al-Yawm 2011). This denomination used by al-Faḍala is the latest official administrative term adopted by the Kuwaiti government to categorize the stateless community in Kuwait.

Al-Faḍala's use of the term is in line with the official standpoint previously articulated by government officials. The term 'illegal resident' was officially adopted by the state in 1993 (Human Rights Watch 1995:17). In an interview with Human Rights Watch (HRW) in 1991, the undersecretary for Foreign Affairs, at the time, Sulayman al-Shahin said that there is no such thing as people 'Bedoon jensiya [*sic*] (without citizenship)' because everybody must have come from somewhere (55). Similarly, in 1993, Saud al-Nasir al-Ṣabaḥ who was the minister of information and official spokesman for the government said in an interview:

> [T]here is no such people as Bedoons [*sic*]. Everybody has an origin; no one comes from a vacuum. Every person has a father and a grandfather and comes from a specific family. This Bedoon [*sic*] phenomenon started in Kuwait many years ago when some people were smuggled here from outside.

> They would throw away their documents – passports and foreign identity cards and live in Kuwait, claiming that they were without any documents, or Bedoon [*sic*].
>
> (55–56)

Abdulatif al-Thuwaini, who headed of the government's central committee on the *Bidun*, said in 1994, '[T]here are no Bedoons [*sic*] in Kuwait, but rather thousands of people who are residing in the country illegally' (56).

Throughout the years, the *Bidun* have been subject to a series of labelling acts practised by the government. They were officially labelled respectively as: *Abna' al-Badiya* (sons of the desert), *Bidun Jinsiyya* (those without citizenship), *Ghayr Kuwaiti* (non-Kuwaitis), *Ghayr Muḥaddad al-Jinsiyya* (those with undetermined citizenship), *Majhuli al-Hawiyya* (those whose identities are unknown) and, since 1990, *Muqimun bi Ṣura Ghayr Qanuniyya* (illegal residents). The final denomination, 'illegal residents', is seen by some as a manipulative tool used by the Kuwaiti government to reduce the *Bidun* issue to a standard migratory issue dismissing its complex historical particularity (Beaugrand 2017).

On the other side of the spectrum, human rights' discourse drives international agencies and activists to adopt the legal denomination '*ʿAdimu al-Jinsiyya*' (those without citizenship or stateless) to refer to the *Bidun*. This adoption is a tactical necessity to recognize a legal status protected under UN conventions concerned with the stateless. It is worth noting that the government of Kuwait is not yet a signatory to the 1954 Convention Relating to the Status of Stateless Persons and the 1961 Convention on the Reduction of Statelessness. Although this adoption aims to offer a legal cover, it inevitably takes away from the historical weight of the term *Bidun* and the very nature of its complexity.

The *Bidun* activist Abdulhakim al-Faḍli, for example, rejects internalizing the term, stating in a seminar organized by the Kuwaiti Democratic Forum in November 2014: '*lasna ʿadimi al-jinsiyya, naḥnu sukkan aṣliyun*' (We are not stateless, we are native residents) (Abdulhalim 2014). Both the official state and human rights discourses, in effect, universalize the *Bidun* issue to fit their specific aims. Thus, using the term *Bidun* in this book is a mark of resistance to such abstraction and universalization, as it is a term that carries its untranslatable distinct historical weight both materially and imaginatively.

The term, following Beaugrand, stands as a reminder of the instability and complexity of the category:

> [T]he category of *Biduns* has thus no coherence apart from the administrative label assigned to them. In spite of some broad attested characteristics like their overwhelming presence in the military, the situations of the *Biduns* in terms of socio-economic conditions, networks and rights enjoyed, are very varied. The *Bidun* category is far from the completely segregated group into which they have been fashioned by years of discriminatory policies.
>
> (114)

While the term *Bidun* is adopted in this book as a present signifier for the stateless community in Kuwait, it is important to acknowledge its capacity to carry new meanings. In different contexts, the term implies derogatory connotations (al-Wugayyan 2009; Beaugrand 2017). It is not uncommon for local newspaper headlines, or indeed novels as will be discussed later in the book, to associate the term *Bidun* with crime, villainy, and lawlessness.

Yet as Mikhail Bakhtin writes 'the word does not exist in a neutral and impersonal language but rather it exists in other people's mouths, in other people's contexts, serving other people's intentions: it is from there that one must take the word, and make it one's own' (Bakhtin 1981:293). *Bidun* activists, for example, appropriated the term by advocating for the appellation 'the Kuwaiti *Biduns*' (al-Kuwaitiyyun al-*Bidun*) to counter the exclusivity of the term. Contrary to the logic of the state, the appellation affirms a double awareness of official exclusion and emotive belonging. Yet more importantly, as will be discussed in the following chapters, the book is mainly concerned with the aesthetic reworking of the term and its connotations through the literary production of the *Bidun*. Italicizing the term *Bidun* aims to materialize its tentative use and resist a sociological-anthropological imprint on the book's literary considerations.

The dialectic of extrinsic and intrinsic powers of naming the phenomenon is one of the main challenges entailed in writing this book. In other words, how can one engage critically with the existing tools, methods and languages that restrict the understanding of the phenomenon? How can one write about '*Bidun* writers' or stateless writers, many who reject to be identified as such? Beginning with their own radical articulations might risk alienating the reader with the lack of ready modes of reception. In view of this intrinsic challenge, the book's main aim is to proceed in understanding the phenomenon through its own language dialogically. To do so, the chapter proceeds first in highlighting how the phenomenon has been historically conceived and linguistically formulated in different relevant discourses.

Global and local contexts

Statelessness is a phenomenon concomitant with the rise of the modern nation state. One of the reasons behind the creation of the now 12 million stateless people in the world is state succession, during which individuals fail to register for citizenship under new legislation or new administrative procedures. The more prevalent reason, however, is the arbitrary deprivation of nationality and discrimination against certain target groups based on ethnic, religious or linguistic differences (Blitz and Lynch 2011:6). Stateless populations such as the Crimean Tatar in Ukraine, or the Nubian community in Kenya, or people of Russian descent in post-independent Slovenia and Estonia, are examples of statelessness induced by ethnic differences. The Bihari Urdu-speaking stateless people in Bangladesh are often accused of maintaining an allegiance to the country adopting their mother-tongue Pakistan and are discriminated against on linguistic basis. While each stateless population has its own particular history, not belonging to the adopted conception of 'the national' is a major factor behind their stateless condition. Yet all three traditionally assumed factors of ethnic, religious or linguistic differences do not necessarily apply easily to the case of the *Bidun* in Kuwait. The *Bidun* are not historically conceived as belonging to a distinct ethnic, religious or linguistic minority. As described by 1995 HRW report, the *Bidun* are:

> [A] heterogeneous group which includes a substantial number of people – perhaps the majority of the Bedoons [*sic*] – who were born in Kuwait and have lived there all their lives .... Sometimes they lack citizenship because a male ancestor neglected to apply for it when citizenship regulation were first introduced in 1948 and later in 1959, in anticipation of independence in 1961 .... Members of tribes whose territory once extended between Kuwait and its neighbours, and whose allegiance was traditionally to the tribe were

> denied citizenship and classified as Bedoons [*sic*], although large numbers of them have long been settled in urban areas in Kuwait.[1]
>
> (Human Rights Watch 1995:10)

Beaugrand highlights the difficulty 'to establish a typology of *Biduns*' as the reasons behind the group's statelessness vary. One group is composed of the children of Kuwaiti mothers married to *Bidun*s who have been denied citizenship as per the 1959 Nationality Law. Another group are who have refused second degree of nationality because they felt entitled to the first degree. Others have never registered with nationality committees while others' files have been rejected. Another group consists of army recruits from neighbouring countries, some who may carry existing nationalities. Finally, there are those who arrived in the 1980s and who took advantage of the stalemate surrounding the issue (Beaugrand 2017:112).

The *Bidun* in Kuwait consist of *de jure* stateless individuals who have never obtained citizenship from any other country and *de facto* stateless individuals, who may have once been citizens of neighbouring countries but are now are effectively stateless. After being treated as quasi-nationals until 1986 and under the prospects of future naturalization through service in the army, many have cut off any links or affiliations elsewhere and have lost the claim for citizenship for their children (al-Anezi 1994:1). In addition, stateless people who once resided in Kuwait include many of the Gazan Palestians who hold Egyptian documents, but are not considered as part of the *Bidun* category (8).

In anthropological approaches to the issue, some argue that even though the *Bidun* are historically not a marked ethnic collectivity, they have been effectively 'ethnicized' as a result of social and economic discrimination (al-Najjar 2001; al-Wuqayyan 2009; Beaugrand 2010). Socially, the *Bidun* are viewed by a large part of Kuwaiti society as described by the 1995 HRW report as 'latecomers', 'coming to milk' the newly established welfare state (Human Rights Watch 1995:56). This depiction has been advanced by official state discourse. In 1993, Saud al-Nasir al-Ṣabaḥ, who was the spokesman of the Kuwaiti government at the time, said: '[I]f they had to pay income taxes and if there was no free medical care or education in Kuwaiti there would be no more Bedoon [*sic*]' (Human Rights Watch 1995:56). Years of denial of citizenship rights have also further 'ethnicized' the *Bidun* into a social underclass because of the economic consequences of lacking citizenship rights.

Beaugrand argues that contending understandings of pre-state sovereignty, territoriality and loyalty is the main reasons behind the continual denial of the *Bidun* from citizenship rights. This impasse preventing the *Bidun* from gaining citizenship rights is due to 'the confusion in the understanding of transnationalism that needs to be better historicized' (Beaugrand 2010:29). While the lack of historicizing transnationalism is one of the main reason behind the impasse, the term 'confusion' implicitly assumes a naïve lack of awareness on the part of the state and of its own history. The lack of historicization perhaps is a more calculated attempt to monopolize the dominant historical representations of the *Bidun* issue on the part of official state discourse. The contention between the transnational and the national understandings of the history of the region and the formation of concepts of belonging has been mainly understood through the dominant dichotomy of *Badu/Ḥaḍar* present in studies on the Kuwaiti social construct. *Badu* is the term commonly used to denote Kuwaiti citizens from Bedouin origins mostly living outside the 1920 town wall, and *Ḥaḍar* denotes the townspeople residing within the wall

The *Badu/Ḥaḍar*[2] discourse has been a dominant paradigm in understanding the prevailing sentiments depicting the *Bidun* as ethnic outsiders undeserving of citizenship rights. In Anh Nga Longva's analysis of this dichotomy, the benefits of the welfare state become a deciding factor in rejecting 'newcomers' from naturalization. *Ḥadari* discourse depicts the *Badu* as newcomers wanting to reap the benefits of the newly established welfare state, where education, healthcare and housing are practically free. The *Badu* are also viewed as people who will not assimilate to 'Kuwaiti Culture' by holding on to their tribal traditions (Longva 2006:172). Thus, naturalization of many of the *Badu* was considered as a 'widening of the nation', in terms of the community of citizens, which 'means – at least in the people's imagination – a reduction or even the end of the welfare state' (183). This view in turn 'sets in motion the process of ethnicization' of the *Badu* community, 'whereby differences between host population and newcomers are systematically emphasized, even invented when need be' (172).

This 'ethnicization' is understood as a result of the government's direct measures relating to housing policies that have kept *Badu* and *Ḥaḍar* segregated; 'fixing them as socio-spatially distinct categories' as argued by Farah al-Nakib (al-Nakib 2014:15). Three-housing schemes were implemented by the government to house its population as decisions were made to demolish the old town quarters and develop a new housing strategy. The first scheme pertained to the *Ḥaḍar* (townspeople), whose homes were relocated from the old town quarters to newly developed *manaṭiq namudhajiyya* (model areas) not far from the old town. Relocation was made possible through the government's land acquisition scheme, whereby land was appraised and purchased by the government at inflated rates (15). The second scheme applied to residents of peripheral villages such as Salmiyya, al-Jahra and Farwaniyya. Their properties were similarly acquired by the government and were given new housing in their respective areas. The third housing scheme was concerned with the *Badu* who had started to settle in what is commonly referred to as *ʿAshish*, or ad hoc shanty dwellings originally established around oil company work sites that offered jobs for many *Badu* (al-Moosa 1976:3). Because of their lack of land ownership, many of the *Badu* missed out on the economic opportunity of the government's land acquisitions. As the government was planning to rehouse the shanty dwellers in the 1970s, it built temporary housing commonly referred to as *shaʿbiyyat, or al-masakin al-shaʿbiyya* (popular housing) in areas such as Jahra, Minaʾ Abdullah, ʿArḍiyya, Jlib al-Shyukh, Dawḥa and Ṣulaybiyya (al-Moosa 1976:294; al-Nakib 2014). The *shaʿbiyyat* are 'constructed very cheaply, using locally made grey concrete bricks without any plastering, painting, or other finishing applied, and the settlement areas contained no paved roads' (al-Nakib 1976:18–19). Compared to the 400–1000 square metres range of houses in the *manaṭiq namudhajiyya*, a *shaʿbiyyat* house was 150 square metres despite the larger *Badu* family's average size (al-Moosa 1976:294). The majority of *Badu* who gained citizenship moved out from the *shaʿbiyyat* and into the Low-Income Housing projects developed by the government in areas such as Riqqa, al-Jahra, Khayṭan and Ṣubahiyya (290). Those *Badu* who did not gain citizenship, that is, the *Bidun*, were excluded from these housing projects and instead moved into the *shaʿbiyyat*, and many are still living there.

While geographically excluded, *Badu* who had gained citizenship rights have been enabled to negotiate their social, economic, political status, while the *Bidun* have been further distanced from Kuwaiti society due to their lack of citizenship rights and the economic privileges associated with it. In comparison with non-Kuwaiti residents, Kuwaiti nationals enjoy a generous welfare system guaranteeing its citizens free education, healthcare and subsidized housing among other benefits. In addition, Kuwaitis are offered economic incentives in the public and private sector, which inflates their salaries significantly in comparison with non-Kuwaitis. Such citizenship privileges create economic disparities between Kuwaitis on the one side as a definite social cluster, and non-Kuwaitis including the *Bidun* in another.

However, the *Bidun* also suffer from unique forms of citizenship-based discrimination due to their lack of citizenship. The *Bidun* have enjoyed a special status of 'quasi nationals' (al-Anezi 1989:257) in-between nationals and expatriates, primarily due to their historical exemption from the 1959 Law on the Residence of Aliens, which allowed them to 'enter Kuwait by their usual land routes for the purposes of carrying out their usual business' (260), and their employment in the Kuwaiti military and police (al-Anezi 1994:9).

Historical development of the *Bidun* issue

Faris al-Wuqayyan presents the development of the *Bidun* issue in Kuwait in three main historical phases: recognition, denial and accusation. The first phase, 'phase of recognition' (1959–1986), stretches from the establishment of the Kuwait Nationality Law No. 15 of 1959 and the Law on the Residence of Aliens No. 17 of 1959 to the year 1986. During that period, the lack of documentation of the *Bidun* community was not considered as an impediment to daily life. The *Bidun* enjoyed access to many of the privileges that were later denied such as public education, public health and government employment. The *Bidun* were officially included as Kuwaitis in the national census up until 1989 (al-Najjar 2003).

The recognition manifests itself legally through the *Bidun*'s historical exemption from the 1959 Law on the Residence of Aliens. The Kuwaiti military and police in its early stages heavily recruited the *Bidun* (al-Anezi 1994:9). In June 1985, the *Bidun*, or those who were legally identified as non-citizen 'Kuwaiti birth certificate holders', constituted 32.7 per cent of the overall Kuwaiti police force (al-Fahad 1989:308).

Recognition of the *Bidun* as a constitutive group within the bureaucracy was overturned in the second phase 'phase of denial' (1986–1991) where life for the *Bidun* in Kuwait took a drastic turn. Because of domestic and regional upheavals, the unsettled position of the *Bidun* was viewed by the state as a 'ticking time bomb' that needed immediate action (Human Rights Watch 1995; al-Wuqayyan 2009). Regionally, the intensification of the Iraq-Iran war exerted pressures on the government to drastically change its security measures towards its stateless population. The presence of undocumented individuals in Kuwait was seen as a pressing security threat in light of increased migration, regional sectarian polarization and the alleged infiltration of the Kuwaiti army by a group of *Bidun* officers brought about by the war (al-Najjar 2003; al-Wuqayyan 2009). On the local level, the issue of mass naturalization has developed into a highly sensitive issue within Kuwaiti political discourse. This was primarily due to what is commonly referred to as *al-tajnis al-siyasi* in the late 1960s, or politically motivated extra-legal naturalization to counter political opposition (al-Ghabra 2011:55; Human Rights Watch 1995:62; al-Hajeri 2014:8; Beaugrand 2017:4). Thus, any attempt at mass naturalization was viewed as an alteration of the electoral body that would ultimately destabilize the 'political balance' (al-Hajeri 2014:8). On the economic level, naturalizing the *Bidun* was and is still presented to the public as an economic burden that would exert significant pressures on the welfare system. Debarring *Bidun* from citizenship rights was also purported to protect the social fabric of society from 'imposters'. The increased presence of expatriates also exerted pressures on the formation of a Kuwaiti national identity. To cement a Kuwaiti national identity, the 'grey area' that the *Bidun* historically occupy had to be eliminated (Crystal 2005:176).

The year 1986 marks the year of extreme transition in the government's dealing with the *Bidun* issue. After being recognized as part of the Kuwaiti population in the national census since 1959, a new government strategy aiming to tighten the living conditions on the *Bidun* denied their right of existence as part of the resident population and deemed them illegal residents. On 20 September 2003, *al-Ṭaliʿa* weekly newspaper published the minutes of a confidential ministerial committee held in December 1986 outlining measures that aimed to make life extremely precarious for the *Bidun*. The shift in the governmental committee's policies is corroborated by the HRW report in 1995 titled: *Bedoons in Kuwait 'Citizens without Citizenship'* which cites excerpts from an interview with the then minister of Interior Affairs Salim Subah al-Salim in the Emarati journal *al-Azmina al-ʿArabiyya* where he outlined the policy shift.

At the legal level, the 1986 measurements called the *Bidun* 'illegal residents'. This meant that they were denied travel documents (driving licenses, passports, and birth, death, marriage and divorce certificates). In 2012, the Central Committee for Illegal Residents came up with a three-colour card scheme to differentiate between *Bidun* cases. Green cards were given to those eligible for nationality. Red cards for those disqualified from naturalization because of a criminal record while yellow cards were given a three-year period to regularize their status on the basis of foreign nationality (Beaugrand 2017:130). These obstacles have had a great impact on the daily life of the *Bidun*.[3] This legal positioning, as unrecognized outsiders, does not allow the *Bidun* to contest their rights to citizenship according to Kuwaiti citizenship law in the judicial system. Citizenship is considered a matter of sovereignty and is a prerogative of the executive branch. This leaves the *Bidun* with limited formal channels to voice their discontent. In March 2017, members of the Kuwaiti parliament proposed amendments to the naturalization law that allow, among other things, the judicial branch to adjudicate citizenship cases. These proposals created polarization in the media and the establishment of reactionary pressure groups such as *Majmuʿat al-Thamanin* (The Group of 80 activists) whose main purpose was to lobby against any 'tampering with Kuwaiti national unity' through undeserved naturalization.

Politically, the *Bidun* lack any officially sanctioned political rights and are denied the right to protest their existing conditions. Starting in February 2011, the *Bidun* have been involved in public protests to advocate their rights and to express their frustration towards the government's lack of initiative and sincerity in finding a solution for their conditions. These protests have been suppressed by the Ministry of Interior Affair's Special Forces and a number of *Bidun* activists have been detained (Human Rights Watch 2011b). Another informal channel to advocate *Bidun* rights is through increasing international pressure from organizations headed by the *Bidun* residing outside of Kuwait such as the Kuwaiti Bedoon Movement led by Muhammad Wali al-ʿInizi in Harrow, London, and Bedoonrights.com led by Mona Kareem in New

York. Locally, many of the *Bidun* pressure members of parliament whose constituencies include Kuwaiti relatives of the *Bidun* to raise the issue of their rights.

The economic consequences of the lack of citizenship rights have effectively left the *Bidun* in the lower strata of Kuwaiti society. The *Bidun* are barred from employment in the public sector and restricted from employment in the private sector except for menial jobs. These restrictions are coupled with the denial of welfare benefits and access to public education and public healthcare, which increases the economic burden on the *Bidun*.

The *Bidun*'s conditions are further reiterated by psychological measures, which Beaugrand refers to as 'administrative violence' defined as the 'use of all possible administrative means to delegitimize the claims to citizenship by anybody feeling some sense of entitlement' (Beaugrand 2017:116). This administrative violence manifests itself in four ways: (1) the imposition of an identity rejected by the concerned persons, (2) a de facto pauperization of this category of the population, (3) a symbolic process of stigmatization, (4) a nerve-wracking absence of transparency (Beaugrand 2017:127).

One important instance embodying these acts of administrative violence is the government's proposal, as revealed in November 2014 by an official in the Ministry of Interior Affairs, to offer the *Bidun* an 'economic citizenship' granted by the Union of the Comoros in return for Kuwait's investments. With this new 'economic citizenship', the *Bidun* would then receive residence permits in Kuwait as Comorians with the added value of enjoying free education and healthcare. Other less serious proposals that circulated in the media included the offloading of the *Bidun* to Sudan which has been ridiculed by *Bidun* activists on social media. Such proposals every now and then intensify the psychological stress on the *Bidun,* ultimately making life more precarious for the community. All of the above measures are materializations of the second phase of denial as described by al-Wuqayyan.

The third phase after the 1986 decree is the 'phase of accusation' (starting from 1991), which came as an aftermath of the Iraqi invasion of Kuwait. Many of the *Bidun* were accused by the state of holding or 'hiding' their original passports. The Iraqi invasion exacerbated the *Bidun*'s already vulnerable position in Kuwaiti social structure. During the invasion, the Iraqi army in some cases encouraged non-Kuwaitis to join *al-Jaysh al-Sha'bi* (the Popular

Army), a 'local' militia under the supervision of the Iraqi forces (Human Rights Watch 1995:23). While many of the *Bidun* were forced to join under military or economic pressures, there were those who joined voluntarily as a reaction to the unfavourable treatment they had received prior to the invasion (23). After the liberation of Kuwait in 1991, the *Bidun* were immediately stigmatized *en masse* for mere suspicion of joining the popular army, while at the same time many of the sacrifices of the *Bidun* in the Kuwaiti military were overlooked. The 1995 HRW report mentions that almost one-third of native inhabitants killed by the Iraqi forces during the invasion were *Bidun* (Human Rights Watch 1995:23). This stigmatization would then be legally materialized in the form of *al-qayd al-amni* (a security hold), which is a legal barrier against naturalization today.

Al-Wuqayyan's presentation of the historical development of the *Bidun* issue emphasizes the extrinsic local and regional forces that have shaped the historical experience of the *Bidun*. While these forces are essential in understanding the historical development of the issue, it nevertheless overlooks important questions relating to the *Bidun*'s agency and their capacity to negotiate their position in society in spite of such forces. If one is to extend the logic of al-Wuqayyan's historical narrative, then the *Bidun*, since 2011, have been witnessing another phase that can be termed 'the phase of visibility'. While all other phases emphasize the external forces that have shaped the *Bidun* experience as a passive collectivity and receivers of governmental policies, this phase is defined by the *Bidun*'s visible assertion of their own agency. This visibility is most clearly materialized in the *Bidun* activists' claim for their rights through public demonstrations. February 2011 witnessed the first *Bidun* public demonstration, which was later followed by a series of public protests between 2011 and 2013. Whereas the *Bidun* issue was historically approached from outside the *Bidun* community by local Kuwaiti activists or local 'middle-men' and representatives of international human rights agencies, in this phase, *Bidun* activists went to the front lines. It is telling that the first public lecture on the *Bidun* issue co-organized by *Bidun* activists in the Kuwaiti Association for Human Rights in November of 2006 was titled *al-Bidun Yataḥadathun* (the *Bidun* Speak). This title highlights a departure from a previously patient and passive stance. Yet to reduce the *Bidun*'s visibility to their engagement in mass public demonstrations, starting in 2011 is problematic and goes against this book's main aim. It is the contention of this book, that in each of the aforementioned phases, visibility and agency were ever-present, taking different cultural forms, particularly literary production, but were often overlooked. In other words, the *Bidun* have been speaking for a long time, but who was listening, or for that matter reading?

An approach which limits knowledge of the *Bidun* to the external political and socio-economic factors, as highlighted throughout the chapter, subjects the *Bidun* to the very exclusionary forces that have upheld the impasse. It is an approach that presents the *Bidun* as a social group that can be understood, contained and controlled solely in terms of legal, sociological or anthropological considerations.

In the scarce studies where agency has been approached, the emphasis is on the collective agency of the *Bidun* as social and political interlocutors within Kuwaiti society creating 'networks of solidarity', or as 'transnational actors' historically influencing the region's geopolitical structure (Beaugrand 2010). What is often left out in the limited approaches to agency is the personal and singular narratives articulated in cultural production, which often operate within different spheres than the human rights, anthropological, international relations or legal discourses. Thus, it becomes a question of accessibility, readership and interpretation; who reads works by *Bidun* writers? What works are read? And how are they read?

Beyond the descriptive

Often, when the sphere of literary production and the social sciences intersect, conclusions regarding questions of the cultural identity of marginalized groups, which require a different set of tools than those offered by the social sciences, are formulated with a socio-anthropological imprint. An obvious example is Faris al-Wuqayyan's characterization of what he terms a distinct '*Bidun* Culture', which arose out of the causal relationship between the *Bidun* and their political and socio-economic positioning (al-Wuqayyan 2009). He writes:

> These government policies, conflicting outlooks in dealing with the stateless, the many enforced changes in the group's label, the increased restrictions to their civil rights, along with the rejection of their historical presence in

> spite of contrary evidence has created a present identity crisis for stateless individuals. The crisis is accompanied with psychological symptoms such as restlessness, pessimism, lack of confidence, anxiety, depression, obsessive-compulsive disorders and aggression among other things.
>
> (al-Wuqayyan 2009)

Bidun culture is then defined as 'a culture of deep feelings of exclusion and loss of the main components of cultural identity', which in turn induces defiant reactions such as 'drawing graffiti, misuse of public space, burglary, crime, brawling and a general sense of cynicism' (al-Wuqayyan 2009). As a way to cement this characterization of *Bidun* culture, al-Wuqayyan refers to the literary production of the *Bidun* as a literature necessarily reflecting those conditions. He adds, what characterizes *Bidun* writers' works is 'a melancholic tone and a tragic use of language that almost always revolves around the loss of rights and the dispossession of identity' (al-Wuqayyan 2009).

Through such unscrutinized characterizations of '*Bidun* culture', the term 'culture' is used as a substantial feature of the community that, as Arjun Appadurai argues, brings 'culture back into the discursive space of race' (Appadurai 1996:12). At the same time, as Appadurai suggests, this substantialization of culture appears to 'discourage attention to the worldviews and agency of those who are marginalized or dominated' (12). Thus, such totalizing characterizations subjects the community to the very exclusionary forces that keep them entirely containable and perceivable.

The approach to *Bidun* literature as a means of extrapolating certain notions of cultural identity poses a question that is central to this book, namely, the interplay or tension between an approach advanced by the demands and concerns of the social sciences and one suggested by a critical engagement with the literary works. The *Bidun*, as discussed in the chapter, have been approached from an international relations perspective as transnational stateless tribal agents (Beaugrand 2010), a sociopolitical and anthropological perspective as marginalized disenfranchised *Badu* (Human Rights Watch 1995; Longva 2006; al-Nakib 2014) and a legal perspective as dispossessed stateless individuals in relation to international Human Rights Law and conventions (al-Anezi 1989, 1994; al-Wuqayyan 2009; Blitz and Lynch 2011). While these descriptive approaches are important in addressing any issue related to any study on the *Bidun*, they simply do not suffice.

These approaches are currently what constitute knowledge on the *Bidun* issue and consequently on the *Bidun* as a people. This chapter, so far as a first step, aimed to highlight the ways in which the issue has been historically conceived and presented in both local and academic discourses. Yet when it comes to reading the cultural production of the community, literary texts do not necessarily strictly operate within the parameters imposed by the considerations of the sociological or anthropological models. Literary works, as will be discussed throughout the chapters of the book, often negotiate and reconsider the parameters and fixities on which the rubric of aforementioned models is structured.

I argue in this book for another type of knowledge, one that, although informed by sociological or anthropological models, is not restricted by it. It aims to broaden the categories of representation through reading literary and cultural articulations that go beyond mere correspondence to material realities of the condition of statelessness or anthropological considerations. In doing so, the book attempts to keep a distance from prevalent practices within scholarship on the Gulf, where restricting knowledge production to descriptive models is only a symptom of a wider pathology.

Dominant approaches to studying societies in the Gulf often involve a methodical process of panoramic mapping of different groups ordered along anthropological or sociological units of analysis: national, sectarian (Sunni-Shiites), tribal, sociopolitical (Badu-Haḍhar) and according to territory of origin (Ajam, Huwela, Najdis, Africans). In *The Persian Gulf in Modern Times* (2014), Lawrence G. Potter emphasizes the need for a new approach in Gulf studies outside of the dominant paradigms that have historically defined the field: the role of the British empire in the region; the oil industry; and rentier state approaches (Potter 2014:1). One of the ways in which this is surpassed, according to the volume's editor, is by focusing on 'Peoples of the Gulf'. As he puts it: 'One aim of this volume is to highlight and recover the history of groups who played an important role historically but have been excluded in the national narratives promulgated by ruling dynasties' (11). While the edited book does not present a study of the *Bidun*, it approaches other communities such as the Baloch, those of African descent and the Hawala, which are described as 'a mysterious group of Arabs who migrated from Arabia to Iran starting around the eighteenth century and later returned to play important roles in places like Bahrain and the UAE' (13). Later, this mysterious people are finally exhibited to scholars on the Gulf.

In the case of the *Bidun*, as in Beaugrand's foundational work, a complete charting of the Kuwaiti social construct is presented as prerequisite for the *Bidun*'s placement in the margins of Bedouin societies. In her analysis, Beaugrand draws a complete panoramic exhibition of Kuwaiti society for the interested reader. The first step utilizes the *Haḍhar/Badu* divide as a primary principle. Within each subgroup, social hierarchies are presented. Within the *Haḍhar*, and '[a]t the top of the social hierarchy' following the al-Sabah, are the tribes from Najd along with others who claim autochthony, Zubara, and Shiite merchant families. The lower classes of the inner city included 'craftspeople, clothmakers, and owners of coffee or grocery shops' along with the pearl-divers (bahara). These are followed by slaves of African descent.

After presenting a social hierarchy, the Haḍhar are then further subdivided along sectarian cleavages. 'On the Sunni side', the community includes those from the Sunni parts of Iran (the Baloch), families with lineages tracing to Hejaz, and Sunni families from Iraq. 'On the Shiite side', the community includes those from Persian descent (*Ajam*), *Hasawis* (from al-Hasa) and the *Baharna* (from Bahrain). The Badu are then categorized into southern tribes including the 'Sunni Ajman, Dawasir, and Mutair' and southern tribes of Zafir, the ʿanaza, and the Shammar which 'include both Sunni and Shiite members'. (50). While Beaugrand's overall work knowledgeably accomplishes to demonstrate the constructed and contingent nature of national identity at large, subnational divisions aren't offered the same scrutiny.

In other more cultural approaches to Gulf societies, such as *The Tribal Modern* (2014) by Miriam Cooke, the author is also keen on producing definite knowledge of existing social hierarchies based on what seems an offhand analysis of Gulf societies. The 'formerly egalitarian tribal society' of the Gulf, has as a result of capitalism and globalization, split into five main 'tribal classes'. At the top of the class pyramid are the ruling families, followed by tribes who stayed during the hunger years and established alliances with the ruling families. The third class are those with Persian connections, being either the Ajam or the *Hawala*. Fourthly, are the ʿ*abid*, or slaves, who remain lower than the previous three classes of citizens. The *Bidun* are conveniently placed at the bottom of the social hierarchy of Gulf societies.

Micheal Herb's invaluable website Kuwaitpoliticaldatabase.com, a comprehensive database providing information on politics in Kuwait, offers a prime example of this urge for the panoramic map. The database presents information on more than 3500 political participants in Kuwait's political history. The names of the local politicians are immediately followed by their sectarian affiliation, then tribal, finally followed by political affiliation and key voting record. While sect and tribal affiliations play a vital role in the local political scene, it simply does not suffice for a more nuanced understanding of the complex political dynamics. Any understanding of the political agents within the local scene is continually pinned back to the panoramic grid of sect, tribe, origin.

The panoramic map, when necessary for a macroanalysis of Gulf societies, becomes more productive when approached from a more relational perspective as in Khaldun al-Naqib's analysis of society in the Gulf and Arab Peninsula. Al-Naqib acknowledges the contingent nature of societal categories and the role of the ruling families in manipulating these categories. Ruling families 'govern by means of unofficial corporations and by manipulating with the social forces under new division of labour'. These 'corporations' include the tribal establishment, the merchants, the sectarian establishment, the religious establishment: the leaders of the religious movements, the middle classes and the workers (al-Naqib 1990:106). In his discussion of the tribal establishment for example, al-Naqib acknowledges how the ruling families 'gradually transformed [tribal clusters] into clearly organized interest groups or corporations'. (63).

This type of societal analysis, where people are primarily understood anthropologically in terms of origins, kinship ties and sectarian affinities, can be attributed, in part, to what the anthropologist Johannes Fabian calls a 'denial of coevalness'; a dominant methodological approach within anthropology; 'a persistent and systematic tendency to place the referent(s) of anthropology in a Time other than the present of the producer of anthropological discourse' (Fabian 1983:31). For example, in Potter's introduction to *Persian Gulf in History* (2009), where he asks

> [w]ho, then, are the *Khalijis*? Historically, they are the descendants of the Ichthyophagi, the 'fish eaters' that lived all around the coasts of East Africa, the Gulf ('Erythraean Sea'), southern Iran, and India who were mentioned

> by Greek and Latin writers. Like the Ichthyophagi, they share a similar lifestyle but not a common identity, except perhaps in the eyes of outsiders.
>
> (Potter 2009:12)

The language used to describe these 'fish eaters' names the origins of a people according to ancient Greek and Latin nomenclatures. An underlying assumption involved in these works is that these societies can be measured by this simple grid, with systematic ontological divisions of *Badu-Haḍhar* and Sunni-Shiʿi among others without attention to subtle nuance after nuance that becomes in many cases the rule and not the exception.

It is also useful to draw on Omar al-Shehabi's critique of the colonial legacy, still very dominant in Gulf Studies which posits societal 'primordial cleavages' as the main units of analysis of Gulf societies. Dating it back to Lorimer's *Gazetteer*, Al-Shehabi questions 'the epistemic validity of the ethnosectarian gaze in Bahrain and the Gulf' which continues to be adopted 'largely uncritically' within recent scholarship on the Gulf (Al-Shehabi 2017).

The idea of the panoramic map in the academic approaches to studying societies in the Gulf is also informed by critiques of orientalism, particularly Timothy Mitchell's *Colonizing Egypt*. Mitchell discusses the role of the panoramic point of view in the representation the Orient in European 'world exhibitions' as an entirely containable and visible whole completely separated from its observer. The orientalist or traveller in the orient needed to 'separate oneself from the world and thus constitute it as a panorama … which required what was now called a "point of view", a position set apart and outside' (Mitchell 1988:24). The panoramic point of view has also been historically associated with the imperial gaze and the surveillance and control of colonial spaces. In their writings, European travellers 'desire for a commanding view that could provide a sweeping visual mastery of the scene' (Ashcroft et al., 2013:208–9). Lorimer's aforementioned *(Gaze)etter* is a foundational text in this regard.

In *Home and Homeland* Linda Layne criticizes the image of the Middle East as a 'mosaic' of ahistoric distinct social groups that 'keep their unique identities and cultures while contributing to a larger structure' (Layne 1994:4). In this mosaic model, collective identities of societal groups are defined ontologically by birth and are assumed to be static and easily identifiable.

Another key assumption to the portrayal of the Middle East as a timeless mosaic is 'the presence of an observer located outside the system in order to see the pattern' (6).

The incessant urge to map, compartmentalize and situate subgroups according to the aforementioned categories restricts knowledge on 'peoples of the Gulf' to essentialized terms. This book is a preliminary investigation into how a literary critical approach to *Bidun* literature could potentially be discussed outside of such assumptions. A study of *Bidun* literature opens up possibilities for a relational and contextual type of knowledge that enquires into the intrinsic articulations of belonging, presence and self-positionality through complex modes of literary and cultural affiliation, beyond official acts of absencing, labelling and ontological representations. In presenting the body of literature analytically and critically, I hope that this book, and some of the tools it proposes, will be useful to understanding how a different type of knowledge on the 'people of the Gulf', more broadly, can be produced.

2

A literary community's struggle for presence

Comprehensive studies addressing the general phenomenon of *Bidun* literature as a literary collectivity have been few and far between. *Bidun* writers have regularly been mentioned in literary criticism and comparative studies but not under the nomenclature of '*Bidun* literature' (al-ʿAbwini 1982; al-Bazei 2001; al-Farsi 2004; al-Juwayyir 2006; Yusuf 2009; Ali 2010; al-Maqaliḥ 2011). As a term, '*Bidun* literature' was first coined by the Kuwaiti novelist Walid al-Rujayb in *al-Watan* newspaper in an article dated 1994 (Salam Ya Kuwait 2011). Generally, it has been casually used to refer to the works of *Bidun* writers.

One of the obvious limitations of approaching *Bidun* literature as a collectivity is that it is based solely on a legal condition without regard to basic differences in the writers' gender, age or affinities to literary schools. *Bidun* writers have been studied in a number of ways but seldom as *Bidun* writers. Sulayman al-Flayyiḥ, who in 1976 was the first *Bidun* poet ever to publish a poetry collection, has been framed within the phenomenon of a Bedouin literary modernism (al-ʿAbwini 1982; al-Ghaythi 2017). Saʿdiyya Mufarriḥ's poetry has been analysed in relation to issues of gender and estrangement (al-Farsi 2004). Other *Bidun* writers have been approached in terms of their thematic expression[1] while others according to their generational association.[2] The diversity of approaches highlights how the literary collective is anything but self-evident.

Within the circle of *Bidun* writers, usage of the term itself is not yet settled. When asked about being a *Bidun* writer, Muhammad al-Nabhan responds, 'I belong to poetry alone and far from established names and terms' (al-Zuhairi 2007). Al-Nabhan finds that such a categorization has the potential of reducing the aesthetic appreciation of the works of *Bidun* writers. As al-Nabhan puts it, 'I am not in favor of such a categorization as it may burden the poet to direct his poem towards purely intellectual, political or social issues without necessary attention to the poetic aspects' (al-Zuhairi 2007).

Similarly, Saʿdiyya Mufarriḥ does not necessarily identify with this term, flatly rejecting '*Bidun* writer' as it is 'void of meaning' (Mufarriḥ 2011:109). For Mufarriḥ, individual creativity is not directly related to her statelessness. The *Bidun* issue in her view is not necessarily a 'cause to fight for', rather it is 'a problem' that needs to be solved (Mufarriḥ 2011:109).

Mufarriḥ also worries that asserting a *Bidun* literary identity implies an exclusion from national literature, an idea which reiterates the general official exclusion of the *Bidun* based on their lack of citizenship rights. Rather, Mufarriḥ emphasizes emotive notions of belonging. To her, being a Kuwaiti is not solely a matter of official documents; it is an emotional attachment that is independent of official recognition. She writes:

> Yes, I am without citizenship, but fortunately I am not without a homeland. In my opinion, there is a difference between a homeland, which is an attachment … a sentiment … a coexistence … and before all else, a faith and a belief that is firm and true … and between citizenship, which is an official document that demonstrates to others that its holder belongs to this or that state. I exist with all my consciousness and all my belief as a Kuwaiti, and, personally, do not need a document to authenticate this feeling, even as my need for the document in facilitating my daily affairs becomes greater. In any case, I have never, in my whole life, stopped before this partial detail, and have never made it an excuse not to achieve. In life, luckily, there are many options that do not require the document in order for us to continue practicing hope.
> (al-Khuwayldi 2012)

On the other hand, the *Bidun* poet Dikhil Khalifa insists on emphasizing *Bidun* literature as a valid literary collectivity within national literature. To Khalifa, being *Bidun* is a mark of an epistemic privilege that allows *Bidun* writers to enjoy a distinct poetic identity unique in its themes and styles of expression (Salam Ya Kuwait 2011). At the same time, *Bidun* writers are 'more creative' within national literary circles and are 'leading the poetic scene' in Kuwait (al-Jaffal 2011; Mufarriḥ 2011:109). Thus, *Bidun* literature is presented as a literary collectivity that is inclusive of Kuwaiti literature and a main component contributing to the Kuwaiti literary scene. Similarly, the *Bidun* novelist Nasir al-Ẓafiri, in an event commemorating his works in 2017, remarked: 'I will fight until the last day of my life for this literature [*Bidun* literature] to remain Kuwaiti' (Suwaydan 2018).

In both views, there seem to be an emphasis on rejecting any form of inclusion-exclusion binary that limits *Bidun* writers' choices of self-definition. This rejection of the Kuwaiti versus *Bidun* binary acknowledges both terms to emphasize emotive belonging to a country of residence while still acknowledging an experience of exclusion from it. In political discourse, this is reflected in the *Bidun* activists' adoption of the term 'the Kuwaiti *Biduns*' to acknowledge both conditions simultaneously marking the *Bidun*'s insistence on creating intrinsic spaces of self-definition.

A shared struggle for presence

The act of writing for many *Bidun* writers carries a certain sense of urgency as it counters a state of unrecognized existence and an officially sanctioned institutional act of absencing. What is meant by institutional acts of absencing are those specific acts of exclusion related to the materialities of publishing, access to spaces of cultural exchange, and questions of inclusion and exclusion from literary histories and anthologies. This urge to defy an absencing act by engaging in literary production and cultural visibility will be examined as a powerful binding force bringing *Bidun* writers together. An exhaustive study of the political economy of publishing, or a detailed analysis of the power dynamics of the literary field in Kuwait, is beyond the scope of this chapter. What will be emphasized is how *Bidun* writers actively negotiate intrinsic affiliative cultural networks and spaces of representation.

In an article published in *al-Wasat* newspaper,[3] the *Bidun* short story writer Karim al-Hazzaʿ writes about what he terms 'the poets of absence'. It is a term denoting those *Bidun* poets, the likes of Ahmad al-Nabhan, Saʿad Farḥan, Fahad al-Rudaini and Ali al-Ṣafi who have completely fallen from the cultural scene for different reasons and whose works have been 'devoured by the fires of absence'. As al-Hazzaʿ puts it, Ahmad al-Nabhan 'forgot how to write', Saʿad Farḥan 'soaked in his tragedy', Fahad al-Rudaini 'got lost in his estrangement' while Ali al-Ṣafi 'departed on the day of Eid' (al-Hazzaʿ 2012).

In introducing these *Bidun* poets, al-Hazza' positions them within a wider generational cluster: the poets of the 1990s in Kuwait. The 1990s generation, writes al-Hazza' was 'mostly made up of the "*Bidun*"', who '*struggled to affirm their presence* in face of the pressures practiced by official cultural institutions' (al-Hazza' 2012 emphasis added). Yet this 'struggle for presence', al-Hazza' argues, was eased by the advent of digital publishing. New technological developments and the internet, continues al-Hazza', 'served as an excellent breathing space for some of this generation's sons, especially the *Bidun*' (al-Hazza' 2012). Yet even with this unprecedented access to these new spaces of cultural presence (i.e. digital publication), many *Bidun* poets still disappeared from the cultural scene altogether for different reasons. There is more to the 'fires of absence' than matters of accessibility. Al-Hazza' directly relates the poets' disappearance to the materialities of everyday life.

In mentioning the biographies of the absent poets, al-Hazza' is keen to present the poets' daily reality as *Bidun* as a default condition of absencing that they are born into. Al-Nabhan was 'born in Kuwait in 1969 … earned his high school diploma … and was unable to continue his education, despite his academic distinction, because he was *Bidun*'. When asked about why he stopped writing, Ahmad al-Nabhan replied sarcastically, 'I don't even know how to hold a pen in my hand anymore' (al-Hazza' 2012). Similarly, Fahad al-Rudaini decided to emigrate to the United States after the Iraqi invasion of Kuwait.

What needs to be stressed in al-Hazza''s article is how the presence of *Bidun* writers by way of publication is depicted as a struggle against official institutionalized acts of absencing that are both political and cultural. In this context, the act of publishing becomes a form substantiating, affirming and articulating a presence for *Bidun* writers. Also apparent in the article is yet another form of struggle for presence through an act of remembrance of other absent *Bidun* poets. This act turns into another, perhaps more potent, struggle for presence. One may ask: If al-Hazza', a *Bidun* writer, hadn't taken on this task of keeping the memory of the absent *Bidun* poets and their works alive, then who would have? It is a double struggle for presence: in the wilful act of writing and publishing and in the act of making present other absent poets by writing about them. Thus, this idea of a 'shared struggle of presence' against the 'fires of cultural absence' will be approached as an intrinsic lens in which a *Bidun* literary community can be envisaged.

Materialities of cultural production: Venues of publication

An overview of the key historical instances related to *Bidun* writers' experience with publishing cannot be fully condensed into a schematic narrative as the experiences vary and span a period of more than thirty-five years. Yet what is of particular interest are the instances of enabling collective publishing by *Bidun* writers, first by local specifically targeted initiatives and second by the establishment of publishing houses by *Bidun* writers themselves.

As highlighted earlier in the book, one of the main challenges involved in researching this body of literature is the limited circulation of the early published works of *Bidun* writers. This is primarily due to *Bidun* writers' particular experiences with publishing outlets. Early venues of publishing for most *Bidun* poets of the 1990s generation were made possible through local journalism. *Bidun* poets have always been highly engaged with the cultural pages of local newspapers. At a time when only five newspapers were officially allowed in Kuwait, prior to the 2006 Law on Press and Publication, *Bidun* poets were involved with each of the five newspapers' cultural pages. Saʿdiyya Mufarriḥ worked at *al-Waṭan* newspaper and then served as head of the cultural page of *al-Qabas* newspaper. Nasir al-Ẓafiri and Saʿad Farhan worked as cultural editors at *al-Waṭan* newspaper, Dikhil Khalifa worked at *al-Anba*ʾ newspaper and later in *Awan* newspaper, Ali al-Ṣafi worked as a cultural editor at *al-Rai al-ʿAm* and Khalaf al-Aslami at *al-Siyasa* newspaper. This active engagement presented many *Bidun* writers with access to publishing opportunities in local newspapers. Dikhil Khalifa and Muhammad al-Nabhan both first started publishing in the readers' pages of local newspapers (al-Nabhan 2013; Khalifa 2013).

Early publications of works by *Bidun* writers (poetry collections, short stories, novels) were mostly privately published by the writers themselves who had limited access to local or Arab publishing houses. Examples of privately published early collections include Sulayman al-Flayyiḥ's *al-Ghinaʿ fi Ṣaḥraʿ al-ʿAlam* (Singing in the Deserts of Agony) (1979), *Aḥzan al-Badu al-Ruḥḥal* (The Sorrows of the Journeying Bedouins) (1980), *Thiʿab al-Layali* (Night Wolves) (1993), Nasir al-Ẓafiri's *Walimat al-Qamar* (The Feast of the Moon) (1990), which was published in Nicosia, Cyprus and Dikhil Khalifa's *ʿUyun ʿAla Bawwabat al-Manfa* (Eyes on the Gate of Exile) (1993).

In 1992, one of the most significant specifically targeted publishing projects for *Bidun* writers was the *Dar Suʿad al-Ṣabaḥ's* (Suʿad al-Ṣabaḥ's Publishing House) initiative run by the poet and member of the Kuwaiti ruling family Suʿad al-Ṣabaḥ. The initiative was successful in giving many previously unpublished *Bidun* writers wider circulation and visibility in local and Arab cultural scenes. The initiative was then headed by two writers who were, at the time, *Bidun*: Ali al-Masudi (now a Qatari citizen) and Ahmad al-Dusari (now a Bahraini citizen). The project encouraged other *Bidun* writers to publish their works with an added financial incentive (Khalifa 2013). Titles published by the project include Saʿdiyya Mufarriḥ's *Akhir al-Ḥalimin Kan* (The Last Dreamer) (1992), Jassim al-Shimmiri's *Ummi, ʿAynan wa Bariq* (The Sparkling Eyes of My Mother) (1992), Ali al-Masudi's *Mamlakat al-Shams* (The Kingdom of the Son) (1992), Nasir al-Ẓafiri's second edition of *Walimat al-Qamar* (The Feast of the Moon) (1992). In a personal interview, Muhammad al-Nabhan recalls refusing the opportunity to publish his work under the sponsorship of Suʿad al-Ṣabaḥ. Retrospectively, he attributes his refusal to an acute sensitivity towards any form of quasi-official patronage since the publishing house was owned by a member of the ruling family. Also, in retrospect, the short story writer Jassim al-Shimmiri describes the short-sighted approach taken by the initiative as it did not truly adopt *Bidun* writers in the long term (al-Shimmiri 2014). It is also worth noting that in 2014, following the death of the Sulayman al-Fullayih (who gained Saudi citizenship), Suʿad al-Ṣabaḥ's Publishing House printed a volume of his complete works.

Other possible publishing venues included Arab publishing houses in Beirut (*Dar al-Jadid*, Arab Scientific Publishers), Cairo (*al-Hayʾa al-Misriyya al-ʿAmma li-l-Kitab* and *Dar Sharqiyyat*) and Damascus (*Dar al-Mada*). Yet these opportunities were mainly restricted to established and previously published *Bidun* poets such as Saʿdiyya Mufarriḥ, Dikhil Khalifa and later Mona Kareem. It is worth noting how within an Arab context, the intricacies of the local are overpowered by a wider Arab discourse. One example is Mona Kareem's poetry collection titled *Ghiyab bi Aṣabiʿ Mabtura* (Absence with Severed Fingers) published by *Dar Sharqiyyat* in Cairo in 2004. In the collection, the Egyptian publisher changed the title of one of the poems originally titled '1965', a significant year relating to Kuwaiti citizenship law, to '1956', a year relevant to a wider Arab readership (Kareem 2014b).

Another initiative at the local level was led by the publishing outlet *al-ʿAlamiya li-l-Nashr wa-l-tawziʿ* (Global Publishing and Distribution), headed by Nasir al-Subai. The initiative published the poetry collections of the *Bidun* poets Ali al-Ṣafi and Ahmad al-Nabhan in 1998 and 1999, respectively. Both writers received twenty copies of their work and no financial compensation (Khalifa 2013). Despite these two collections' influence on the local literary scene (Ali al-Ṣafi's work will be discussed in this context in detail later), the two poetry collections were limited in circulation and have not been reprinted since. Other local initiatives for young *Bidun* poets included *Dar Qirṭas*' Fahad al-ʿAskar initiative for young creative writers which published Mona Kareem's first poetry collection *Naharat Maghsula bi Maʾ al-ʿAṭash* (Mornings Washed by Waters of Thirst) (2002).

With the advent of digital publishing, the dynamics of publishing naturally shifted. Online literary magazines and online cultural forums provided new spaces of visibility, cultural exchange and publishing for *Bidun* writers. As this was a crucial turning point, a survey of the digital publishing scene will be provided below in the discussion of spaces of cultural exchange and a more detailed analysis will be offered in Chapter 6.

Returning to print publishing, two important publishing projects have been established by *Bidun* writers to publish their works and the works of other *Bidun* poets. First was the establishment of *Dar Masʿa* by Muhammad al-Nabhan in 2008. While not exclusively for *Bidun* writers, *Dar Masʿa* has become their main publishing venue. More than ten works by six *Bidun* writers were published between 2006 and 2015.[4] In addition to publishing the works of well-established *Bidun* writers such as Muhammad al-Nabhan, Saʿdiyya Mufarriḥ, Dikhil Khalifa and Nasir al-Ẓafiri, *Dar Masʿa* became a space for young *Bidun* writers to publish their works, with examples such as Hanadi al-Shimmiri's novella *Ṣafih* (A House Made of Tin) (2015) and Shahad al-Faḍli's poetry collection titled *Faṣila Manquṭa* (Semicolon) (2015).

The second publishing house established by *Bidun* writers is *Dar Masarat*, which was established in 2014 by *Bidun* writers Dikhil Khalifa, Jassim al-Shimmiri and Saʿad Karim. While not exclusively a publishing house for *Bidun* writers, it provides an accessible space for young *Bidun* writers to publish their works. Works by *Bidun* writers published through *Dar Masarat* include Ashwaq al-Khalifa's *Jahraʾiyya* (2015) and Jassim al-Shemmiri's *Yatasalaqun Ajlisu Munzawiyyan li Aghfu* (They Ascend. I Sit in Solitude to Sleep) (2015).

These key examples provide an understanding of the historical specificity of *Bidun* writers' experience in publishing. Most early publications of *Bidun* writers were published collectively through specifically targeted initiatives, namely, Suʿad al-Ṣabaḥ's Publishing House's initiative in 1992 and Global Publishing and Distribution's initiative in 1999. Later, *Bidun* writers established publishing houses such as *Dar Masʿa* in 2008 and *Dar Masarat* in 2015 that provided accessible venues of publication for young and established *Bidun* writers alike.

Placement in national literary histories and anthologies

Another debate relating to the institutional act of absencing, or forgetting in this case, is that of the placement of *Bidun* writers within national literary histories and anthologies. A detailed study of the question of placement of *Bidun* writers will be presented in the following chapter. The following section will provide a cursory overview of how the dialectics of an extrinsic official absencing and the struggle for a presence play out in writing national literary histories and anthologies.

The placement of *Bidun* writers within national literature is ambiguous, to say the least. In national literary histories and anthologies they may be both included in some and excluded from others.[5] The *al-Babtain Glossary of Contemporary Arab Poets* (1995) perhaps is an apt example of this ambiguous inclusion/exclusion status of *Bidun* writers. Profiles of the *Bidun* poets Ahmad al-Nabhan (al-Babtain 1995a:258), Dikhil Khalifa (al-Babtain 1995a:312), Saʿad Farhan (al-Babtain 1995b:514), Saʿdiyya Mufarriḥ (al-Babtain 1995b:522) and Sulayman al-Flayyiḥ are included in the glossary which is arranged in alphabetical order. However, they are entirely absent from the table of contents which is organized according to nationality (al-Babtain 1995f:340). In other words, *Bidun* writers do 'exist' in the actual content of the dictionary as published contemporary Arab poets but are officially unrecognized by the national table of contents, which perhaps mirrors the *Bidun*'s political and social status as unrecognized residents.

As to their placement within national literary histories, it is important to mention that most national literary histories were written in, or concerned with, a period that precedes the emergence of the *Bidun* issue as a social and political phenomenon, namely, before 1985. However, the most recent comprehensive work on Kuwaiti literary history, Sulayman al-Shaṭṭi's *Poetry in Kuwait* (2007), gives a general sense of the ambiguity of the placement of *Bidun* writers within a national narrative. Al-Shaṭṭi does not omit *Bidun* writers from the national narrative but rather places them in a separate final chapter under the title of '*al-Adab al-Mujawer*' (Adjacent Literature). This placement only compounds the question of belonging. The official stateless status of *Bidun* writers is transposed to a literary statelessness situated in a convoluted conception of adjacency.

Both cases provided above attest to the particular paradoxical position of *Bidun* writers within national literary histories. They are outside and inside at the same time; inside the book but outside the national table of contents, inside the geographic space, yet outside, or 'adjacent' to, the national space. Such an in-between position has allowed *Bidun* poets to articulate their own presence within literary histories and anthologies, national or otherwise. One key example is Saʿdiyya Mufarriḥ's Kuwaiti literary history and anthology titled *The Cameleers of Clouds and Estrangement* (2007). In this literary history and anthology, which will be the subject of discussion in the next chapter, Mufarriḥ dedicates her attention to the contributions of *Bidun* writers presenting them as constituents of national literature and an organic extension of the national literary history narrative.

Spaces of cultural exchange

Similar to *Bidun* writers' peculiar placement within national literary histories, their relationship with official spaces of cultural exchange is also contentious. This ambiguous relationship urges *Bidun* writers to forge alternate spaces of cultural exchange outside of official circles. What is meant by spaces of cultural exchange are those spaces (both physical and virtual) where writers gather, exchange thoughts and organize cultural events. One of the main spaces, which illustrates the general attitude of the official cultural institution towards the

Bidun, is the Writers' Association *Rabiṭat al-Udaba'* (henceforth referred to as *Rabiṭa*), a government funded civil society. In many ways, the *Rabiṭa*'s attitude towards *Bidun* writers in Kuwait followed the general official governmental stance towards the *Bidun* in Kuwait. It is also important to note how such spaces are necessarily gendered in that women writers, in particular, confront other forms of implicit exclusion beyond the official. Surveying a number of historical markers can shed light on the relationship between *Bidun* writers and the *Rabiṭa*.

The *Rabiṭa* was first officially established in 1965 under the name of *Rabiṭat al-Udaba' al-Kuwaytiyyin* (The Kuwaiti Writers Association). However, the founders opted to change the name to *Rabiṭat al-Udaba' fi-l-Kuwait* (The Writers Association of Kuwait) to allow broader participation from Arab poets residing in Kuwait (Mufarrih 1997a). Prior to the Iraqi invasion and the shift in governmental policy, *Bidun* writers were actively engaged in the *Rabiṭa* and were accepted for what they were. One of the most important marks of acceptance, which will be discussed in further detail in Chapter 5, is the *Rabiṭa's* enthusiastic reception of the *Bidun* poet Sulayman al-Flayyiḥ in 1976 at the annual poetry festival. Al-Flayyiḥ was not received as a *Bidun* poet *per se* as the *Bidun* issue did not carry much resonance at the time, but as a promising Bedouin poet writing modern Arabic poetry in *Fuṣḥa*. Following his first participation, al-Flayyiḥ regularly contributed to the annual poetry festival up until 1982. In addition, al-Flayyiḥ was a regular contributor to the *Rabiṭa*'s literary periodical *Majallat al-Bayan* between 1976 and 1982.[6]

For many years after that, a number of *Bidun* writers such as Dikhil Khalifa, Karim Hazza' and Ahmad al-Nabhan were regular weekly attendees at the *Rabiṭa's* events (Khalifa 2013). Along with the weekly gatherings, *Bidun* poets Dihkil Khalifa and Ahmad al-Nabhan participated in poetry nights organized by the *Rabiṭa* (al-Nabhan 2013). As the *Bidun* issue developed into a more visible social and political phenomenon, formalized in exclusionary official policy, the welcoming stance of the *Rabiṭa* shifted.

The *Rabiṭa*'s stance towards *Bidun* writers took a drastic shift following the Iraqi invasion of Kuwait in 1991. Even though *Bidun* writers were never officially and explicitly denied participation in the *Rabiṭa*'s events, they were denied active membership cards, which limited their engagement. In 1992, the *Rabiṭa* held a poetry night to commemorate the anniversary of the liberation of Kuwait in which *Bidun* poets participated. Yet this participation was a contentious matter within the *Rabiṭa*, as the repercussions of the Iraqi invasion complicated the *Bidun* writers' already vulnerable position. Muhammad al-Nabhan recalls that the Iraqi novelist and long-time organizer in the *Rabiṭa*, Faysal al-Saʿad 'fought for our participation' in the event. At many times, the official stance of the *Rabiṭa* towards the *Bidun* was not final and was a matter of contention counterbalanced by sympathetic influential figures within the organization, such as Khalifa al-Wuqayyan and Sulayman al-Khulayfi (al-Nabhan 2013).

For another generation of *Bidun* poets, the ambiguous relationship with the *Rabiṭa* persisted. One example is the *Rabiṭa*'s establishment of Layla al-Uthman's Prize for Young Writers of Fiction in 2004. Under the auspices of the *Rabiṭa*, the organizers initially restricted the call for applications to young Kuwaiti writers. This was later overturned to include *Bidun* writers as well, after *Bidun* poets exerted pressure on the prize board (Kareem 2014b).

The general non-accepting stance of the *Rabiṭa* prompted responses from *Bidun* writers. Commenting on his relationship with the *Rabiṭa*, Dikhil Khalifa says, 'I do not recognize any institution which associates the creative act with citizenship' (al-Khuwayldi 2012). Similarly, Muhammad al-Nabhan maintains that 'the *Rabiṭa* does not represent writers in Kuwait' as it is not open to diversity of literary expression and is xenophobic towards non-Kuwaiti Arab communities (al-Jaffal 2012). Nasir al-Ẓafiri mentions his resentment towards the ineffectual role of the *Rabiṭa* as 'the only breathing space for writers', which 'refused to organise any cultural event related to young *Bidun* writers'. The *Rabiṭa*'s excuse was that it considered itself a civil society association that abided by the rules of the ministry of social affairs and work which did not recognize the *Bidun* (al-Hindal 2009). Mona Kareem highlights what she calls a 'double marginalization', of a political and an aesthetic kind. Firstly, because of their 'illegal' status and secondly because of the *Bidun* poets' adoption of the modernist form of *Qaṣidat al-Nathr* (the prose poem), which was considered radical within the circles of the *Rabiṭa* (Kareem 2014b).

In light of such explicit and implicit distancing from the official institution, *Bidun* writers worked on establishing other spaces of cultural exchange, or 'breathing spaces', outside of the official radar. Most important of all is the establishment of *Multaqa al-Thulatha*ʾ (The Tuesday Gathering) in 1996. The

Tuesday Gathering, founded by Muhammad al-Sa'id (a Kuwaiti writer), Dikhil Khalifa (a *Bidun* poet), Nadi Ḥafidh (an Egyptian writer), Karim Hazza' (a *Bidun* short story writer) and Falaḥ Dabsha (a Kuwaiti poet), boasted a diverse body of Kuwaiti, *Bidun* and Arab expatriate members who felt the need to create an alternative, sometimes oppositional, space of cultural exchange (Khalifa 2013). It is important to mention that the Tuesday Gathering is not immune to exclusionary practices and internal contention between its members.

The focus of the activities of the Tuesday Gathering was different in approach to that of the *Rabiṭa* as it focused on a wider audience of Kuwaiti, *Bidun* and Arab expatriate communities. Yet with time, and as Khalifa puts it, Kuwaiti writers were slowly 'lured back by the *Rabiṭa*, and we, the *Bidun*, were left with Syrian and Egyptian poets' (Khalifa 2013). One of the Kuwaiti founders, Muhammad al-Sa'id, attempted to persuade the members of the Tuesday Gathering to hold their events within the physical premises of the *Rabiṭa* but was unsuccessful as they were adamant about operating outside the official institution (Khalifa 2013).

As opposed to the fixed meeting space of the *Rabiṭa*, the Tuesday Gathering's events were held in various spaces such as cafes, the personal office of the Kuwaiti novelist Ismail Fahad and the campuses of social associations such as the Gulf Theatre Troupe's building, the Women's Cultural Association and the Graduates' Association. At times, the Tuesday Gathering had to stop its activities, sometimes for more than three years, primarily due to lack of funding and lack of a meeting space. As to its funding, it was initially supported by donations from the members and at times by outside funding. In 2008, the Kuwaiti merchant Anwar al-Qatami financially sponsored the Tuesday Gathering without imposing any conditions (Khalifa 2013).

With the advent of Arabic online literary magazines in the latter part of the 1990s, new spaces of virtual cultural exchange opened up to *Bidun* writers. Initially, online literary magazines such as *Jihat al-Shi'r* (The Direction of Poetry) (www.Jehat.com) established by the Bahraini poet Qassim Ḥaddad, *Kika* (www.Kikah.com) by the Iraqi poet Samuel Shimon and *Ufouq* (Horizons) (www.Ufouq.com) by the *Bidun* writers Muhammad al-Nabhan in Canada and Saleh al-Nabhan and Karim Al-Hazza' in Kuwait, offered new 'read-only' publishing opportunities for Arab poets. In addition, online cultural forums (muntadayat) such as *Jasad al-Thaqafa* (The Body of Culture) (http://aljsad.

org/forums.php), *Madina ʿAla Hadab Ṭifl* (A City on a Child's Eyelids) (www.madeenah.net), *al-Shiʿr al-Muʿaṣir* (Contemporary Poetry) and *Shathaya Adabiyya* (Literary Fragments) (www.shathaaya.com) offered a chance for *Bidun* writers to maintain a literary presence. These forums were not merely publishing sites, but spaces of immediate social and cultural exchange that could bring together writers across geographical spaces in real time.

More recently, there has been a surge in the number of local cultural platforms, commonly referred to as *Manaṣat* (sing. Manaṣa), typically associated with local bookshops that have had an active role in the cultural scene. Most notable is *Takween*, headed by Buthayna al-ʿIsa, which worked on co-organizing 'The *Bidun* Cultural Week' celebrating the works of *Bidun* authors before it was officially prohibited by the ministry of interior affairs.

In each of the examples relating to the materialities of cultural production above the dialectics of extrinsic official absencing and intrinsic acts of cultural presence are at play. While the earlier discussion of *Bidun* literature focused on the extrinsic binding forces that bring a literary community into view, the following analysis will shift the focus towards the poetics of this struggle for presence.

Poetics of presence: The death of Ali al-Safi

The poetics of presence manifest themselves most notably in the specific case of the late *Bidun* poet Ali al-Ṣafi, whose death was emblematic of the absence of a whole community and whose remembrance was symbolic of a community's shared struggle for presence. The literary responses (public mourning, elegies, dedications) to al-Ṣafi's death, particularly from within the *Bidun* community, will be examined as instances of crystallizing the idea of a literary community orbiting around a poetics of presence. These instances of remembrance will be read not only as personal elegies, but more importantly as urgent public instances of affiliation and association with a wider literary community asserting its presence.

While the absence of other *Bidun* poets described in al-Hazzaʿ's aforementioned article was merely a metaphor for disappearance from the cultural scene, al-Ṣafi's absence was real. In January 2000, the then 32-year-old

Bidun poet Ali al-Ṣafi was killed in a tragic car accident. More than a year earlier, he had published his only poetry collection titled *Khadija la Tuḥarrik Sakinan* (Khadija Doesn't Move). The orphaned collection is dedicated to his sister Khadija, who was born with cerebral palsy leaving her immobile and mute. Al-Ṣafi writes in his dedication: '[T]o Khadija, who sheltered me from fear and accompanied me in my estrangement' (al-Ṣafi 1998:3). Al-Ṣafi identifies and empathizes with Khadija's mental and physical condition that represents an extreme manifestation of absence and silence. This empathy with Khadija's condition highlights one of the main stimuli for his poetry collection, namely a concern with the wider issue of voicing a personal and communal silence and articulating the presence of those who are absent. The representational overtones of his poetic voice are pronounced in his often-quoted two-line poem titled *I*, where he writes: 'I am the thump on the chest of the oppressed, and the aggrievement of those who are absent' (67). Al-Ṣafi's poetry, perhaps even more acutely after his death, was received by *Bidun* poets as representative of a whole community's voice. This is illustrated by Dikhil Khalifa's characterization of al-Ṣafi as someone who 'expressed the voice of his group searching for its face in the crowded night' (Naṣr 2010).

Khadija Doesn't Move is written in three main sections titled 'the sleeping cities', 'the coastal road' and 'the confined rooms'. Two distinct spaces (the 'sleeping cities' and the 'confined rooms') are defined by the distance of the 'coastal road' between them. The distance between those two spaces can be read tentatively as that distance between an established central space, perhaps national space, (sleeping cities) and the poet's fractured space of exclusion (confined rooms). The physical and psychological journey along the coastal road from one space to another is a re-enactment of al-Ṣafi's attempts to understand his own positionality between the two. Yet this tension between the two spaces is left unresolved, both metaphorically and literally. Metaphorically, al-Ṣafi's voice is described in his poem *Fḥaiḥil Expressway* as always 'in-between two possibilities' (59). In real life, al-Ṣafi's metaphorical in-betweenness became reality when his fatal car crash occurred on the *Fḥaiḥil Expressway*: that physical and metaphorical space between the sleeping cities and the confined rooms.

A recurring trope in the collection is that of the poet wandering at night alone. This occurs in both the 'sleeping cities' and the 'confined rooms'. The poet is always at a reflective distance from both spaces attempting to find his personal voice. In each, the poet is burdened by a heightened sense of awareness of his estrangement amid 'people who have forgotten themselves in sleep' and who have 'forgotten their faces in desk jobs' (87). He addresses himself:

> O noble son,
> Who witnesses my sadness when people are absent?
> In the land that has cast its fingers into the sea
> So that it does not point at me.
>
> (30)

In the solitude of the sleeping cities, the poet's voice is most pronounced in his repetitive announcement of arrival in the city. He writes:

> I came from the silver of words to expose their pitch-black …
> To hurl the lightning astray in the dark
> I have the path that I know well
> They have their overcrowded roads.
>
> (26)

The poet expresses a multidimensional awareness and unique experience of the sleeping cities. He knows a unique path that remains unfamiliar to those dwellers who are asleep. At the same time, the poet's multidimensional experience of the city allows him to radicalize the very meaning of that space. This is most clearly illustrated through the poet's unique engagement with the image of the sea, which is one of the main symbols of the national space. Of the image of the sea, he writes: '[T]he sea departs if it does not find those who can cross it' (al-Ṣafi 1998:33). Here, al-Ṣafi inverts the image of the sea, presenting it as a place that is a means in itself to achieve human potential instead of a static end. When a human is denied any opportunity to cross that sea, the sea loses its potential and departs. Similarly, the 'land that has cast its fingers into the sea' is depicted as a static site of exclusion that prevents people from fulfilling their potential. The image of the poet wandering around at night in the sleeping city hurling thunder captures the relationship between the total neglect of the poet's presence and his incessant assertion of it.

The second section, titled 'the coastal road', is made up of personal moments and encounters with the everyday realities as the poet drives his car along the *Fḥaiḥil Expressway*. The poet is neither in the 'sleeping cities' nor is he in the 'confined rooms'. Rather, he is in that liminal space between the two.

In this space, the poetic voice is most accentuated where the phrase 'I am' is emphasized and repeated. The aforementioned two-line poem titled *I* stands as a clear marker of the poet's voice. What is most significant in this section is the symbolic resonance of the poems as it foretells his own death. The section includes two poems one titled *Impala '82*, the car he crashed in, and the other titled *Fḥaiḥil Expressway*, the actual site of his death. In *Fḥaiḥil Expressway*, the poet addresses the expressway:

> Of coal and beauty,
> A Sufi in an outstretching night:
> Aren't you tired of accidents and anticipation? …
> O guardian of anticipations, absences, and pavements:
> How does life pass by like a storm?
>
> (59)

These lines illustrate the symbolic resonance of al-Ṣafi's almost prophetic expression as it anticipates his personal death while hinting at a communal absence.

In the third section, titled 'the confined rooms', an overarching theme is that of death and absence. In the poem titled *You Walk into My Funeral a Stranger*, the poet imagines his funeral (71). He writes, 'I saw the grave digger carry me in a shroud every day, while they curse me' (74). In another poem he writes: '[W]e were killed yesterday, and we will die in an appointed time' (82). Again, this metaphorical death is also a marker of a heightened sense of awareness of exclusion. He writes:

> I know that people have forgotten themselves in sleep,
> And I forget that which allows death to be simple in my country,
> Ask the dead.
> And do not ask those who have survived death,
> They have forgotten their faces in their occupations.
>
> (87)

Those who are dead in confined rooms are juxtaposed with those who have forgotten themselves in sleep in the sleeping cities. It is as if 'the dead' are the ones who are truly awake. In the confined rooms, death stands as a metaphor for the experience of the confined rooms as a unique space of exclusion.

The symbolic resonance of al-Ṣafi's death was made more acute as he was killed on the first day of Eid. Al-Hazzaʿ recalls '[his] departure … was a shock to the cultural circles. For more than ten days, newspapers wrote about him in a rare humane contribution'. Mourning, as Freud puts it, is not only a reaction to the loss of a loved one, but also to 'the loss of some abstraction which had taken the place of one, such as one's country, liberty, an ideal, and so on' (Freud 1975:243). The wider abstraction that al-Ṣafi resembled was absence as a metaphor taken to its extremity; a literalization of absence. Almost instantly, al-Ṣafi was turned into an icon for a generation of *Bidun* writers.

The many deaths of Ali al-Ṣafi

In his poem titled, *I Hide My Eyes at Home* Ali al-Ṣafi writes:

> My soul gasps its last breath in my hands
> And Khadija does not move
> Die, you last bit of my soul
> We were killed yesterday, and will die in an appointed time
> Many times, I was killed, many times crucified
> My hands and feet were cut off, one then the other
> And I was banished from the land.
>
> (al-Ṣafi 1998:82)

In the preceding excerpt, al-Ṣafi speaks of his previous deaths in the figurative sense. He expresses a familiarity with death that is both communal and personal. It is a figurative death that can be read as a metaphor for a real condition of 'absencing'. This condition is first mentioned in the plural ('we were killed … and will die') as a shared communal act of murder. Within the overall condition of absencing, he then points out his singular death: 'many times, I was killed, many times'. This singularity can perhaps signify the personal death and banishment of al-Ṣafi *the poet*. It is through the poetic voice that this singularity is expressed. At the same time, this voice is the subject of another, more personalized act of absencing.

In other words, as the *Bidun* community is made absent from the political institution, the *Bidun* poet is also repeatedly killed, muted, banished and made absent culturally. The absence of official documentation of the *Bidun* pushes official cultural institutions to 'make absent' the voices of *Bidun* writers. One way in which al-Ṣafi's 'repetitive murder' and 'banishment' can be interpreted is in his total absence from what can be termed the official national cultural memory propagated by state sanctioned cultural institution.

In the particular case of al-Ṣafi, he is absent from *all* national literary histories or anthologies written by non-*Bidun* writers. One exception would be the quasi-presence of al-Ṣafi in *al-Babtain's Glossary of Contemporary Arab Poets* (1995). While an entry on al-Ṣafi is provided in the glossary, he is absent from the table of contents that categorizes writers according to their nationality as mentioned earlier in the chapter.

Al-Ṣafi is also omitted from official commemorative literary publications such as the National Council for Culture, Arts and Literature annual series titled *Manarat*. This series celebrates the memory of deceased national poets. More than a decade and a half after his death, al-Ṣafi has not been considered for the Council's *Manarat* series. His influential impact on his generation as a poet who lived and died in Kuwait would make him at least eligible for such an inclusion. Yet it seems he is perceived as being located beyond the official national radar.

Again, similarly to al-Hazza''s article mentioned earlier, the onus of conserving and upholding the memory of al-Ṣafi has fallen solely on other *Bidun* poets. Al-Ṣafi is only included in national anthologies and literary histories produced by *Bidun* writers. At work in this inclusion is the shared struggle for presence against a backdrop of cultural absencing. Firstly it is manifested in the insistence of some *Bidun* writers on producing and compiling national literary histories and anthologies to defy an officially imposed narrative. Secondly, the act of inclusion of *Bidun* writers such as al-Ṣafi makes present these otherwise muted voices. This is evident in the works of *Bidun* poets Saʿdiyya Mufarriḥ and Dikhil Khalifa concerning literary history and anthologies.

Saʿdiyya Mufarriḥ's *The Cameleers of Clouds and Estrangement* (2007) is an anthology of Kuwaiti poetry preceded by a long introduction offering an overview of Kuwaiti literary history for the uninitiated reader. In the introduction, a specific section is devoted to the works of *Bidun* poets who are presented as an essential component of Kuwaiti literature. Mufarriḥ comments that the *Bidun* issue 'has been totally absent from the *Diwan* of Kuwaiti Poetry' until the 1990s generation made it present when they responded poetically to their own conditions of daily life. Within this 1990s generation, al-Ṣafi stands out as an influential figure. The act of inclusion by Mufarriḥ is not to be read simply as a struggle for mere presence, or simply as a strategic act of solidarity, but as testament to his aesthetic resonance of a generation. Mufarriḥ comments:

> Al-Ṣafi, who was gone before his experiment reached its artistic apex, formed a significant mark in the history of the generation that he so strongly belonged to .... It wasn't only the experimentation that he immersed himself in, whether this was conscious .... but also his sudden departure, which acted as a symbol for the absence that had enveloped his contemporaries.
> (Mufarriḥ 2007)

Here yet again 'the insistence of producing literary works' is read against a backdrop of the 'cloak' of absence that enveloped a generation. This insistence on writing can be reworded as a struggle for presence against an act of absencing. Al-Ṣafi's iconic status is informed by his representation and literalization of the overarching generational metaphor of absence.

Al-Ṣafi is also included in the UNESCO-sponsored anthology titled *The Diwan of Arabic Poetry in the Last Quarter of the Twentieth Century: The Arabian Gulf (Kuwait and Bahrain)* compiled by Saʿdiyya Muffariḥ. Out of a total of fourteen poets in the Kuwait section three *Bidun* poets (Ali al-Ṣafi, Dikhil Khalifa and Saʿdiyya Mufarriḥ) are included (Mufarriḥ 2008). This insistence on the inclusion of al-Ṣafi and other *Bidun* poets further affirms the political urgency of cultural presence.

Similarly, Dikhil Khalifa's online contribution, published in the cultural forum *Jasad al-Thaqafa,* titled *A Portfolio of the New Kuwaiti Poem* highlights the role of the 1990s generation in innovating and introducing new poetics to Kuwaiti literature. In this work, Khalifa presents an online anthology of twelve poets from the 1990s generation, out of which six are *Bidun.* It is an attempt to first cement a subcategory within Kuwaiti literature (i.e. the 1990s generation), and to present their works as a distinctive voice within Kuwaiti literature. The emphasis on the 1990s generation is perhaps driven by how little attention this generation has received from the cultural institution, especially as its majority is formed of *Bidun* poets. Thus, the burden of writing about this generation is on one of its sons. As for al-Ṣafi, he is included in the anthology and introduced in these words: '[H]e is the wound of poetry, we lost him when we weren't looking ... he was adored by all ... the unpolluted, charming, kind, loyal, talented young man … everyone expected him to become an illustrious knight of poetry' (Khalifa 2003). Again, Khalifa hints at al-Ṣafi's centrality to the generation both in terms of his literary persona and in terms of his poetic talent. In such works, the inclusion of *Bidun* poets is a marker of a communal struggle for presence against an act of absencing in which al-Ṣafi is a central iconic figure. The struggle for the presence of al-Ṣafi in national anthologies and literary histories is at the same time representative of a struggle for the presence of a whole literary community.

The tenth anniversary of al-Ṣafi's death

In January 2010, the Tuesday Gathering, one of the unofficial cultural circles discussed earlier, held a commemorative event celebrating the tenth anniversary of Ali al-Ṣafi's death. In his coverage of the event, Yusuf Adam, the Kuwait-based Mauritanian literary critic, lamented the cultural institution's total neglect of al-Ṣafi. Al-Ṣafi's distance from the cultural institution is seen by Adam as a direct result of al-Ṣafi's status as a *Bidun*. Al-Ṣafi 'was never a member of the cultural institution nor was he a member of any civil society in Kuwait because his paperless condition prevented him from being one' (Yusuf 2010). Thus, al-Ṣafi is only remembered by his friends, 'those who sing to a different tune than that of the institution' (Yusuf 2010).

Celebrating the memory of a writer ten years after his death immediately forces one to reflect on the symbolic significance of holding such an event. Muhab Naṣr, an Egyptian poet residing in Kuwait and an active member of the Tuesday Gathering, writes in his coverage of the event in *al-Qabas* newspaper:

> The poet, who is regarded by some as an icon, was finally celebrated the 10th anniversary of his death this Tuesday. Companions, peers and those who consider his life a symbol of an era, all remembered him as a friend whose blood has not dried yet, who only exited their gathering an hour earlier with his shadow lingering at the doorstep. After that, the conversation was closer to a personal memorial of a friend than a search for his singularity as a poet. The conversation hid behind a mask of rebellion that was used as testimony to condemn this present that is not present.
>
> (Naṣr 2010)

The event seems to transcend the memory of al-Ṣafi to be representative of a political and cultural urgency of a literary community. This urgency is related to a condemnation of a 'present that is not present'. What is at work primarily in this event is a literary community affirming its presence through the use of al-Ṣafi as a mask.

When speaking of presence and absence in the light of such an event, both terms become physically manifested in a space of communal gathering. This space of cultural exchange is situated beyond the official radar and consists of the members of the Tuesday Gathering. What emerges is a physical manifestation of the idea of a *Bidun* literary community with al-Ṣafi's absence as its focal point. Attending and participating in such an event can be read as a form of claiming membership in, and association with, a wider literary community.

In the event, al-Ṣafi's poetry collection and life were presented in allegorical terms. In his opening speech, the *Bidun* poet Muhammad al-Nabhan directed his speech to al-Ṣafi, asking him, '[W]hat absence is this Ali?' ('Allam 2010) In his contemplation of al-Ṣafi's absence, al-Nabhan spoke of it with a shared sense of familiarity, 'it hunts us while we hunt it, it pursues us while we pursue it. It enters our homes while we enter its cold confined houses', alluding to al-Ṣafi's poem titled *Confined Rooms* (ibid). This condition of absence is not sudden or momentary, but depicted as a familiar ongoing encounter of a community expressed in a collective voice.

Al-Nabhan then turned to al-Ṣafi's poetry collection and reads it as semi-autobiographical:

> Ali, when you were absented by death, it didn't know that it took away a handsome poet … a poet who stirred the cultural scene with an orphaned collection of poetry … honest and genuine … that resembles you like an autobiography of what has been and what will come, and disguised, resembling us also.
>
> (Allam 2010)

Al-Ṣafi's life and poetic voice are both retrospectively personal and prospectively collective. It is about 'what has been' and 'what will later happen' to a whole community facing an absencing act.

It is important to mention that al-Nabhan's words and most elegies recited at the event never explicitly mention the term *Bidun* or mentioned al-Ṣafi's status as *Bidun*. The condition is rather expressed in metaphor and framed within the general theme of absence. This however is not the case with other Arab poets who participated in the event. Abbas Mansour, an Egyptian poet, is quite direct in his identification of al-Ṣafi as a *Bidun* poet, describing him as a '*Bidun* of regal blood'. This distinction highlights the reluctance of *Bidun* poets to directly associate themselves with the term and their reflective distance from it. To al-Nabhan, the metaphor of absence suffices not only to describe al-Ṣafi's death, but to self-identify as a community struggling for a presence through the mask of al-Ṣafi.

At the end of the event, there were calls by the attendees to reprint al-Ṣafi's out-of-print poetry collection *Khadija Doesn't Move* (1999). This suggestion was received enthusiastically by the owner of *Dar Masʿa* Muhammad al-Nabhan. These calls to reprint *Khadija Doesn't Move* can be read as another material manifestation of making al-Ṣafi present. Even though the collection has not yet been reprinted, *Dar Masʿa* in 2014 announced the inauguration of 'The Ali al-Ṣafi Fund for Poetic Creativity' which publishes works by young talents from the Arab world.

The ten-year anniversary is a visible instance of a literary community emerging around the figure of al-Ṣafi. This is best summed up in the title of one of the poems recited at the event: *Khadija Has Finally Moved*. It is as if the memorial event is a reassertion of the presence and mobilization of a literary community.

Al-Ṣafi intertextual presence

Another significant way in which al-Ṣafi is made present is through other *Bidun* writers' intertextual engagement with al-Ṣafi's literary works. Since his death al-Ṣafi has been present in a number of works by other *Bidun* writers in the form of citations, direct quotes and dedications. These intertextual engagements at the intra-*Bidun* level span from the time of his death to recent works by *Bidun* writers. Some examples include Laṭifa Buṭṭi's short story *al-ʿAdhab Waraqa* (Torture is a Paper) (Buṭṭi 2000), which is dedicated to the memory of Ali al-Ṣafi, Ahmad al-Nabhan's poem titled *Ali al-Ṣafi* in his collection titled *An Introduction to the Biography of the Father*, Muhammad al-Nabhan's poem titled *Another Estrangement* from his eponymous poetry collection in 2004 and Shahad al-Faḍli's *Two Steps towards Ali al-Ṣafi* from her poetry collection *Semicolon* in 2014. The continual remembrance of al-Ṣafi throughout the years attests to his symbolic and poetic resonance for *Bidun* writers. These intertextual works invoke the singularity of al-Ṣafi's poetic voice which continues to influence and stir the poetic consciousness of a whole community.

Muhammad al-Nabhan and Shahad al-Faḍli's elegiac poems give some insight into al-Ṣafi's purely textual presence. The two poets attempt to go beyond the symbolic resonance of al-Ṣafi as a mask to emphasize and celebrate his singular voice and unique poetics. Both poems engage in an intimate poetic dialogue with al-Ṣafi's own work through the many uses of direct quotes and images such as the 'departing sea', 'the sleeping cities' and 'Khadija'.

In Muhammad al-Nabhan's *Another Estrangement*, the poem starts off with the invocation of al-Ṣafi's voice: 'you said once, my friend: "the thump on the chest of the oppressed" (al-Nabhan 2004:51). Similarly, in *Two Steps towards Ali al-Ṣafi*, al-Faḍli begins the poem with the same line taken from al-Ṣafi's poem *I*, 'I am the thump on the chest of the oppressed and the aggrievement of those absent' (al-Faḍli 2013:76). This particular line is used as an emblem of al-Ṣafi's poetics of presence. The common use of this particular line at the beginning of the poems signifies how al-Ṣafi's poetics become a stimulus for the poets' own works.

More importantly is the way in which al-Ṣafi's poetics seem to offer solace and hope. Al-Nabhan describes al-Ṣafi's words as a 'green dream … still on the cross of promise, waiting' (Al-Nabhan 2004:53). To al-Faḍli, al-Ṣafi's poems 'offer silence a prayer' (al-Faḍli 2013:77). Al-Faḍli further describes the personal influence of al-Ṣafi's poetics on her:

> Every morning
> he opens, in his innocence, windows of hope
> rearranges the sea so that he would smile
> draws a sky and birds
> offers me his purity
> and teaches me how I can create a 'homeland'
> He incites me to become a wheat seed that grows in the seasons
> of frustration
> despair
> and non-belonging.
>
> (78)

Al-Faḍli emphasizes how al-Ṣafi's opens up possibilities of presenting an intrinsic subjective relationship to the homeland. Al-Ṣafi's poetics incite al-Faḍli to reorder reality by images of rearranging the sea, drawing a sky and creating a 'homeland'. It also incites her to 'become a seed' that grows in seasons of 'frustration, despair and non-belonging'. This description signals the capacity of language and poetry to resist an extrinsic 'absencing' and to articulate a presence.

A shared struggle for a cultural and literary presence of a community manifests itself most clearly in the many instances of remembering Ali al-Ṣafi by *Bidun* writers. Al-Ṣafi is made present through his inclusion in literary histories and anthologies. At the same time, his literary presence is highlighted through intertextual engagement with his unique poetic voice which stirs a communal consciousness of articulating a presence.

3

Cameleers of the national spirit: *Bidun* poets and Kuwaiti literary history

In his article 'My Experience with Kuwaiti Literature', the Kuwaiti literary historian Khalid Saud al-Zaid (d. 2001) recounts a disheartening encounter in 1965 with a new generation of Kuwaiti literary enthusiasts in the newly established Writers' Association (*Rabiṭa*). Many of these young poets, he recalls, doubted the very existence of Kuwaiti Literature, 'if there were poets and a literary tradition from the time of the founding of Kuwait, we would've certainly heard of them', they said (al-Ḥaddad 2002:137). He goes on, 'I defended the literary tradition in Kuwait … opposed their accusation by reciting the poetry of Khalid al-Faraj, Abdulatif al-Niṣf, the bold stances of Abdulaziz al-Rushaid as well as the poetry of Saqir al-Shibib' (137).

What left al-Zaid saddened was this upcoming generation's total unawareness of Kuwait's literary past. Returning home after the incident, al-Zaid writes:

> I returned home after a storm of discussion sad and disheartened. I reclined on my cushion by the wall. No one around me knew of my grief. I then quickly leapt up as if I had a planned rendezvous with old papers crammed in a timeworn cabinet in our house, a jumble of worn-out old Kuwaiti journals. I didn't know exactly what they were … journals without cover pages, cover pages without journals. Everything seemed scattered and sad. I left them on the ground and ordered that no one touch them …. After a short break, I took a deep breath and asked myself: *Where to start? And How?*
>
> I then returned to face the scattered journals … it is my duty now … to create out of this heap I am surrounded by something that could be remembered. For these old journals are the *diwan* of literature and poetry in Kuwait.
>
> (137–8 emphasis added)

In 1967, two years after this foundational moment, al-Zaid published the first comprehensive work on Kuwaiti literature titled *Kuwaiti Writers in Two Centuries*, a literary history and anthology, which would develop into a relatively stable narrative for later works on national literary history.

Reflecting on al-Zaid's anecdote, one can begin to visualize what is at stake in approaching national literary history generally and in the Gulf specifically. The challenges could be summed up in the two questions articulated by al-Zaid as he stood amid the heap: Where to begin? And how? In other words, when does the history of national literature begin? And how can this history be narrativized?

These questions highlight how the endeavour of writing national literary history is inextricably linked to the impulses and urgencies of nation building. To ask the question: who is the first Kuwaiti poet, requires one to first ask: who is Kuwaiti and when does Kuwaiti history begin. Forging a new national literary history probes into the very meaning of both the 'national' and the 'literary' in national literary history. The words (national and literary) are generally studied under two different, often antagonistic, modes of enquiry. The national, in the current approaches to the Gulf, often operates within the logic, methods and considerations of area studies and the social sciences, while the critical paradigms in the humanities emphasize the intrinsic affiliative networks that often destabilize the fixities of such categories. Thus, any work that revisits the arena of national literary history, whether affirming a narrative or contesting it, is necessarily also an enquiry into the parameters of the national category both spatially in terms of geographic boundaries and temporally in terms of national beginnings. At the same time, it poses questions related to what constitutes the literary across different times.

This chapter reads national literary history writing in Kuwait as a site of opposition and contestation. It begins by highlighting the modalities of national literary history writing in Kuwait in its earlier stages focusing on questions of beginnings and periodization. The chapter then shifts the focus on the question of the placement of *Bidun* (stateless) writers, within recent national literary history narratives. The *Bidun* poet Saʿdiyya Mufarriḥ's work on Kuwaiti literary history titled *The Cameleers of Clouds and Estrangement* (*Ḥudat al-Ghaym wa-l-Waḥsha*) (2007) will be read as a revisionist work of Kuwaiti literary history that emphasizes literary and cultural affiliations of *Bidun* writers beyond the official demarcations.

Kuwaiti literary history: Beginnings and periodization

Traditional practices of literary history tend to narrate the history of the 'unfolding of an idea, principal, suprapersonal entity, or Geist as its subject' (Perkins 1993:5). This subject is presented as a hero who goes through linear transitions (with a definite beginning and a life story). The teleology of the narrative or plot can then only be assumed in retrospect. As David Perkins puts it, the 'function of literary history is to produce useful fictions about the past' to 'project the present into the past ... while taking the past to reflect our concerns and supports our intentions' (182). In the case of Kuwaiti literary history, the 'hero's' untold story that needed to be narrated was the post-independence state of Kuwait, a hero in search of a deeply rooted sense of cultural continuity emerging in a moment of political and cultural exposure to a wider Arab and global context.

One of the main anxieties associated with traditional national literary histories is the tension between the national and the literary in national literary history, which usually tends to gravitate towards the ascendancy of the national over the literary. Commenting on the rise of English literature as a politically induced discipline, Terry Eagleton writes: '[W]hat was at stake in English studies was less English *literature* than *English* literature' (Eagleton 1996:25). With an emphasis on the national, the literary becomes a function of the national. Shakespeare's works become genealogical descendants of Beowulf and not necessarily Dante or Homer, regardless of their literary influence as pointed out by Anthony Appiah (Lentricchia and McLaughlin 1995:285).

For early literary historians in the Gulf, delineating the contours of the national was a significant challenge as they needed to negotiate notions of 'national' belonging within local vernacular, regional, pre-national and transnational affinities. Early literary historians, such as al-Zaid, grappled with two main questions related to national history writing in Kuwait. The first relates to debates over national beginnings: or, simply put, who is the first Kuwaiti poet? The second relates to questions of periodizing narratives of national literary history.

Khalid Saʿud al-Zaid's foundational literary history and anthology *Kuwaiti Writers in Two Centuries* (1967) considered Abduljalil al-Ṭabṭabaʾi (1776–1853) as the founding figure of Kuwaiti literature. Published just six years after the independence of Kuwait, the impulse of nation building in al-Zaid's work cannot be overlooked. At the same time, writing literary history at this critical historical juncture stemmed from a need to position Kuwaiti literature within a wider Arabic cultural context. In contextualizing the question of beginnings at a time preceding the emergence of the nation states, al-Zaid writes:

> You do not need a passport or a travel document to travel from Kuwait to any other Arab or Muslim land. There are neither borders nor barriers. There is no belonging but to the town or city of your birth.
>
> You are free to travel wherever you desire in God's vast land. You are free to reside in any land your heart desires.
>
> Nobody will ask: where have you come from? Why do you reside here? You are welcome as a newcomer and resident or as a departing guest. This had been the case until the end of the First World War.
>
> (al-Ḥaddad 2002:26)

Without such an acknowledgement of the historical context, the newly established official notion of the national would leave Kuwaiti literature as a nascent literature void of any historical continuity, and al-Zaid's mission to inform the young poets of a tradition would certainly have failed.

The year 1776 marks the birth of al-Ṭabṭaba'i as the first Kuwaiti writer and founder of a Kuwaiti literary tradition. Born in Basra, Abduljalil al-Ṭabṭaba'i arrived in Kuwait in the year 1843 at the age of sixty-seven, spending the last ten years of his life in the country. He was the first to 'plant the seed of intellectual revival (*nahḍa*) in Kuwait' (al-Zaid 1967:35). Previously, he had settled in Zubara (in modern-day Qatar), and Bahrain, where he served as a secretary for the al-Khalifa rulers (al-Zaid 1967:42). Al-Ṭabṭaba'i is now claimed by Iraqi, Qatari, Bahraini and Kuwaiti national literary histories (Abdullah 1986:10; al-Wuqayyan 2011:341, 2012:30). This definite beginning set by al-Zaid was later reiterated by other writings on Kuwaiti literary history (al-Ṣabaḥ 1973; Abdulfattaḥ 1996).

The narrative of *Kuwaiti Writers in Two Centuries* is organized chronologically in accordance with the birth years of the writers and is divided into four main periods. The first period was inaugurated with the arrival of Abduljalil al-Ṭabṭaba'i (1776–1853) in Kuwait in 1844. Before al-Ṭabṭaba'i, there was 'no documented poetry' (al-Zaid 1967:34).

The second period is associated with Abdulaziz al Rushaid, a seminal figure in Kuwaiti intellectual history, author of the first book on Kuwaiti history,

Tarikh al-Kuwait (The History of Kuwait) (1926). Born in Kuwait, al-Rushaid travelled through different parts of the Islamic world including Zubayr, al-Hasa, Baghdad, Madina, Istanbul, Cairo and Indonesia (al-Zaid 1967:95-6; al-Hijji 1993). Whereas al-Ṭabṭabaʾi was the first to 'plant the seed of intellectual renaissance (*nahḍa*) in Kuwait', al-Rushaid then 'nurtured and developed' that seed (al-Zaid 1967:35). Influenced by his travels, al-Rushaid founded *Majallat al Kuwait* in 1927, which brought the Kuwaiti reading public into the different discourses on revival (*iṣlaḥ*) in the wider Arab and Islamic intellectual circles.

Then comes the Pan-Arabist tide as the main feature inaugurating the third period. This period is concerned with the years between 1936 and 1958 marked by important events such as the arrival of Palestinian teachers in Kuwait in 1936, the commencement of the first Kuwaiti educational scholarships to Cairo in 1939 and the establishment of the cultural magazine *al-Biʿtha* in 1946 among other events. The fourth and final period in al-Zaid's narrative coincides with the founding of *al-ʿArabi* magazine in 1958, which is a further development of the Pan-Arabist tide.

Following al-Zaid's work, Muhammad Hasan Abdullah published another important work on Kuwaiti literary history titled *The Literary and Intellectual Movement in Kuwait* (1973). Commenting on the first Kuwaiti poet, Abdullah writes that al-Ṭabṭabaʾi

> is not a Kuwaiti. He only settled in Kuwait in the final ten years of his life. However, this matter can be forgiven, as Kuwaitis did not differentiate between the sons of the Gulf and the Arabian Peninsula in general, especially before the establishment of the state and defining citizenship by formal documents. Many Kuwaiti poets are regarded as Bahraini poets and are placed with the poets of al-Hasa or Najd, such as the poet Khalid al-Faraj among others.
> (Abdullah 1973:116)

In *Poetry and Poets in Kuwait* (1987), Abdullah also comments that the beginnings of Kuwaiti poetry might seem self-evident but are unacceptable from a methodological point of view since the founding figures of Kuwaiti poetry are not exclusively Kuwaiti (Abdullah 1987:9–10). These founding poets can be 'officially found in the literary histories of Najd, Qatar, and Bahrain' (Abdullah 1987:9–10). Again for a beginning to be conceived, Abdullah sees it necessary to attach a caveat reminding the reader of the differences between a more fluid historic notion of belonging and a modern one substantiated by official documentation.

Abdullah criticizes al-Zaid's logic of periodization, proposing instead two main periods in Kuwaiti literary history resulting in the political, economic and social rupture caused by the production of oil (*ma qabl al-nafṭ wa-ma baʿdahu*). In the pre-oil production period, literature was 'conservative and traditional, holding on to a past rather than future', while the 'concerns of Kuwaiti intellectuals and poets were restricted to their limited worlds' (120). Abdullah mentions that problems with writing Kuwaiti literary history are not only methodological, but pertain to the question of the existence of 'Kuwaiti literature' in the first place (109). A main reason behind Abdullah's interest in writing Kuwaiti literary history is 'the fierce dispute over the existence of this [Kuwaiti] literature' as a valid category.

Al-Ṭabṭabaʾi's pioneer status was contested in Khalifa al-Wuqayyan's *The Arab Cause in Kuwaiti Poetry* (1977). Al-Ṭabṭabaʾi is left out of the Kuwaiti literary history altogether, as 'the period of his residence in Kuwait was not sufficient enough and his influence on Kuwaiti poetry was minute' (al-Wuqayyan 1977:26). Al-Wuqayyan continues: '[W]hen we try to find any reference to Kuwait, or any of its emirs or of the events occurring during his stay or before it, we are left empty-handed' (21). It would be 'more honest' to consider him as belonging to other countries in which he resided in such as Iraq, Bahrain or Qatar (al-Wuqayyan 26). Instead, the 'true beginning' of Kuwaiti literary history starts with Khalid al-ʿAdsani (1834–1898) and Abdullah al-Faraj (1863–1901).[1]

Al-Wuqayyan periodizes Kuwaiti literary history into three main periods. The first is between the 1850s and the 1920s, a period characterized by its 'backwardness' and the lack of outside cultural influences, when poetry was limited in form and content (al-Wuqayyan 30). The second period, between the 1930s and the 1940s, coincides with the establishment of governmental schools, the first public library, first literary club and the first newspaper. The poet Fahad al-ʿAskar is considered the highlight of this period along with poets Abdulaṭif al-Niṣf (1906–1971) and Abd al-Muhsin al-Badir (1927–2008). The third period commences after the beginning of the Second World War as the tide of Arab nationalism surges.

In *Culture in Kuwait: Beginnings-Currents-Pioneers* (2003), Khalifa al-Wuqayyan revisits the question of the beginnings of Kuwaiti literature. Instead of al-Ṭabṭabaʾi, ʿUthman bin Sanad (1766–1827) is introduced as the founding poet in Kuwaiti literature because of his historic precedence and longer residency in Kuwait. Born on the island of Failaka (in modern-day Kuwait), Bin Sanad settled in Basra, al-Hasaʾ, and Baghdad where he is buried (al-Wuqayyan 2011). He has been referred to in different works as *al-Failakawi* (in reference to his birth place), *al-Waʾili* (tribal origin; descendent of Bakir ibn Waʾil), *al-Najdi* (the place of his family's origin: Najd in modern-day Saudi Arabia), *al-Basri* (his place of residence in modern-day Iraq) and resident of *al-Qurain* (a historical name for Kuwait). In one biography, he is referred to as ʿUthman bin Sanad bin Rashid bin Abdullah bin Rashid of the Maliki *madhhab* (school of jurisprudence), the Qadiri *mashrab* (Sufi order), born in Failaka, and resident of al-Qurain (319). Here are multiple layers of belonging that challenge a facile nationalizing claim. However, it is important to note that al-Wuqayyan acknowledges that Bin Sanad was not primarily a poet but a religious scholar (*ʿalim*) who 'from an aesthetic perspective … was below the level of his contemporaries' (334) and not so influential on the literary movement in Kuwait. This perhaps reflects the urgencies of finding a historic national beginning at the expense of a more formal literary beginning.

A number of general trends can be identified in the literary history writings surveyed above. The first relates to the question of contentious beginnings and the search for a deeply rooted historical sense of cultural continuity. For a national beginning to emerge, for al-Zaid to reply to those sceptic young poets, the literary historian needed to address the differing pre-state notions of territoriality, sovereignty and belonging that give legitimacy and meaning to the national present. In almost every literary history, caveats were necessary to define a point of departure for national literary history. This allowed an *act of naturalization* or nationalization of key transnational figures including ʿUthman Bin Sanad, Abduljalil al-Ṭabṭabaʾi and Abdullah al-Faraj among others.

The national appropriation strategies of early poets in the Gulf are best exemplified in the cultural skirmishes over the publication of al-Ṭabṭabaʾi's *diwan* titled *Rawd al-Khil wa-l-Khalil* (The Garden of the Beloved and the Companion) (1883). Al-Ṭabṭabaʾi's *diwan* was first published in Bombay by al-Tabtabai's grandson Musa'ad Ahmad al-Ṭabṭaba'i 1883 (1300 h.). In 1964 (1384), the *diwan* was reprinted by the emir of Bahrain Sheikh Salman Bin Hamad al-Khalifa. Simultaneously in 1965 (1385), the *diwan* was reprinted under the patronage of the emir of Qatar Sheikh Ali bin Abdullah. A fourth edition, published in Damascus in 1964, reprinted the *diwan* from the original 1883 Bombay manuscript. Finally in 2011, the Diwan was edited and printed by Muhammad al-Ṭabṭaba'i, one of Al-Ṭabṭaba'i's great grandsons in Kuwait (al-Wugayyan 2012).

Nationalizing the transnational does not only pertain to the beginnings of Kuwaiti literature but extends to later periods. One example is Khalid al-Faraj (1898–1954), who is commonly referred to as 'the Poet of the Gulf' (*Sha'ir al-Khalij*). Born in Kuwait, al-Faraj spent some time in India, then worked in Bahrain, al-Qatif, and al-Hasa' in the eastern Arabian Peninsula. He is also to be found in Kuwaiti, Bahraini and Saudi literary histories (Idris 1960:170; al-Zaid 1967; al-Ansari 1970; Ḥalibi 2003; al-Ḥaddad 2012).

A second general trend relates to how national literary histories discussed earlier have been keen on conceiving Kuwaiti literature within a broader Arab literary context. As al-Zaid puts it:

> Arabic poetry in Kuwait – the old and the contemporary – is a branch of this Arab tree and a fruit of its many endeavours … carrying its characteristics. Even though it maintains its own noticeable specificity … this specificity is lost if taken outside of its general Arab essence.
>
> (al-Ḥaddad 2002:52)

Similarly, al-Wuqayyan's title *The Arab Cause in Kuwaiti Poetry* attests to that affinity. National literary history writing stems from a need to historically and territorially position national literature within a wider Arabic literary context. The conception of national literature in Kuwait is inextricable from a Pan-Arab ideological outlook prevalent at the time of publication of the respective literary histories. It can be argued that a Pan-Arab outlook allowed for a more inclusive approach to transnational poets and a more fluid conception of national belonging.

The third general trend in Kuwait's literary histories relates to the steady continuity of the narrative revolving around the establishment of national institutions and the influence of key figures. The metaphor of al-Ṭabṭaba'i's sowing and al-Rushaid's reaping used by al-Zaid captures the essence of this continuous narrative. The narrative begins with an inclusionary attitude that legitimizes fluid notions of territoriality and belonging, which allow for national literature to emerge. The linear development of the narrative is then steadily focalized and consolidated within a narrowing official national framework.

Yet this necessary inclusionary outlook of early works on national literary history recedes as the narrative develops in time. The national begins to take a more official and concrete form. Unlike the pre-national times described by al-Zaid, God's vast land cannot be traversed now without travel documents. Belonging is reduced to an official paper and a fixed border. Without this paper, one will be constantly interpellated: When did you arrive? Where have you come from? What are you doing here? Within these new official proscriptions, *Bidun* writers, those excluded from national belonging, emerge into the national cultural scene posing the question of their placement within national literature.

The placement of *Bidun* literature as an 'adjacent literature'

The works on Kuwaiti literary history discussed above precede the emergence of the *Bidun* issue as a social phenomenon. The question of the placement of *Bidun* writers can only be investigated after Sulayman al-Flayyiḥ's first poetry collection *Singing in the Deserts of Agony* in 1979. The first comprehensive work on Kuwaiti literary history to deal with the question of the placement of *Bidun* writers is Sulayman al-Shaṭṭi's *Poetry in Kuwait* (2007).

Al-Shaṭṭi's narrative does not divert from the relatively stable narrative suggested by early historians such as al-Zaid and al-Wuqayyan. Al-Shaṭṭi's main contribution is in extending the narrative by incorporating new developments in national literature. As to the question of national beginnings, al-Shaṭṭi confirms that ʿUthman bin Sanad is the first Kuwaiti poet. Yet the Kuwaiti literary movement did not truly commence until after the arrival of Abduljalil al-Ṭabṭabaʾi (al-Shaṭṭi 2007:7). On al-Ṭabṭabaʾi, al-Shaṭṭi writes, '[W]e will not enter into a debate about his belonging or background' (7). Rather, what is important to al-Shaṭṭi is al-Ṭabṭabaʾi's actual influence on the Kuwaiti literary scene regardless of his 'national' belonging. Yet this criterion, which establishes a national beginning, does not necessarily apply to *Bidun* writers appearing towards the late stages of the narrative, as will be discussed later.

Al-Shaṭṭi advances a teleological view of the national literary narrative. National literature goes through a series of linear progressions starting from the first period titled *Rawafid Tatashakkal* (Tributaries Take Shape) around the end of the nineteenth century to the last chapter titled *al-Shi'r 'Ala Bawwabat al-Qarn* (Poetry at the Gates of a New Century). The metaphor of tributaries forming assumes a general sense of continuity, progression and steady flow of the narrative. The chapter on the poets of the 1960s is titled *al-Ḥaṣad* (The Harvest), where poets reap what the founders sowed. Similarly, some chapter titles can give a general sense of that progress: *al-Mar'a Tataqaddam* (The Woman Advances), *Qadim Yatajaddad* (The Old Becomes New), *Jil Jadid Yataqaddam* (A New Generation Advances) and *al-Shi'r 'Ala Bawwabat al-Qarn* (Poetry at the Gates of a New Century).

Within that continuity, there are diversions from the norm. Immediately after the first period, titled 'Tributaries Take Shape', the second period is titled *al-Khuruj 'An al-Ma'luf* (Outside of the Norm), featuring the estranged poetics of Fahad al-'Askar and Abd al-Muhsin al-Badir. Similarly, another chapter later in the narrative is titled *Kharij al-Nasaq* (Outside of the Dominant Mode), featuring Fawziyya al-Salim and 'Alia Shu'ayb, who 'leap into the arena of free experimentation unhindered by any poetic restriction' (401). What is emphasized is a general sense of national continuity and stability of the national literary narrative. Estrangement, transgression and subversion are presented as deviations that ultimately do not obstruct the river's steady flow. While these estranged and subversive poets divert from the norm, their belonging to the national literary history narrative is unquestioned. This, however, is not the case with *Bidun* poets.

Al-Shaṭṭi advances an official view of national belonging that suspends *Bidun* writers from belonging to that narrative. *Bidun* writers are placed in a separate chapter under the title of *al-Adab al-Mujawir* (Adjacent Literature). On *Bidun* writers, al-Shaṭṭi writes: '[T]here exists a social phenomenon that clearly and directly impacted the literary movement in Kuwait leaving a distinctive achievement that cannot be overlooked or neglected.' The chapter includes just two well-known *Bidun* poets, Saʿdiyya Mufarriḥ and Dikhil Khalifa, who reside in Kuwait. Other *Bidun* poets who have settled elsewhere, such as Sulayman al-Flayyiḥ and Muhammad al-Nabhan among others, are left unmentioned.

Al-Shaṭṭi's proposed placement reflects a notion of belonging that strictly conforms to an understanding of the national as official; like a border officer, permitting only those with a passport to enter the national literary history narrative. The question of the *Bidun* poets' impact on the Kuwaiti literary movement is unquestioned, yet what is a matter of contention is their national belonging. They are presented not as a continuation of a national plot line, but as some adjacent or parallel phenomenon that cannot be overlooked. Al-Shaṭṭi does not offer any further insight into the meaning of that adjacency and its relation to the national perimeter or any other perimeters. The term 'adjacent' (*mujawir*) perhaps implicitly hints at the poets' alleged affinity and connection with Iraq, be it in literature or belonging.

Within the *Bidun* literary community, the term 'adjacent literature' has been flatly rejected. The *Bidun* poet Dikhil Khalifa deems it offensive as it is 'a form of expulsion from the Kuwaiti border' (Salām Ya Kuwait 2011). Sulayman al-Flayyiḥ, a main contributor to the cultural scene in the 1970s and 1980s, is also critical of al-Shaṭṭi's total neglect of his contributions and his general stance on *Bidun* writers:

> A 'litterateur' friend denies my chirps in the sky of Kuwait and my humble contributions to the literary arena … he knew well that I have not missed a single poetry night organized by the *Rabiṭa* for three continuous decades … my five poetry collections distributed all over Kuwait bookshops are not even enough for him … he invented, out of his own whim, a label for his colleagues who hold no citizenship that even the most racist person could not come up with.
>
> (al-Flayyiḥ 2008b)

More importantly, al-Shaṭṭi's placement, and the position of *Bidun* writers within national literary history narratives in general, is contested in revisionist works of national literary history such Saʿdiyya Mufarriḥ's *The Cameleers of Clouds and Estrangement*.

National *literary* history: *The Cameleers of Clouds and Estrangement* (2007)

In 2007, the same year in which al-Shatti published *Poetry in Kuwait*, Saʿdiyya Mufarriḥ (b.1964) published *The Cameleers of Clouds and Estrangement* (*Ḥudat al-Ghaym wa-l-Waḥsha*). The title can also be translated to the Urgers or Guides of Clouds and Estrangement. The word *ḥadi* refers to the lone cameleer who both sings to and guides the camels in a desert journey. The publication is primarily an anthology of Kuwaiti poetry, preceded by a lengthy introduction, a 'brief historical survey' titled 'Reading the Memory of Poetry in Kuwait'. In the introduction, Mufarriḥ provides an overview of Kuwaiti literary history for the uninitiated Arab reader. A close reading of the introduction can help in highlighting the implicit ways in which Mufarriḥ's literary history can be read as an intervention into the modalities of writing national literary history in Kuwait. Mufarriḥ's perspective on Kuwaiti literary history can be understood as a perspective that aims to reread and reconstruct Kuwaiti literary history through emphasizing the affiliative literary and aesthetic aspects of belonging over official notions of national belonging, which allows *Bidun* poets to be a natural and organic extension of Kuwaiti literary history.

While early literary historians were primarily concerned with the question of national beginnings, Mufarriḥ seems to be less concerned. She rather undermines the nationalizing claims of past poets by stressing the unresolved tensions between a transnational past and a national present. She comments:

> If we are still contesting … whether Abdullah al-Faraj [1836–1901] was a Najdi, a Bahraini, a Kuwaiti or an Iraqi relying on the time he spent in each country, then the dispute over other poets preceding al-Faraj would certainly be more intense. Of those poets is Abduljalil al-Ṭabṭabaʾi, who only lived in Kuwait during the last ten years of his life.
>
> (Mufarriḥ 2007:10)

Instead of participating in the debate over the first Kuwaiti poet, Mufarriḥ abandons a historical approach altogether, starting with neither al-Ṭabṭabaʾi nor bin Sanad. Her criterion is less conventional, emphasizing what she calls 'poetic talent' over historical precedence. She begins her anthology with the most talented Kuwaiti poet in her view: Fahad al-ʿAskar (d. 1951). The book is also dedicated to al-ʿAskar, who she describes as 'a poet, witness and martyr'. Justifying her selection of al-ʿAskar as the first Kuwaiti poet, she writes:

> I have chosen willingly to start my historical selection with the most important poet in the Kuwaiti poetry scene, Fahad al-ʿAskar. This is not only because of my inclination towards his unprecedented poetics, but also because he was one of the turning points in the Kuwaiti and Gulf literary movements.
>
> (9)

A number of reasons make Fahad al-ʿAskar the most important poet in Mufarriḥ's view. He is an iconoclast in both his life choices and his poetics. Because of his non-conformist rebellious attitudes towards societal norms, al-Askar was considered a social outcast. His relatives 'rejected his life choices that went against their choices and the choices of their traditional society' (19). Al-ʿAskar's main biographer, al-Ansari, gives insight into the poet's confrontational attitude:

> From being religious to leaving religiosity, from having a conservative outlook to free progressive thought, from his sternness in conserving religion, inherited customs and traditions to a total break from it … he rushed into reading and enquiry, tracking the social and political movements, then to compulsive consumption of wine which he often wrote beautiful poems on.
>
> (al-Ansari 1997:81)

Al-Ansari notes that on al-ʿAskar's death, none of his relatives or friends attended his funeral (85). It is also purported that the majority of his poetry was burned by his close relatives after his death (al-Ansari 1997:75; Mufarriḥ 2007:18).

As for his iconoclastic poetics, al-ʿAskar brought about 'a new variation on the content of Kuwaiti poetry where the homeland, as a political entity, is a matter of direct criticism' (Mufarriḥ 2007:20). Al-ʿAskar's poetry decoupled belonging to homeland from official notions of belonging, an impulse shared by many *Bidun* writers. Similarly, Mufarriḥ has always been keen on decoupling belonging from acquiring official documentation. Despite her status as *Bidun*, she regards herself as a Kuwaiti poet:

> Whether others like it or not … I am a Kuwaiti in my existence, belonging and inclinations. This truth is unrelated to that paper called 'passport' … whether I gain citizenship from Kuwait or any other country, or if I never gain citizenship, Kuwait will remain my first, last and eternal homeland, simply because it is my only homeland.
>
> (Fawwaz 2012)

Al-Askar's critique of homeland embodies a poetics of estrangement that becomes a central theme of the Kuwaiti literary history narrative.

It is important to highlight what Mufarriḥ means in her use of the term 'estrangement' (*waḥsha*) when discussing al-ʿAskar by juxtaposing her analysis with previous studies concerning al-ʿAskar's alienation (*ightirab*) and discontent (*shakwa*). In *Alienation in Kuwaiti Poetry*, Suʿad Abdulraḥman writes that alienation (*ightirab*) is a phenomenon that 'is not prominent in the [*sic*] Kuwaiti poetry' (Abdulraḥman 1993–4:172 original translation). She adds that alienation 'is not assumed to be an "exceptional state", conditioned by a [*sic*] temporary situations, such as war or worries regarding [the] future' (172). It is rather 'a state of sharp awareness of time, recognition of what occurs in life and responding to individual misfortune' (171). The category of estranged Kuwaiti poets is limited to a few, such as Saqir al-Shibib, Fahad al-ʿAskar and Abd al-Muhsin al-Badir. Alienation in Kuwaiti poetry is presented as resulting from an individual impulse of self-reflection stemming from a critical mind and rebellious soul (172). Similarly, Nuriya al-Rumi locates the roots of al-ʿAskar's discontent (*shakwa*) in what the romantic school calls 'sickness of the Geist' (al-Rumi 1978). Mufarriḥ, however, offers a historical reading of al-ʿAskar's estrangement. She writes that the 'reasons behind his [al-ʿAskar's] hardship, sadness and true estrangement lie in the harsh life that he had experienced in his homeland, surrounded by those who suffocate him, standing as obstacles to his personal and national aspirations' (Mufarriḥ 2007:24).

Mufarriḥ presents Al-ʿAskar as a precursor to the Arab modernist literary movement in Kuwait. Her narrative of literary history following al-ʿAskar is guided by a notion of literariness embedded in an affiliation to the poetics of Arab literary modernism. Particular attention is given to those poets who adhere to that notion of literariness embodied in al-ʿAskar. Others perceived as 'traditionalists' or 'classical' are given less attention. After al-ʿAskar, Mufarriḥ introduces ʿAli al-Sabti (b.1936) and Muhammad al-Fayiz who inaugurate the 'new poem' (*al-qaṣida al-jadida*) influenced by the Arab literary modernity movement embodied in the figure of the Iraqi poet Badir Shakir al-Sayyab. Al-Sabti is the first to introduce modernist poetics (*al-ḥadatha al-shi'riyya*) while al-Fayiz's use of free verse poetry (*taf'ila*) in his epic poem 'Memoirs of a Seafarer' registered him a place within the poets of the modern Arabic literary movement. Yet both poets are criticized in the latter stages of their poetic life as they fell back into a more traditionalist outlook. In addition, the period includes Khalid Saud al-Zaid, whose poetry 'did not fall into the pits of traditionalism … as many of his contemporaries' (37–8).

Mufarriḥ brushes over a number of poets previously emphasized by al-Shaṭṭi's *Poetry in Kuwait*, including Khalifa al-Wuqayyan, Abdullah al-Utaybi, Ya'qub al-Subai'i, Ya'qub al-Rushaid, Ahmad al-Saqqaf and Abdullah Sinan, as 'their poetic attempts … did not step out of the general framework' (40). Particular attention is given to those who 'stepped out of the general framework' in the later stages such as the *Bidun* poet Sulayman al-Flayyiḥ (40). It is worth noting that al-Flayyiḥ is not introduced as a *Bidun* poet.

The bulk of Mufarriḥ's literary history is focused on what she terms the 'nineties generation' (*al-tis'iniyyun*), which includes the majority of *Bidun* poets. This generation 'found refuge in a style that rebels against all previous experimentations in writing in a more bold and intensified manner' (51). The content of this generation's writing tended to gravitate away from the 'grand issues' of the previous generations and into personal articulations of troubled identities. Mufarriḥ excludes a number of poets from the nineties generation as they wrote from within 'the trench of the classical musicality of the *qaṣida*' (64).

Before analysing the placement of *Bidun* writers within the narrative, it is important to identify a number of overarching themes in Mufarriḥ's narrative that allow *Bidun* writers to be an organic extension to the narrative. Firstly, in speaking about al-'Askar as the 'first' Kuwaiti poet, Mufarriḥ begins at a literary moment, rather than a chronological one. The notion of literariness guiding the narrative is embodied in the founding figure of al-'Askar as a precursor of modern literature. Al-'Askar's historical exclusion, rebellious attitude, poetics of estrangement and constant critique of homeland embody the spirit of the national poet and become the benchmark for inclusion for successive poets.

Secondly, estrangement is presented as a central theme in Kuwaiti literary history. It is not necessarily a reliable sense of belonging to the nation that gives the narrative its unity. Rather, it is the poets' unsettled sense of belonging and the inherent estrangement associated with the poetic vocation. As discussed earlier, the impulses of nation building tend to reinforce a stable sense of belonging in national literary history. Whereas al-Shaṭṭi reads al-ʿAskar's poetry as a 'departure from the norm', and a digression from the national literary narrative's relative stability, Mufarriḥ establishes al-ʿAskar as the norm. Al-Shaṭṭi's moments of rupture are Mufarriḥ's moments of continuity. Estrangement and exclusion here are not simply matters of paperwork and citizenship, but poetic identities that speak to a larger social and psychological condition that is at the heart of national literature and the literary vocation. In stressing the dominance of the theme of estrangement in Kuwaiti poetry, Mufarriḥ makes way for the *Bidun* poets, and their poetics, to become a natural extension of that history.

Thirdly, the emphasis on 'poetic talent' at the expense of historical precedence is a claim against the concept of authentic belonging. Simply put, belonging is not necessarily related to the question of how long one has been there, but a question of what one has given to the homeland. Transposed to political discourse, this position can be also read as a way to challenge the common political and social topos of 'bona fide', or first class Kuwaiti, based on the legal distinction between (Kuwaiti *bi-l-taʾsis*), those 'original Kuwaitis' who had maintained an established residence in Kuwait prior to 1920 and (Kuwaiti *bi-l-tajnis*) those who were naturalized without having maintained an established residence; a topos still strong in Kuwaiti political and social discourse.

The hero of Mufarriḥ's national literary history, it seems, is that individual poet who is constantly struggling with the established societal and poetic norms. With such a notion of literariness, or criteria for belonging to the national literary narrative, *Bidun* writers become an organic extension of the narrative.

The *Bidun*'s placement within Mufarriḥ's narrative is incontestable. Mufarriḥ does not place *Bidun* writers in a special category. Rather, they are placed within their generational clusters. Sulayman al-Flayyiḥ is introduced as part of the few poets from the 1970s generation who wrote their poetry 'outside of the general framework'. Al-Flayyiḥ was also a

> reminder of the other half of Kuwaiti society … if Kuwait was established as a maritime city par excellence, it couldn't have soared without that accord between its two wings of sea and desert … and from the depth of the desert, al-Flayyiḥ emerged.
>
> (41)

With no mention of his *Bidun* status, al-Flayyiḥ is placed within a wider context of a Bedouin poet from the desert whose contributions cannot be overlooked.

The majority of *Bidun* poets are placed within the nineties generation. She writes, '[T]he loss of identity is one of the main problems facing this generation as part of the Kuwaiti cultural scene within a wider Arab topography' (66). This loss of identity is primarily a result of the shock of the Iraqi invasion that necessitated major ideological revisions to the idea of a unified Arab national identity. Yet, within the nineties generation, Mufarriḥ specifically singles out *Bidun* poets as suffering from a more acute sense of loss that goes beyond ideological revisions, as they 'search for an identity on the margins of a present that refuses to recognize their identity' (66). The question of the loss of identity of the *Bidun* is thus presented as an intensification of the dominant literary *theme* of estrangement within the Kuwaiti literary history narrative. These conditions imposed on the *Bidun* writers give rise to a new unique poetics, which is considered an essential contribution that adheres to the very founding spirit of Kuwaiti literature.

In her discussion of *Bidun* poets, Mufarriḥ includes former *Bidun* poets who no longer reside in Kuwait and have become citizens of other countries such as Sulayman al-Flayyiḥ (Saudi), Muhammad al-Nabhan (Canadian) and Ahmad al-Dusari (Bahraini) among others. Whereas early literary historians needed to contextualize and acknowledge the fluidity of the notion of belonging of past poets to understand a national past, Mufarriḥ suggests an extension of this logic to understand a national present. The inclusionary or contextualizing attitude expressed by early literary historians in approaching the question of beginnings is extended in Mufarriḥ's reading of a national present. In forging national literary histories, a certain spirit of a nation is projected through its poets and poetry. The essential spirit of national literature, as Mufarriḥ seems to suggest, is that forsaken inclusive attitude and openness towards those who contribute. Any exclusionary approach, based on non-literary principles, then becomes a deviation from the very spirit that constituted Kuwaiti literature in its formative stages. A literary approach to literary history heeds to the realities of literary affiliations beyond the traditional borders of the nation state.

In her literary history, Mufarriḥ does not propose to abandon a national platform, nor does she essentialize the *Bidun* as a marginal literary community having a distinct identity or tradition that is independent of the national narrative. While *Bidun* writers specifically are emphasized and made visible, they are not excluded by excess visibility through writing a *Bidun* literary history, for example. Mufarriḥ carefully treads the fine line between recognizing the uniqueness of the *Bidun* writers and their inclusion within the national narrative. Her point of departure is precisely national literary history. However, what is at stake is the concept of the national itself, which is reworked through an emphasis on the inclusivity of literary and cultural affiliation over the exclusivity of the limiting notions of official belonging.

A final radicalizing tool in Mufarriḥ's revisionist work is the question of language style. Instead of a more pedagogical use of language found in other literary histories, Mufarriḥ uses a highly stylized poetic language. The title stands as a marker of that poetic use of language. When compared to other literary history titles such as *Kuwaiti Writers between Two Centuries, The Literary Movement in Kuwait, Modern Poetry in Kuwait, Poetry and Poets in Kuwait, Culture in Kuwait* and *Poetry in Kuwait*, the title *The Cameleers of Clouds and Estrangement* seems like a methodological shift and a departure from that genealogy of Kuwaiti literary history titles.

The question of 'proper' titles for literary histories is brought to light by the Kuwaiti poet and critic Abd al-Razzaq al-Baṣir (1919–1999), who once criticized al-ʿAlawi al-Hashimi's 1981 study on Bahraini literary history titled *Ma Qalat al-Nakhla li-l-Baḥr* (What the Palm Tree Told the Sea) (1981). On the title, al-Baṣir comments:

> I don't know why Dr. ʿAlawi al-Hashimi has selected this title for his book. It is more suited for a story or a poem. But to be a title of a broad and in-depth work of literary criticism is a matter over which I see myself in disagreement with the author.
>
> (al-Baṣir 1986:117)

Al-Baṣir's comment perhaps reflects a general classicist attitude and expectation of language use in approaching works of national literary history within the region. A clear distinction is made between literary histories' factuality and seriousness and literature's playful subjectivity, which are both realized in 'proper' respective discourse.

This contrast between Mufarriḥ's literariness and al-Baṣir's insistence on an objective use of language can be read in a number of ways. One can read it in light of postmodern approaches to historiography, where as Mark Currie argues 'the neutral tones of traditional historicism have yielded to a rampantly tropological language: language pervaded by metaphorical, analogical, and associative modes of connection and argumentation' (Currie 2004:77). Mufarriḥ's use of tropological language can also be read in light of a gendered approach to rewriting history. Literary history is a site of contestation, not only as it relates to an inclusion of a marginalized group in the national framework, but also as a gendered space subject to another form of hegemonic masculine discourse. Indeed, one can entirely read Mufarriḥ's work in such light. The playful use of a poetic language in writing literary history blurs the lines between a seemingly neutral, masculine and objective writing usually associated with nation-building and a subjective literary approach capable of resisting hegemonic discourses in both its national and masculine guises.

Conclusion

Mufarriḥ's revisionist work radicalizes national literary history writing in Kuwait while opening up spaces for articulating a presence and a belonging beyond questions of official exclusion. The title of the publication encapsulates the capacity of the literary to intervene: the individual cameleer in the desert urging the camel, always with an effort, a song or a poem to follow her trail. Mufarriḥ plays on the Arabic word *hadi* which when used in the form *Hadwa*ʾ becomes another name for the northern winds that urge the clouds like a cameleer urges his camels with songs. The poet, like the northern winds becomes a cameleer of the spirit of the nation, imprinting her meaning while contesting its limiting demarcations.

Similarly, the capacity of the literary to intervene can be transposed to the general study of modern societies in the Gulf. An investigation into the often neglected arena of literary history writing in the Gulf offers critical insight into how notions of belonging can be analysed beyond the logic of conventional descriptive and anthropological methodologies of approaching modern societies in the Gulf, where societies are primarily understood along anthropological units of analysis: national, sectarian (Sunni-Shiites), tribal, sociopolitical (*Badu-Haḍar*) or according to territory of origin (*'Ajam*, *Hawala, Najdis*, Africans). The critical and analytical perspectives emerging from within literary and cultural articulations widen the categories of representation whether it be an isolated 'stateless' literature, or an 'adjacent' literature excluded from any placement within national literatures.

4

The desert apocalypse: The last bedouin, the first *Bidun*

In June of 1976, the 25-year-old poet Sulayman al-Flayyiḥ (1951–2013) was invited to participate in the annual poetry festival organized by the Kuwaiti Writers' Association (*Rabita*). There, he debuted poems from his first poetry collection *Singing in the Deserts of Agony* (1979), the first poetry collection to be ever published by a *Bidun* poet. On that night, the Kuwaiti poet and literary historian Khalid Saud al-Zaid, previously encountered in Chapter 3, enthusiastically introduced the young poet with the following words:

> Whenever the streams of the city dry out, the desert brings forth its streams. Whenever life in the city becomes more perplexed, the desert gushes with the intuition of Bedouin life, which is like the sun in its purity and serenity. The desert is forever a merciful mother and its prophet is now carrying to you some of its fragrant flowers .... In this man sitting on my right, the intuition of the desert and the experience of the city converge.
>
> (Majallat al-Bayan 1976:10)

In this moment of reception, al-Flayyiḥ's voice was elicited to represent a long-lost and romanticized space, an idealized desert against which modernity and the city are contrasted. The desert space as described by al-Zaid is site of intuition, purity, authenticity, origin and serenity that is unpolluted by the perplexities of modernity afflicting the city. These short introductory lines, albeit intended as praise, celebrate an ahistoric arrival of the desert poet. The Bedouin poet emerges like a 'prophet' from the desert and is made visible in history at the precise moment of encounter with the city. The desert space, unlike the perplexed city, is a space of ontological void, outside of linear time altogether.

Contrary to al-Zaid's description, al-Flayyiḥ, in the poems recited on the night, and in his literary works more broadly, continually depicts a desert space that is itself subject to the disturbances of modernity and in need of rejuvenation. In these poems, al-Flayyiḥ disrupts the communal projections of his city dwelling, nostalgic audience by articulating a desert space that has been subjected to the very same material realities as theirs, of the modern imposition of borders and the demise of the authentic life. A year prior to the *Rabita's* annual poetry event, Al-Flayyiḥ published his first poem, which he considers to be his true poetic birth titled 'Apprehensions of the Lakhmid Knight in Corrupt Times'. In this poem, the poet gives a powerful poetic rendering of the apocalypse of the desert and the displacement of its inhabitants. While his reception depicts the desert as an established ahistorical space of origin, al-Flayyiḥ rather represents the desert as a space of alternate historical beginnings. The contested literary representations of the desert space, outlined in the poetry night, are central to an historicized understanding of the *Bidun* issue at large. In the works of al-Flayyiḥ, which are the main focus of this chapter, the desert space is utilized poetically as a pre-national site where modern statelessness is historicized and particularized and where the historicity of the desert is restored.

Stateless sons of the desert

The depoliticized and dehistoricized representations of the *Bidun* have been instrumental to their continual denial of citizenship rights. Beaugrand's contends that 'the history of the *Bidun* cannot be written without placing it back into the broader framework of the desert, constructed as a place of lawlessness and legality – which is somehow the reality to which the official designation of the *Biduns* as "illegal residents" refers' (Beaugrand 2018:16). Any attempt to historicize the issue is inextricably linked to an understanding of the history of the desert and its inhabitants. In the face of an overpowering national narrative concomitant with the development of modern states, the desert as an alternative material and cultural space of belonging was overlooked, which in turn rendered many of its inhabitants stateless.

The 1959 Nationality Law defined 'original' Kuwaiti nationals as those who maintained an established residence in Kuwait prior to 1920. The year 1920 marks the construction of *al-Sur al-thalith* (the third wall) around the town of Kuwait to protect it from external threats. As al-Nakib puts it, the wall became 'a new physical barrier separating the town from the desert, it developed over time into a psychological obstacle dividing the *hadhar* on the inside from the Bedouin tribes and villagers on the outside' (al-Nakib 2010:384). The 1959 Nationality Law's requirement of providing an established residence within the walls of the town of Kuwait prior to 1920 laid the foundations of the modern-state's notions of belonging and territoriality.

To validate citizenship claims, the 1959 Nationality Law established Nationality Committees. Originally, four committees were established each including five prominent members of Kuwaiti society 'who were considered to have reasonable knowledge of most Kuwaiti families' (Al-Anezi 1989:182). The evidence for establishing a proof of residence prior to 1920 included providing official documentation (including ownership of real-estate deeds, Kuwaiti passports based on the 1948 Nationality Law, birth certificates and marriage contracts), and other subjective evidence such as statements made by witnesses who can validate the applicant's claim and the applicant's accent and appearance (181). Such criteria, which favour those living within the town wall, made it especially difficult for Bedouin applicants to provide evidence of their citizenship claims. As al-Anezi puts it:

> The task of the Nationality Committee was made more difficult by the fact that thousands of Bedouins applied for Kuwaiti nationality on the ground that they lived and had for long lived within the territorial limits of Kuwait but not within a city or town. Similarity of culture, traditions, appearance, dialect and costume existing between the Bedouins of the Arabian Desert, which extends between Kuwait, Saudi Arabia, Iraq, Syria and Jordan, made it more difficult still for the Committee to distinguish between dwellers of the Kuwaiti Desert and others. Proof of belonging to a tribe settled within the territory of Kuwait was furnished through a statement from the leader of the tribe that the individual person was a member of the tribe.
>
> (256)

As a result of such measures, the work of the National Committees 'resulted in the creation of a large number of people who insist that they are Kuwaiti nationals notwithstanding decisions of the Committees to the contrary' (257). Many of the *Bidun*, who at the time of the establishment of the committees were officially labelled as *Abna' al-Badiyya* (sons of the desert), were not incorporated into the national imaginary. Indeed, one can trace the roots of the *Bidun* issue to the critical historical juncture of the 1959 Nationality Law and the subsequent assessment of citizenship claims performed by the Nationality Committees between 1960 and 1963.

In subsequent years, the *Bidun*'s official label was changed from 'sons of the desert', which designated an historicized positionality, origin and historical space of belonging, to other labels that fixed the *Bidun* within the discourses of the state bureaucracy: *Bidun Jinsiyya* (those without citizenship); *Ghayr Kuwaiti* (non-Kuwaitis); *Ghayr Muḥaddad al-Jinsiyya* (those with undetermined citizenship); *Majhuli al-Hawiyya* (those whose identities are unknown) and finally *Muqimun bi Ṣura Ghayr Qanuniyya* (illegal residents).

Such labels dehistoricized the issue by positioning the *Bidun* within the hegemonic historiographical discourses of the state. Pre-national notions of belonging, territoriality and sovereignty embedded in the desert space have been forcibly rendered superfluous by an overpowering official narrative. The history of the sons of the desert, as a collective group, then becomes restricted to the history of modern statelessness. In light of the above, the significance of the desert space in many works of *Bidun* writers cannot be overstated.

Bidun writers often utilize the desert as a space where modern statelessness and uprootedness are contested. It is often returned to, poetically, as both a real and an imaginative space to reclaim a sense of uncontested origin and belonging prior to the inception of the modern nation state. At the same time, it is a space where pre-national conceptions of belonging, territoriality and sovereignty are historicized and legitimated.

A brief note on statelessness and the desert

The desert has long been a site of many imaginations in literature. It is a space that has been often synonymous with timelessness, emptiness, sacredness, silence, innocence and spirituality. In her study of the representations of the desert in the literary imaginary of the Americas, Maria del Pilar Blanco traces the desert imagination back to European romanticism which 'dealt with this spatial tabula rasa as a site for renewal, reinvention, and regeneration' (61). The desert has been 'perversely allegorized … vulnerable to attributions of immense meanings and suspensions of human history' (69). Similarly, this romantic streak has dominated the representations of the Arabian desert in orientalist literature. As Said points out, the Arabian desert particularly 'has been an especially privileged place for the Orientalist ... considered to be a locale about which one can make statements ... devoid of historical grounding' (Said 1978:235). European travellers often shared a sentiment of disappointment and lament of a lost orient, a common trope in romantic literature (100). The disappointment relates to the failure of the modern orient to match up to the transcendent orient existent in the orientalist imaginary. The influence of European romanticism may have been instrumental in the literary representations of the deserts by modern Arab poets. Al-Zaid's aforementioned depiction of the desert cannot be viewed in isolation from latent orientalist-romanticist representations.

In the context of modern Arabic literature, the desert space has often been utilized as a space where questions of displacement, identity and belonging are tested and refigured. In the works of Ibrahim al-Kuni, for example, the desert is 'a timeless microcosm that allows for a re-enactment of the story of creation and the everlasting struggle between good and evil' and 'as a stimulus for existential quest and Sufi struggle' (Fouad 2013:39). On the depiction of the desert in the modern Arabic novel, Wen-Chin Ouyang comments, 'the historical ambivalence towards the desert makes it possible for the Arabic novel to portray the desert as stateless and situate statelessness there' (Ouyang 2012:73). Particularly, Palestinian writers such as Ghassan Kanafani, Ibrahim Nasrallah and Mahmoud Darwish often depict the desert as a space of 'journey and transformation' and at the same time 'a metaphor for displacement, homelessness, and statelessness' (76).

The case of Palestinian writers' representations of the desert space carries special relevance to *Bidun* writers. Firstly, both Palestinian and *Bidun* writers share an experience of displacement in its different manifestations. Secondly, Palestinian writers such Kanafani and Nasrallah write of the desert of the Arabian Peninsula, a geographic and imaginative space often revisited and shared by *Bidun* writers. In both cases, the desert space is closely related to questions of identity and displacement, yet, in significantly different ways.

Khalida Saʿid describes the desert in Kanafani's *Men in the Sun*, as a 'geography of danger' (cited in Ouyang 2012:77). The desert is portrayed as a space of absolute unfamiliarity, failed journeys and hostile death. Similarly, the desert in Nasrallah's *Barari al-Ḥumma*

> spreads, stretches endlessly, covers everything and swallows anything on its path. It engulfs like its night, day, and silence, leaving nothing and nobody immune to its overpowering hegemonic immensity ... it is the home of wolves, foxes, hyenas, snakes, carnivorous vultures feasting on human remains, and wild dogs barking incessantly.
>
> (77)

The desert, in such works, becomes a metaphor for ultimate displacement and a liminal space of inhabitability, unfamiliarity and statelessness. However, in the works of *Bidun* writers, specifically in the work of Sulayman al-Flayyiḥ as will be discussed, the desert is represented as a familiar space of abode and a site where modern statelessness is historicized and particularized.

The desert of national belongings

As mentioned above, al-Flayyiḥ's collection titled *Singing in the Deserts of Agony* (1979) is the first poetry collection to be published by a *Bidun* poet. The poetry collection inaugurates the body of what this book reads as *Bidun* literature. Even though al-Flayyiḥ is considered the first published *Bidun* poet, the term *Bidun* did not at the time carry the connotative weight that it carried in later periods. When Al-Flayyiḥ first contributed to the national literary scene in the mid-1970s, the *Bidun* issue had yet to emerge in clear material form as it did in the post-1986 era. Only preliminary features of statelessness were perceivable, mostly restricted to the lack of official documentation, denial of political rights and spatial marginalization as mentioned in chapter one. Yet statelessness was not a serious impediment to everyday life in the city. Many of the *Bidun*, such as al-Flayyiḥ were integrated into the state's structure by enlisting in the Kuwaiti army.

Before arriving in Kuwait in the late 1960s, al-Flayyiḥ lived and received his education in Jordan where his uncle served in the Jordanian army under Sir John Bagot Glubb, commonly referred to as Glubb Pasha. He later moved to Kuwait to enlist in the Kuwaiti army, which was facilitated by a tribal identifier (*mu'arrif*) who would authenticate applicants belonging to his tribe. In the army, al-Flayyiḥ was chosen to serve as part of the communications bureau, which offered him a chance to train as a journalist in *al-Siyasah* daily newspaper. The army later dispatched him during the 1973 Arab-Israeli War to serve as a war correspondent. During his career, al-Flayyiḥ was highly active in journalistic circles and a prolific commentator on cultural affairs. Between 1975 and 2013, the year he died, he continued to write his column *Hatharologia* ('the science of blabbering') in different newspapers including the Kuwaiti papers *al-Siyasah, al-Ṭali'a, al-Waṭan, al-Rai al'Am, Awan* and *al-Jarida* and the Saudi papers *al-Riyaḍ, al-Jazira.*

While living in Kuwait between the late 1960s and 1990, and despite his service in the army and established journalistic and literary career, al-Flayyiḥ continued to live in Kuwait as a *Bidun*. Interestingly, in Sami al-Flayyiḥ's biography of his father, there is no explicit mention of al-Flayyiḥ's *Bidun* status. It is only hinted at as 'facing daily bureaucratic problems' (al-Flayyiḥ 2013:31). In 1999, al-Flayyiḥ was granted Saudi citizenship by Salman Ibn Abdulaziz, who was the governor of Riyadh at the time. Along with his family, al-Flayyiḥ settled in Riyadh where he passed away in August 2013.

Given his biography, al-Fulayyih's 'national belonging' cannot be understood solely through official documentation and recognition. In a newspaper article titled 'I Have Two Homelands', al-Flayyiḥ does not just speak of a national belonging, but of national belongings. He writes:

> Here I am for the first time writing about *umi al-waṭan* (my mother-homeland), Kuwait, since I have left her to *al-waṭan al-um* (my homeland-mother), the Kingdom of Saudi Arabia. Dear readers, have you ever witnessed a man with two mothers and two homelands despite living most of his life homeless? Travelling on his camel in the desert, he has been tossed from one to another. Without a passport, he wakes up in one homeland and sleeps in another heeding to his camel's will in search for sustenance.
>
> (Al-Flayyiḥ 2007)

His description transcends official notions of belonging by emphasizing his belonging to the more fluid space of the desert. Situating himself in the desert, travelling on his camelback without a passport, allows him to belong to more than one homeland simultaneously and interchangeably or to none.

Al-Flayyiḥ constantly refers back to the desert as a space of uncontested belonging where official notions are challenged. Of his birth, al-Flayyiḥ writes:

> I am Sulayman bin Flayyiḥ al-Suba'i al-'Inizi. I was born, according to the tribe's narrative between 1951 and 1952 .... Under a desert tree, my mother gave birth to me. She wrapped me in her *Abaya* and continued to sing along the journeying tribe's trail moving towards the brink of the clouds in search of water and fodder.
>
> (al-Khaldi 2013: 11)

The description, albeit in metaphorical language, emphasizes notions of temporality and spatiality associated with the desert space. Al-Flayyiḥ is born into movement in the undisclosed vastness of the desert. The fluidity of the desert space is given precedence over territorial and temporal fixities.

The spatial fluidity of the desert is emphasized by al-Flayyiḥ's description of his tribe's semi-nomadic movement and the abrupt shift that occurred in the 1950s. Al-Flayyiḥ was part of a generation who had experienced a transition from a semi-nomadic mode of life in the desert to an enforced process of sedentarization at the peripheries of cities. He describes this collective transition:

> I have moved to and fro on my camel's back across many homelands that share the vast *Ḥamad* region reputed to be one of my tribe's lands since pre-Islamic times. Its vastness extends to parts of the Kingdom of Saudi Arabia, the Hashemite Kingdom of Jordan, the Syrian Arab Republic and Iraq. My journeying tribe has always slept within one country's borders waking up in another ... in search of rainfall, and fodder, and other sources of water.
>
> This constant movement lasted till the mid-fifties when years of drought ... hit that part of the region. Thus, my tribe (greater 'Iniza) dispersed in all cities and countries that overlapped or are part of that land.
>
> (Al-Flayyiḥ 2007)

Al-Flayyiḥ historically identifies with the *Ḥamad* area of the northern Arabian Desert, which spills over four modern national borders. It is a space that both extends over and transcends official national borders. The *Ḥamad* area is depicted as a witness to an uninterrupted sense of origin and belonging since 'pre-Islamic times'. At a particular moment in history, the tribe's historical seasonal movement in between the different national borders halted due to the restrictions imposed by modern state borders in the postcolonial era. At work in such a description is a legitimation of the differing notions of territoriality, sovereignty and belonging of the desert space.

Edward Said describes the life of the displaced exile as life 'led outside habitual order … nomadic, decentered, contrapuntal' (Said 2001: 149). Said speaks of a modern conception of exile in a postcolonial world where one is forcibly taken 'out of place' into an alien place. However, the notion of displacement takes on a different light when viewed in the context of al-Flayyiḥ's own postcolonial reflections. Displacement as a modern phenomenon occurred precisely at the time when restrictions on transnational movement took place and when life became forcibly *centred* and *sedentary.* Al-Flayyiḥ's insistence on reclaiming the desert space as a site of belonging is also evident in his literary persona as the 'last Bedouin'.

The 'last Bedouin' in the city

Throughout the book, other proximate terms for the term 'Bedouin' have been used interchangeably depending on different contexts and discourses. Terms such as *afrād al-ʿashāʾir* (tribesmen) or *abnāʾ al-badiyya* (sons of the desert) have been used in legal discourse to refer to a group of people who come from a Bedouin background. The term *Badu,* as opposed to the *Ḥaḍar,* has also been used as an anthropological unit of analysis within the Kuwaiti social structure (Longva 2006; al-Nakib 2014). In such works, the term 'Bedouin' is used as a classifier of origin, as opposed to Badu which refers to a sociopolitical category, of Bedouin origin, but 'are no longer technically Bedouin' (al-Nakib 2014:8).

The particular choice of the term 'Bedouin' to describe al-Flayyiḥ is based on his own use of the term as a self-identifier. Similarly, his reception as will be discussed, emphasizes his experiences a Bedouin poet belonging to the desert. However, as the chapter aims to demonstrate, al-Flayyiḥ problematizes the category of the Bedouin in both its legal and its anthropological guises. Al-Flayyiḥ posits 'Bedouinness', like the modern formulations of nomadism, as a subjectivity rather than solely a question of anthropological origin. At the same time, 'Bedouinness' becomes a question of a relational alterity and a set of values, as opposed to a fixed notion of identity.

In her newspaper article titled *Bidun Literature*, Najma Idris considers al-Flayyiḥ the 'godfather of *Bidun* literature' who uses the literary mask of the *Ṣaʿalik* to confront his marginalization (Idris 2012). Throughout his literary career, al-Flayyiḥ affiliated with the deep-rooted literary tradition of the *Ṣaʿalik* (sing. *Ṣuʿluk*) poets in classical Arabic literature. The *Ṣaʿalik*, who will be examined in more detail later in the chapter, are a band of excommunicated poets who sustain a sense of self-sufficiency outside of the dominant social order by taking refuge in the desert. In terms of their poetic expression, the poetry of the *Ṣaʿalik* valorizes *ṣaʿlaka*, or the act of living as a *Ṣuʿluk*, as a mode of life and a subjectivity that defies communal consensus.

Yet the critical reception of Al-Flayyiḥ's works has seldom been read in light of his statelessness. Instead of being identified as a *Bidun* poet, al-Flayyiḥ's literary persona as expressed in his early works and reception is encapsulated in the image of the 'last Bedouin' who is experiencing an acute sense of estrangement amid the perplexities of the modern city. Khalil al-ʿAbwini and Abdulfattaḥ read al-Flayyiḥ's return to the desert in light of modern Arabic poetry's Pan-Arab aspirations. The desert, in al-Flayyiḥ's works, offers a deep-rooted sense of identity that can guide the awakening of the Arab nation (Abdulfattaḥ). The desert is also utilized to warn against the return of neocolonial forces threatening the aspirations of Arabs (Al-ʿAbwini 1982:205). Within the context of literature in the Gulf, al-Bazei reads al-Flayyiḥ's merging of Bedouin imagery with modernist techniques as an embodiment of the transformation in modernist poetics in the Gulf (al-Bazei 1991:148).

In al-Zaid aforementioned introduction to the 1976 poetry night, al-Flayyiḥ is described as a rejuvenating 'prophet from the desert' in whom 'the intuition of the desert and the experience of the city converge'. This contrast between desert and city as analysed earlier in the chapter carries some semblance with Raymond Williams' reflections of the city-country divide in the English literary imaginary. Williams writes:

> On the country has gathered the idea of a natural way of life: of peace, innocence, and simple virtue. On the city has gathered the idea of an achieved centre of learning, communication, light. Powerful hostile associations have also developed: on the city as a place of noise, worldliness and ambition; on the country as a place of backwardness, ignorance, limitation.
>
> (Williams 1975:1)

It is through this negative association with the country, that the city gathers its relevant meanings. The lost authenticity of the complex city is legitimated by the stagnation of an authentic 'other'. Such divisions created fictions that 'served to promote superficial comparisons and to prevent real ones' (54). Similarly, al-Zaid's desert of authenticity becomes the space of 'nature' and nostalgic moorings where a lost 'organic' society can be recovered.

Regina Bendix's insights on the search for authentic culture, particularly within the discipline of folk studies, are helpful in understanding al-Flayyiḥ's reception as a desert poet. In her book titled *In Search of Authenticity*, Bendix contends that the pursuit for authentic culture, within German and American folklore studies, has been inextricably linked to nationalist ideologies and the processes of modernization. Authenticity has long served as legitimizing tool for nationalists' claim of returning to a 'true spirit' of the nation (Bendix 1997:8). At the same time, the search for authenticity is 'oriented toward the recovery of an essence whose loss has been realized only through modernity, and whose recovery is feasible only through methods and sentiments created in modernity' (8). The object of this pursuit, or the ideal folk community, is that which is 'pure and free from civilization's evils … a metaphor for everything that was not modern' (7). Authentication is a two-way process. As Bendix puts it, '[d]eclaring something authentic legitimated the subject that was declared authentic, and the declaration in turn can legitimate the authenticator' (7).

The reception of al-Flayyiḥ as a representative of a communal desert imaginary can be read in light of both Williams and Bendix's insights. As presented by al-ʿAbwini and Abdulfattaḥ, al-Flayyiḥ's desert is read from an Arab nationalist outlook as a space of authentic national origin where an essential identity for the Arab Nation can be found and resurrected. Al-Flayyiḥ's desert is also depicted, as in the reception of al-Zaid, as an authentic 'other' to reflect on the nature of modernity afflicting the city. The desert's intuition, purity and serenity are juxtaposed with the city's perplexities and experiences.

The *Rabita's* poetry festival in 1976 was a stage from which al-Flayyiḥ disrupted a communal desert imaginary. While his reception emphasized the moment of arrival in the city, al-Flayyiḥ's poems were instead absorbed in the moments of displacement and departure from the desert abode.

Two poems exemplify this contrast between al-Flayyiḥ's conception of the desert space and his audience's. In the first poem *The Journeying Bedouins*, published in the poetry collection *Sorrows of the Journeying Bedouins* (1981), the poet articulates the experiences of a generation of last Bedouins as they complete their final journey from the campsite to an uneasy arrival at the city gates where they are faced by fierce politics of exclusion. In the second poem *Apprehensions of Corrupt Times*, published in al-Flayyiḥ's first poetry collection *Singing in the Deserts of Agony* (1979), the poet thematizes the apocalypse of the poet's campsite and the total demise of desert life and the displacement of its people. Both poems will be read against al-Flayyiḥ's reception as a representative of the communal desert imaginary. The analysis aims to expose the mediation between the poet's reception and his poetic articulation, labelling and self-positionality, eliciting the communal desert voice and act of attentive listening to the poet.

A journey of displacement: *The Sorrows of Journeying Bedouins*

Here they are-my tribe descending from the heights of the past- dust-colored gray eyed
Winds of the future lash them towards oases populated with rainwater
Here they are – like locusts of imminent drought coming from the last lands of the world
They arrived and scattered in this sandy desert like stones
Here they are- sleeping at the borders of the blue clouds
Impoverished they bed down in bramble bushes
They dreamt of dawn and wept as they saw a thunderbolt tearing the darkness
limping in the circle of shut horizons, receding gradually
At dawn, their tears wetted the wind, the earth, and the trees,
Here they rise to their feet walking towards the limits of big cities
Hungry, thirsty, eating parched bread, drinking putrid water and fire
Here they are at the borders of big cities with hunched backs, broken spirits, overspread in their shabby worn-out garments,
Here they are, whiplashed by the horsemen of the Tatar army driving them away from the gates of big cities.

> Here they are before the gates, laying down like pieces of hollowed wood.
> There they are, extinguished stars at the horizons of the blue clouds,
> so that in this era, a final curtain comes down on the tales of the journeying Bedouins.
>
> (al-Flayyiḥ 1981:71–3)

The poet's voice narrates the last journey of his tribe from the desert campsite to the peripheries of cities. The poet is at once a participant in the journey and an onlooker. The journey is described from a bird's-eye viewpoint: 'here they are descending'. This panoramic view allows for an understanding of the tribe's history prior to the encounter with the national borders and their imminent displacement. In this poetic narration, the poet traces the enforced displacement and uneasy arrival of the last generation of Bedouins.

The enforced displacement in the desert is twofold. It is induced by the desert's 'imminent drought' and unsustainability and by the modern impositions on movement that rendered a known way of life obsolete. The desert's unsustainability is symbolized by the theme of water, or the lack of it. The tribe's journey is essentially in search for oases filled with rainwater as the imminent drought besieges them. In sight, blue clouds and thunderbolts in the horizon promise rain, but are now, like the desert as an abode, short of their potential.

The image of blue clouds is returned to in the final part of the poem. Before the city gates, the tribe are like 'extinguished stars at the horizons of the blue clouds'. This double usage evokes the two 'blue' limits of the desert. On the vertical side, the blue clouds in the sky promising rain and life and horizontally alluding to the blue sea, a metaphor of the city, as a geographical limit of the desert. Besieged by limitation and lack of water, the only instance of water in the poem is found when the tribe's own tears wet the winds, earth and trees. The relationship between the desert and its inhabitants is now inverted. A new relationship emerges where the desert can only be cried for as it is rendered obsolete as a space of habitat. Whatever is left of that mode of life is past and unattainable. Tears, laments and elegies of the desert now give meaning and life back to the desert, at the level of the poetic imaginary. The *Sorrows of the Journeying Bedouins* is itself elegiac; an instance of those tears wetting the desert with meaning. The lack of water, as a pressing theme throughout the poem, stands as a signifier of the desert's unsustainability inducing the tribe's displacement.

Concomitant with the desert's own rejection of its inhabitants is the imposed restriction on movement by the modern inception of state borders. This is expressed in the discrepancy between the desert's promised spatial capacity and a modern inability to fathom it. The vastness and fluidity of the desert as a site of journey is underplayed by a vocabulary charged with a sense of limitation and a general ambience of confinement. In the desert, the tribe is confronted with 'shut horizons', 'limits', 'edges', 'borders' and 'city gates'. This sense of limitation transforms the desert from a space of familiarity and habitability to a space where its inhabitants are estranged. In their own abode, they now undertake their last journey as interlopers, as 'locusts' seeking rain and refuge. They travel as disempowered broken individuals 'lashed by the winds', 'impoverished' and 'limping' towards water-filled oases. More so, the tribe is scattered in the desert like stones. This juxtaposition of sand and stone is indicative of the divide between the desert's unbounded potential and modern borders' imposing reality on the tribe's movement. These two forces, drought and modern restrictions, coerce the tribe to undertake their last journey from the desert into the peripheries of cities. They arrive at the city gates hungry, thirsty, broken and powerless. It is an uneasy, destabilizing and unwelcome arrival. At the city gates, they are confronted with violence and exclusion.

Displacement started with the desert's rejection of its people and is then finalized at the city gates when the tribe is denied entry into the city. They are not only denied entry, but more importantly, denied a journey back. Even more, they are denied the journey as an essence of the journeying Bedouins as the title of the poem suggests. The inherent adjective 'journeying' of the Bedouins is usurped leaving them as extinguished stars, pieces of hollow wood, contained and controlled at the mercy of 'the army of Tatar'. The end of the journey represents the end of an era, where the 'final curtain comes down on the tales of the journeying Bedouins'.

At work in the poem is a historicization of the communal arrival of the last Bedouins. This arrival carries its own particular historical process outside of ready-made histories. Most importantly, it narrates an enforced displacement represented in a destabilizing desert journey and an uneasy arrival at the city gates. Read against al-Flayyiḥ's reception in the *Rabita*, the poem highlights a destabilizing and disempowering arrival to the city. The poet's arrival from the desert is received as a source of rejuvenation, like the desert bringing forth its water streams, intuition and a sense of repose from the perplexities of the city. Yet the poet instead articulates a desert space that is itself perhaps even more perplexed, in dire need of water and rejuvenation.

While the national reception celebrated promising beginnings and inevitable harmony, it is countered by another history of ends and beginnings, an end of an era of the last Bedouins and a beginning of a new history of a displaced people. In retrospect, one can read the arrival of the last Bedouins as the very arrival of the first *Biduns*. In a broader sense, al-Flayyiḥ's historicization of the collective journey of the tribe can also be read as offering a more nuanced understanding of the transnational nature of the region and more importantly of the particular history of the *Bidun*. In the poem, the desert space is returned to as a site to claim a historical narrative that precedes an overpowering national narrative.

While *The Sorrows of the Journeying Bedouins* follows the trail of the journeying Bedouins as they complete their last journey from the campsite to the city's periphery, the next poem in this analysis *Apprehensions of Corrupt Times* thematizes the moment of displacement of the poet in the desert abode.

The Apocalypse of the Desert: *The Apprehensions of Corrupt Times*[1] (1979)

And I have dreamt today, mother
of winds storming the grazing lands
holding back my horses
expelling my camels
lashing me in public with a snake
tying me behind my tribe's campsite
and when thirsty, it serves me my blood
mother, it has stretched in its tyranny

* * *

And yesterday I saw, mother, horses with severed heads
invading my tribe

And I saw a woman over a banner hoisted
chanting my name
naked, blood-ridden
I saw ruby coloured clouds racing over our campsite
Showering our tribe's men with firewater and the spirit of poison.
And I saw you, mother, in anguish
spreading sand between the dead
gathering left over flesh
and I saw a crow as great as the night
crowing around me
circling around the tent, neglecting my presence
stealing my child
and flying far away
leaving me wallowing in the black sand
I lost my sanity
I saw lions roaring whispers
I saw dogs barking at the sun
I saw voracious wolves
I saw crowds of black ants on flowers
I saw drunken goats

***

And I have dreamt today, mother, of the long tamarisk branches
protruding out of the horses' corpses
turning into yellow buds
smelling of a stony scent
intertwined like the horns of deer
mushrooming like a terminal anxiety
the teeth of the night chews on it
vomiting it on the flowery face of dusk
in the face of whorish times
spitting on a generation's face
and I saw the big cities running across the desert's mirage
hunted by a tiring sense of fear
chased by a terrifying sickness
the devil of estrangement and evil
breaking it stone by stone.

* * *

And I saw falcons, black-ear kites, and penguins hovering over the cities
I saw the blood of its kin
dripping from the vulture's claws
I saw an eagle hijacking a palace
and saw snakes in the horizon
drawing rainbows
I saw faces on terraces
wearing ghostly masks
I saw minds on the streets
drinking a salty toast

***

Mother, is this a nightmare or an illusion?
or is it something approaching, or …
is this isolating restlessness a dream?
but, since awakening, I felt when laying my head
on the tent's cord
feeling the grass
like spikes it stings me
the cord severs the neck
and it moves from *wasiṭ* (middle column) towards the *'uqda* (the knot on the peg)

***

And I have dreamt, mother, that I was blindfolded
And my tribe's campsite pilfered
And the heads of my men plastered to the wall
And I saw you mother not crying
Because tears are crucified
and because the *'uqda* is now tied to the *wasiṭ*.

(al-Flayyiḥ 1979:2–7)

The imminent apocalypse of al-Flayyiḥ's desert campsite is a recurrent theme in many postcolonial sites narrating the demise of authentic life. In the context of modern Arabic literature, the apocalyptic theme has been one of the main subtexts in Abdulrahman Munif's quintet *Cities of Salt* (1984). The novels trace the gradual demise, not just of the desert life, but of the very environment of subsistence for societies in Arabia. The radical shift propelled by the oil age helped create new cities that have ever since been marked by an unsustainable character and imminent collapse.

In his reading of Munif's *Cities of Salt*, Rob Nixon explores the effects of this radical shift on the inhabitants of desert, 'the lower-class Bedouin' especially, the likes of al-Flayyiḥ. As Nixon puts it,

> [n]omadic Bedouin culture had been inscribed on the land through movement; theirs was a belonging- in-motion shaped to an arid world. But the deracinations of the oil age plummeted them into a rootlessness that was nomadism's opposite. Driven from their lands, increasingly urbanized, repressed and exploited by a corrupt sepoy class in cahoots with American oil interests, many lower-class Bedouin found themselves culturally humiliated and politically estranged.
>
> (Nixon 2011:76)

This radical shift in the life of the desert inhabitants is condensed in al-Flayyiḥ's depiction of the moment of the desert apocalypse. From the outset, the storming winds, an allusion to a sweeping and overpowering change, disrupt the familiar setting of the campsite and the grazing lands. It transforms the campsite from a site of familiarity and habitability to one of total displacement and disintegration of meaning as the desert environment turns against its people. Prior to the moment of disruption, the poet can affirm a sense of meaningful relationship with the campsite. This familiarity is marked by the use of the possessive pronoun: my horses, my camels and my blood. Yet, as the disrupting winds storm, the poet's horses and camels are expelled from the campsite while the poet himself is displaced outside of it.

Thereafter, the campsite loses its sense of wholeness and is only described in fragmented images. This fragmentation is expressed through a series of grotesque, surreal and absurd images. The poet's vision includes horses with severed heads, crows as great as the night, drunken goats, tamarisk branches protruding out of horses, penguins in flight, eagles hijacking a palace and snakes drawing rainbows.

While everything in the apocalypse lacks meaning, the figure of the mother, who is addressed throughout the poem, acts as a referential point. Unlike the poet, the mother is situated amidst the fragmentation of the campsite. As the poem approaches its end, only the mother remains intact amidst the carnage. In repeatedly addressing the mother, the poet is invoking her to make sense of the vision. The mother is 'in anguish, spreading sand between the dead, gathering left over flesh'. This image alludes to the mother's attempts at piecing together the fragments to make sense of the carnage and to possibly restore it. Yet the mother is not even capable of shedding tears, 'because tears are crucified' and because the tent has collapsed. The campsite, as an intelligible form of life, has totally disintegrated. The figure of the mother can be read as a symbol of what is left of the desert life: an enduring sense of origin, belonging and memory that contests notions of uprootedness brought about by the apocalyptic times.

Another potent way in which meaning is created out of the chaos is through the poetic utilization of the apocalyptic form. It useful here to refer to Peter Child's analysis of the theme of fragmentation and disintegration in T. S. Eliot's *The Wasteland*. While the two poems come from different literary and historical trajectories, they both share a compulsive sense of apprehension towards their present moments expressed through mythical and sacred language. Childs suggests that:

> [w]hile history, reason, logic had failed the modern world as organising principles, aesthetics had not. Using mythology and pre- to early modern culture .... Eliot creates a form in the poem which aims to both master the content and to patch together all the many scraps of experience contained in the five parts.
>
> (Childs 2000:183)

While fragmentation and disorientation dominate the poem, Eliot achieves 'a kind of design in his poem through ... mythology' (Childs 1999:73). Similarly, al-Flayyiḥ in *The Apprehensions of Corrupt Times* resorts to sacred language embodied in the trope of the apocalypse. The utter demise of desert life seems to be only articulated and comprehended in the familiar form and language of the apocalyptic vision. The use of the apocalyptic trope also attests to al-Flayyiḥ's association with predominant modernist aesthetics in Arabic poetry which has been highly influenced by both Eliot and what Shomekh calls the repertoire of 'biblical echoes', in modern Arabic Literature (Somekh 1995).

The form of the apocalypse allows the poet to bring together the series of fragmented images in an intelligible manner. In the apocalyptic vision, all creation is brought to a sudden end. At the same time, all creation is summoned before the reader's eyes as a reminder of what once was. While everything is disintegrating in the desert, it is at the same time paraded before the poet's eyes. The poet exhibits the material archive of the desert: horses, camels, snakes, lions, dogs, wolves, ants, goats, deer, vultures, eagles and tamarisks. In addition, the tent's components are also detailed in footnoted terms such as '*al-ʿuqda*' (the knot on the tent's peg) and '*wasiṭ*' (the main middle column of the tent). The exhibited material archive of the desert is also a reminder of the desert as a lived space with a distinct cultural memory.

The apocalypse of the familiar life of the campsite also alludes to the paradox of literary modernity in the context of the Arabian Peninsula. In his readings of modern Arab poets in the Arabian Peninsula, Saʿad al-Bazei highlights the dual meaning of the word *bayt*, which refers to both the Bedouin's tent and the basic unit of classical poetry. The classical (*ʿamudi)* form in Arabic poetry is derived from the pole of the tent (*ʿamud*). Al-Bazei reads modern Arab poets' break away from the classical form (*ʿamudi*) to free verse (*tafʿila*) poetry as a form of 'tension in the house'. This tension is taken as a metaphor of the challenges of literary modernity. Modernist poetic forms shake the basic unit of poetry holding together the poem, and ultimately a known way of life.

In *The Apprehensions of Corrupt Times*, the *bayt*, or tent, which is the focal point of the campsite implodes. As the poet awakens from his vision, he lays besides his tent. The grass stings 'like spikes' while the 'tent cords sever the neck' as it moves from the peg towards the middle column. The collapse of the campsite's *bayt* also signals the necessity of finding a new language to face modern impositions. This new language is manifest in the poet's use of the *tafi'la* form, a sign of a modern aesthetic back then, and his utilization of the apocalyptic trope to face new realities.

Unlike apocalyptic literature's ultimate promise of a post-apocalyptic vision of salvation, the poem ends with utter carnage. The poet describes the end of the world as he knows it while offering no vision of salvation or a fresh beginning. The poem ends with a sense of lingering shock as the mother stands enervated amid the carnage unable to cry for what she has witnessed. The poet is blindfolded and unable to see beyond the apocalypse he is witnessing.

It is in this impasse where al-Flayyiḥ differs from other Arab modernist poets. The theme of rebirth, or a post-apocalyptic vision, has been central to modernist Arab poets connected with the *Tammuzi* movement. Within their different social and political contexts, poets including the likes of Adonis, Salah Abd al-Ṣabur and Badir Shakir al-Sayyab have often utilized the theme of rebirth to face their present realities (Asfour 1988). This rebirth is actualized in a particular form of modernity that manifests itself culturally in modern Arabic poetics and politically in the form of a modern Arab nation emerging from the rubbles of history.[2]

Within Kuwaiti national literature, one prime example, which is highly influenced by Badir Shakir al-Sayyab's *Hymn of the Rain* (1954), is Muhammad al-Fayiz's epic poem *Memoirs of a Seafarer* (1964). The poem tells of the perils of the Kuwaiti pearl diver whose perseverance of the hardships of seafaring is symbolic of a historical national spirit. It is written as both a celebration of and an elegy to maritime culture. Like the desert, maritime culture has also witnessed a radical transition that 'rendered obsolete an entire traditional system of manual skills, maritime knowledge, commercial practices and cultural forms built up over centuries' (Al-Hijji 2010:134). Yet, unlike al-Flayyiḥ's disintegrated desert, al-Fayez anticipates a vision of salvation and rebirth. The seafarer's values of perseverance, honour and sacrifice become the seed for the new beginning for the modern nation and its people (al-Rabei 2014).

The post-apocalyptic in al-Flayyiḥ's work is a vision of the carnage in corrupt times. It is a source of apprehension as it may render superfluous al-Flayyiḥ's desert and what it offers, as a history, a people, a set of values and a subjectivity. The desert, as an archive and an alternative subjectivity, can only now be sustained through poetic articulation. All that is left at the end of the poem is the poet's apprehension of what is to come for a displaced community, which later materialized in the statelessness and disenfranchisement of many of the desert's inhabitants.

The poet, while using mythical language, demythologizes the desert space. The romanticized desert space of serenity and purity is disrupted by an apocalyptic vision. The perplexities of modernity, afflicting the city, are extended to the desert space. Both desert and city are enveloped in the historical moment of apocalypse. This perplexity does not simply extend to the representations of the desert, but to the language of its articulation as well. As the cord, the pillar that holds up the tent snaps and severs the poet's neck, he must find a new abode in a new language, one that is more indebted to modernist aesthetics than to the classical forms from which he is expected to speak in. The event of the apocalypse restores the historicity of the desert as a pre-national site of alternate historical beginnings, while simultaneously reinforcing the desert's own vision of modernity.

In 1978, al-Flayyiḥ was again introduced by al-Zaid in the *Rabita's* poetry festival. While acknowledging al-Flayyiḥ's own disruptive poetic voice, al-Zaid introduces al-Flayyiḥ again with these words:

> A Bedouin who defied, like a rock, stubborn and unmasked, the cruelty of the city and the winds of avarice. He fought hard with a pen dripping pain bellowing at the city: Wake up! He was about to nod off, the city never awakened. I urge you, Bedouin man, to return to your original intuition .... Have mercy on the voice of your inner intuition.
>
> (Majallat al-Bayan 1978:40)

In the 1981 annual poetry festival, al-Zaid introduced al-Flayyiḥ once again with the following words:

> [A] poet who carried in his beginnings the soul of intuition. Thus, we loved and blessed him. He still carries remnants of it. Will he return to his original intuition and uninhibited tendencies? Or will life's paths lead him astray from his intuition ... I still hope that he returns for I have loved him and long-awaited him.
>
> (Majallat al-Bayan 1981:22)

Year after year, Al-Zaid insists repeatedly that al-Flayyiḥ returns to his unpolluted intuition, purity and authenticity of the desert voice. Al-Flayyiḥ is constantly reinstated to his romanticized ahistoric desert space. He is representative of the communal desert imaginary; a rejuvenating prophet bringing forth fragrant flowers and streams of water. Instead, al-Flayyiḥ in his poetic voice sounds like a tired displaced broken prophet who has something else to say. Indeed, like a prophet, al-Flayyiḥ came into the *Rabita* not to affirm continuity or expectations but ultimately to rupture a communal imaginary and disrupt perceived reality through aesthetic articulation.

Nomadology to *Ṣaʿlaka*

From within the communal arrival of a generation of last Bedouins emerges al-Flayyiḥ's personal poetics guised in the figure of the modern *Ṣuʿluk*. Throughout his literary career, al-Flayyiḥ wilfully affiliates with the *Ṣaʿalik* poets in the Arabic literary tradition. The modern *Ṣuʿluk* is utilized as a literary mask that situates the poet within a deep-rooted Arabic literary tradition with contemporary resonance. The *Ṣaʿalik* tradition can also be viewed in relation to wider discussions on nomadology within postcolonial discourse.

The nomad has been initially conceived as a spatial signifier within the context of empire, as 'an intermediate figure between the primitive society without a state on the one hand and the so-called civilized imperial state on the other' (Buchanan 2010:354). As put by Gilles Deleuze, nomad thought works as a force of 'deterritorializing' the ordered 'striated (metric) space' of the state in order to produce a notion of space that is 'smooth (vectoral, projective, topological)' (cited in Tally Jr 2013:159). The figure of the nomad has been often used as signifying a transgressive subjectivity within feminist and postcolonial discourses. A nomadic subjectivity is an 'intellectual position' (Noyes 2004:163), 'a metaphor for critical thinking' (al-Saddah 2012:166), 'a suitable theoretical figuration for contemporary subjectivity … an epistemological and political imperative for critical thought' (Braidotti 1994:1–2) and a 'useful critical figure … that interrupts the persistently binary schemas which tend to condition the way we read and discuss not only postcolonial literature, but postcolonial situations in general' (Lowe 1993:47 cited in Noyes 2010:164). Within the context of Arabic literary studies, al-Saddah reads the postcolonial nomadic Arabic novel in Egypt as a 'state of mind, an intellectual project, and a style of life not as ends in themselves, but as strategies to negotiate new, more liberating identities' (al-Saddah 2012:189). The abstraction of the figure of the nomad, as illustrated above, allows it to become an easily accessible tool for spatial readings of deterritorialization in disparate contexts.

In her critique on the prevalent use of nomadism as a conceptual tool within feminist studies, Caren Kaplan highlights the dangers of the 'privilege of universalizing theories' (Kaplan 1990:194). Kaplan warns against inattentiveness on behalf of first world critics to questions of positionality within existing power relations where 'the margin becomes a linguistic or critical vacation, a new poetics of the exotic' (191). The abstractness of the notion of the metaphorical nomad often overlooks the particular realities of the represented marginal space.

Rather than starting with an abstract universal notion of the metaphorical nomad to read the literary thrust of al-Flayyiḥ, the chapter works on understanding how a particular subjectivity emanates from within al-Flayyiḥ's literary works and the linguistic and literary tradition from which he writes. Al-Flayyiḥ's situates himself within a particular tradition of *Ṣaʿalik* poets that has an untranslatable resonance within a specific linguistic and spatial context. The term *Ṣaʿalik* has been translated in a number of ways including: 'robber-poets' (Treadgold 1975), 'brigand-poets' (Stetkevych 1986), 'destitute poets' (Jones 2011) and 'outcasts' (Farrin 2010). Yet these translations fall short of capturing the connotative weight of the term and its cultural and political resonance in the Arabic literary tradition.

In *The Poetry of Ṣaʿalik: Method and Characteristics*, Abdulhalim Ḥifni defines the *Ṣaʿalik* as a group that is distinct from the rest of society; having a sense of self-sufficiency sustained by an active engagement in marauding and thievery (Ḥifni 1979:27). The figure of the *Ṣuʿluk* is conventionally associated with the following connotative terms: a wolf (having 'wolfish tendencies'), the *khaliʿ*,[3] the *fatik*[4] and the *shaṭir*[5] (Ḥifni 1979).

As to their poetry, the most distinctive aspects of the *Ṣaʿalik* poetic tradition are the semi-autobiographic nature of their poetry and the emphasis on the poet's subjective experiences of his surroundings (374). On the communal level, the poetry of the *Ṣaʿalik* valorizes the act of *ṣaʿlaka*, which works as a defiant force against the status quo and social immobility of the social tribal structure (184). Through the act of *ṣaʿlaka*, the poet gains his self-sufficiency and his sense of inner coherence by withdrawing into nature and outside of the impositions of the social structure.

Kamal Abu-Deeb reads the *Ṣuʿluk* poem as inaugurating a sense of agency of the individual poet in the face of communal consensus. Read against the classical *qasida*, the space of the *Ṣuʿluk* poem is a 'stage for the individual's event' (Abu-Deeb 1986:576) and not the abode of the tribe. Juxtaposed with the classical *qasida's* emphasis on ruins and lamentations over the campsite of the beloved, the space of the *Ṣuʿluk* poem is a space of presentness and action, laden with future potentiality and possibilities of 'creating a new world' (578). Another distinction in Abu-Deeb's analysis relates to the depictions of time between the cyclical and mythological time of the classical *qasida* and the historical notion of time of the *Ṣu 'luk* poem (584). The notion of historical time gives way for the poet to exercise his agency and will.

In comparison with the classical *qasida's* evocation of place names as a marker of the poet's abode, the *Ṣu 'luk* remains elusive about his whereabouts. As Raymond Farrin writes, 'the poet comes out of nowhere, strikes civilization, and then slips back into the obscurity whence he came' (41). The lack of territorial attachment gives the *Ṣu 'luk* a fluid notion of belonging to the vastness of the desert.

From another, more structural-anthropological angle, the *Ṣu 'luk* poem has been analysed through the anthropological modality of 'rite of passage' proposed by Van Gennep. This modality was later appropriated by Suzanne Stetkevych to read the classical Arabic *qasida* (Stetkevych 1983). In Stetkevych's reading of the classical *qasida*, the anthropological subject, or passenger, is the classical *Jahili* poet. His poem is read as a tool to consummate a rite of passage into a wider sense of community. The tripartite structure of the classical *qasida* consisting of *nasib-raḥil-madiḥ/fakhar* is seen as analogous to the three stages involved in the rite of passage (separation–liminality–reintegration). The *nasib*, where the poet laments the traces of his beloved's campsite, represents the first stage of separation. In *raḥil*, where the poet describes his journey and his she-camel, the poet enters into a liminal phase. Finally in *fakhr*, or *madiḥ*, the poet reintegrates into the tribe's value system by reiterating and valorizing shared values through self-pride or panegyrics of tribal leaders (Stetkevych 1983).

In light of such an approach, Stetkevych suggests that the *Ṣu 'luk* poem, with reference to al-Shanfara's *Lamiyyat al- 'Arab* (L-poem of the Arabs), is rather:

> [A] failed or aborted rite in which the passenger does not achieve reintegration into the community or tribe, but rather, the hardships and perils of the liminal state are realized and become a permanent way of life instead of a temporary transitional stage.
>
> (Stetkevych 1984:662)

In other words, the *Ṣuʿluk* naturalizes and reintegrates into the liminal phase by withdrawing into nature.

The *Ṣaʿalik*'s transgressive, subjective and self-sufficient attitude carried connotative resonance that attracted modern Arab poets to recourse to *ṣaʿlaka* to face their present conditions. With this in mind, Hassan Nuriddin views *ṣaʿlaka* in the modern times as enabling a form of agency against new 'ideologies of the tribe' manifest in the hegemonic forces of globalization and global empire (Nurridin 2007b:361).

In a more localized context of the Arabian Peninsula, the Saudi literary critic Saʿad al-Bazei sees that the utilization of *Ṣaʿalik* is prompted by an 'unrelenting estrangement' experienced in the modern social settings (al-Bazei 1991:58). This estrangement is due to the modern city's abandonment of the 'noble neglected values' of the desert, which the *Ṣuʿluk* embodies. The evocation of the *Ṣaʿalik* by modern poets and contemporaries of al-Flayyiḥ, such as the Saudi poets Muhammad al-Thubaiti and Abdulkarim al-ʿUda, is read by al-Bazei as part of a poetic discourse that modern poets confront their societies with (58). These modern *Ṣuʿluk* poets present themselves as upholders of the 'noble neglected values' of the desert. More importantly, the poetic evocation of the *Ṣuʿluk* provides an immediate sense of identity and belonging to the desert of the Arabian Peninsula. The *Ṣuʿluk* is 'not only that exiled Arab *Jahili* persona. He represents, before everything else, the desert's material history (its stones, flora, animals, aura and its harshness)' (59). Thus, a poetic evocation of the *Ṣuʿluk* is also an evocation of the fluid desert topography, which carries an immediate and deep-rooted sense of belonging.

Sulayman al-Flayyiḥ: The modern *Ṣuʿluk*

In a 2008 newspaper column, al-Flayyiḥ introduces himself to his readers as a 'desert wolf', a synonym of the *Ṣuʿluk*:

> To those 3rd or 4th generation Kuwaiti readers who do not know me, I am one of the wolves of the desert who came down to the cities of oil when the desert so blatantly rejected its people with its terrible drought. Kuwait has absorbed me and allowed me the chance to practice all of the wolves' honourable traits (nobility, loyalty, sincerity, generosity and love).
>
> (al-Flayyiḥ 2008a)

More so, poem titles such as *Songs of the Ṣaʿalik* (al-Flayyiḥ 1981:26), *The Last Will of the Son of Oil Ṣuʿluk* (al-Flayyiḥ 1993:53), *From the Diary of a Ṣuʿluk* (al-Flayyiḥ 1979), *The Lone Wolf* (al-Flayyiḥ 1993: 20), *Just Ṣaʿalik* (30), *The Ṣaʿalik Let Go of ʿUrwa ibn al-Ward* (al-Flayyiḥ 2013:342), *Howls of the Restless Wolves* (al-Flayyiḥ 2013:394) and the title of his 1993 poetry collection *Night Wolves* (1993) attest to his strong poetic affiliation with the *Ṣaʿalik* as his historical literary forbearers.

In the context of modern Arabic poetics, Muhsin al-Musawi reads the modern Arab poet's recourse to historical figures as literary masks as 'prompted and coloured by the politics of urgency' (al-Musawi 2002:179). The mask serves 'as a foil for his present status as a modern poet in trying circumstances' where the poet 'emphasises differences, variants and displacements, between his situation and that of his forebears in order to obliquely enhance his achievement' (205).

An example of this use of a literary mask as a foil, which al-Musawi calls 'dialogisation', can be found in the poem *The Songs of Ṣaʿalik*. The poem is written in five 'poem-songs' each dedicated to a *Jahili Ṣuʿluk* poet: Taʾabbaṭa Sharran, al-Shanfara, al-Sulayk ibn Sullaka and Abu al-Ṭamḥan al-Qayni, respectively. In each of these short and highly intertextual poems, al-Flayyiḥ situates the historical *Ṣuʿluk* poet in the present to highlight the challenges and impositions of modern times on the *Ṣuʿluk*. The *Ṣuʿluk* in the 'now' seems more vulnerable and bereft of his sense of inner coherence and self-sufficiency. What space is left for the *Ṣuʿluk* when his refuge, the desert, is overcome by the disturbances of modern times?

Before presenting the individual *Ṣuʿluk*, the song of the *Ṣaʿalik* opens with the following lines under the title of *uhzuja* (anthem):

> Because of our refusal,
> As any true man would, to remain your captive slaves,
> your concubine whores presented at night to the tribe's *shaykh*,
> we have been excommunicated,
> lost, dispersed, and starved
> while the dogs of the tribe continue to whine at us.
>
> (al-Flayyiḥ 1981:26)

From the outset, the use of the first person plural pronouns 'we' and 'us' marks al-Flayyiḥ's alignment with the *Ṣaʿalik* poets as part of and an extension of that tradition. This mirrors the *Ṣaʿalik*'s prevalent use of the first personal plural pronoun in their poetry, which refers to the community of excommunicated *Ṣaʿalik* and not their tribe (Khulayf 1978:206). The space of the poem allows al-Flayyiḥ to join the band of *Ṣaʿalik* in a communal anthem. This choral performance reproduces a sense of the transhistorical brotherhood of the *Ṣaʿalik* and sets the ambience of the poem. One is reminded of the *Lamiyyat al-Arab* of al-Shanfara's where the pack of wolves sing in unison with the poet.

The anthem starts with the shared act of refusal 'because of our refusal …' that leads to shared consequences 'we have been …'. The poets refuse to succumb to the social injustices and subjugation. They find a way out of through engaging in *ṣaʿlaka* while enduring its consequences. The conditions and social triggers of *ṣaʿlaka* are not necessarily related to a specific historical era but persist throughout. *Ṣaʿlaka* then is articulated more as an embodied stance and a defiant attitude that sustains a sense of dignity and communal pride beyond the imposed social order.

In his treatment of the Jahili *Ṣuʿluk* poet, Taʾabbaṭa Sharran, al-Flayyiḥ writes:

The one with evil under the pit of his arm (Taʾabbaṭa Sharran)
is chased by the whirlwind
he races the sound grouse birds to the water streams
which will soon be engulfed by the whirlwind
Taʾabbaṭa Sharran comes, without evilness under his arm
save for his sword of sorrows
and the hunger of the *Ṣaʿalik* and the deprived
He turned back and ran as an arrow racing his fleeting days.

(al-Flayyiḥ 1981:26)

Taʾabbaṭa Sharran, which translates to the one who carries evil under the pit of his arm, now comes with 'no evil under the pit of his arm'. The conditions of *ṣaʿlaka* persist: the whirlwinds, the hardships, the sorrows and hunger. Yet what is lacking now is his nickname, that 'evilness' or panache that is necessary for his survival as a *Ṣuʿluk*. Taʾabbaṭa Sharran then swift-footedly disappears as he realizes the limitations of practising *ṣaʿlaka* as he has known it.

Al-Flayyiḥ then turns to another *Ṣuʿluk* poet, al-Sulayk ibn Sullaka, conversing with him and informing him of the betrayals of his fellow *Ṣaʿalik* in modern times. He writes:

O deviously shrewd man.
Do you know that your companions have now pushed you into your demise?
Your blood is still trickling over the sand.
They returned your sword to its sheath, after you were injured
And before the end of the battle, they surrendered.
While you have saved last winter's water for them
In ostriches' eggs
And you carry on, noble one, practicing *ṣa'laka.*

(al-Flayyiḥ 1981:26)

The noble act of *ṣa'laka* is conceived as a battle that is getting increasingly more difficult in the present. While al-Sulayk holds on to his noble values, his comrades in the 'now' leave him wounded and surrender. That which defines al-Sulayk's historical legacy as a *Ṣu'luk* poet, his honourable values of courage, sense of justice and generosity to his fellow comrades becomes the source of his demise in the present.

In the two readings, the historical *Ṣu'luk* is inserted into the present scene, and after a realization of the imposed limitations on his life as a *Ṣu'luk*, depart the scene. Despite the realization, they both attempt to continue practising *ṣa'laka*. Ta'abbaṭa Sharran 'turned back and ran as an arrow' as it is the characteristic of the swift-footed *Ṣa'alik* while al-Sulayk carries on 'practicing *ṣa'laka*'. The historical *Ṣu'luk* resorted to the desert to practice his values outside of the established social structure. Yet it seems that *ṣa'laka*, in the absence of the desert as refuge, can only be sustained as a defiant attitude or subjectivity in poetic expression.

This is most evident in the way al-Flayyiḥ enacts a recognition of contemporary *Sa'laka* as a necessary stance that transcends its historical scene (i.e. the desert). As the historical *Ṣu'luk* joins a band of excommunicated *Ṣa'alik*, al-Flayyiḥ affiliates with a literary network of contemporary modern *Ṣa'alik* poets in the Arab world more broadly. Unlike the traitorous companions of al-Sulaik, these contemporary *Ṣa'alik* persist in their own doomed *ṣa'laka.*

For example, his elegiac poem *The Wind's Silver Wings* is dedicated to the soul of Naguib Surur (1932–1978), an Egyptian poet and playwright known for his rebellious and non-conformist attitude. Another poem titled *Bows on the Rababa for the Journeys of Shlaiwiḥ al-'Atawi* is dedicated to another *Ṣu'luk* poet from the *Nabati* tradition of the Arabian Peninsula Shlaiwiḥ al-'Atawi. In a footnote to the title, al-Flayyiḥ notes that Shlaiwiḥ al- ʿAtawi is one of the most famous, brave, and noble *Ṣaʿalik* poet knights of the Arabian Peninsula in the nineteenth century known for his infamous unaccompanied raids[6] (al-Flayyiḥ 1981:74).

In *Night Wolves*, one poem's title is dedicated to the *Bidun* poet 'Misfir al-Dusari and the wolf' (7). Al-Dusari is a contemporary of al-Flayyiḥ, was also *Bidun* at the time of the poem's publication. In the poem, al-Flayyiḥ refers to al-Dusari as a ' beautiful crow' alluding to his dark skin complexion and drawing an analogy with the group of 'poet-crows' (*aghriba*), or dark-skinned poets in Arabic literary history, the likes of the *Ṣuʿluk* poets al-Sulayk ibn al-Sullaka, and Taʾabbaṭa Sharran (Khulayf 1978:113; Ḥifni 1979:114; Lewis 1985).

Outside of his poetry collections, al-Flayyiḥ's affiliation with the *Ṣaʿalik* tradition is not less obvious. In 2011, more thirty-five years after debuting his first poetry collection, al-Flayyiḥ was invited by the *Rabita* as a speaker. In his lecture titled 'A Comparative Approach between *Ṣaʿalik* poetry and the Late Desert *Ḥanshal*', 'a band footmen whose nightly exploits and adventures are the subject matter for Bedouin tales' (Jabbur 1996:354), he presents himself as belonging to the last generation of the dying tradition of *Ṣaʿalik* in Kuwait and the Arabian Peninsula. Within the national literary scene, al-Flayyiḥ mentions the poets Fahad al- ʿAskar and Sagir al-Shibib, and his contemporaries Misfir al-Dusari, Fahad ʿAfet, Ibrahim al-Khaldi and Fahad Duhan as part of that dying breed of *Ṣaʿalik*. Interestingly, he points out that while the *Ṣaʿalik* tradition has died away, resonances of it remain in the culture of internet hackers, or the internet *Ṣaʿalik*.

The contemporary network of *Ṣaʿalik* transcends geographical, political and linguistic registers. A *Ṣuʿluk* recognizes another *Ṣuʿluk* whether he is Naguib Surur practising *ṣaʿlaka* in Egyptian colloquial, Misfer al-Dusari, a *Bidun* poet writing *Shaʿbi* poetry, Shlaiwiḥ al- ʿAtawi practising *ṣaʿlaka* in the *Nabaṭi* tradition, or Fahad al-Askar, a Kuwaiti poet writing in *Fusha* Arabic. What establishes the act of recognition is a shared critical stance towards political, societal and often literary norms; an expression of an ascetic desire to return to a self-sufficient life free and far from any form of dependency; and a deliberate will to excommunicate oneself. In his affiliation, al-Flayyiḥ abstracts *ṣaʿlaka* as a concept beyond its desert constraints. It is not just the 'noble neglected values of the desert', as al-Bazei posits, that the modern *Ṣuʿluk* is a reminder of. *Ṣaʿlaka* is a defiant attitude and a set of values that is sustained primarily through poetic expression.

In conclusion, al-Flayyiḥ problematizes the categories that might seem empowering to him, such as the 'desert prophet' and the 'godfather of *Bidun* poetry'. Through his autobiographical reflections, literary works and literary affiliation, al-Flayyiḥ eludes such categories. Firstly, the desert space is depicted as a site that has witnessed an apocalypse and can no longer be represented in romanticized terms. Secondly, in his deliberate alignment with the *Ṣaʿalik*, al-Flayyiḥ engages in an act of claiming and forging a literary history. Instead of the extrinsic bonds (tribal, national or stateless) as being central and constitutive of literary history, al-Flayyiḥ builds on older moments that exist within a literary tradition. The affiliation with the *Ṣaʿalik* offers a deep-rooted sense of belonging to a literary tradition that has historically been associated with the desert, yet is not restricted to it. At the same time, it forges a transnational network of *Ṣaʿalik* poets built on contemporary aesthetic and individual practices.

5

Representations of the *ʿAshish*

One of the often-neglected spaces within the historical spatial imaginary and urban memory of Kuwait is the space of the *ʿAshish*. In the immediate sense, the *ʿAshish* (*ʿIshash* in standard Arabic) (sing. *ʿIsha*) directly refers to the 'squalid slums' (Human Rights Watch 1995), 'squatter settlements' (al-Ḥaddad 1981:109), 'shacks … old dwellings' (al-Eisa 1985) or 'shanty-towns' (Freeth 1972; al-Moosa 1976:75) where the majority of the *Bidun* and other naturalized Bedouins once resided.

Shantytowns were first established around the Kuwait Oil Company work sites that offered jobs for Bedouins (al-Moosa 1976:58–9). According al-Moosa, the existence of shantytowns has been noted in 1936 in the area of Magwa near the oil fields and continued to sprout throughout the 1950s and 1960s (58).

As al-Moosa put it,

> [t]hese shanty Bedouins form a separate community with personality characteristics peculiar to themselves. The shanty areas in which they live are known in Kuwait as 'ishish' [*sic*] areas or Bedouin areas …. The shanty Bedouins are new immigrants who were attracted by the improved conditions of a wealthy developing state, and in that way they are at least different from the old itinerant Bedouins.
>
> (88)

Many of the Bedouins referred to by al-Moosa considered Kuwait's territory as 'part of their own wide-spread homeland' (68). The increased settlements of Bedouins in shanty towns were driven by the prospects of gaining Kuwaiti citizenship which would grant them access to free housing, health and education services, as well as guaranteed employment (68). It is estimated that 12.3–25 per cent of Kuwait's population in 1970s, which was at the time 738,662, lived in shanty towns (al-Ḥaddad 1981:109). In 1975 the Bedouins constituted 80 per cent of total shanty population of 131,275 (al-Moosa 1976:61). However, a field study conducted by al-Moosa in 1974 sampling three major shanty areas revealed that 78.3 per cent of the population were not granted Kuwaiti citizenship (92).

Writing in the early 1970s, Zahra Freeth, the daughter of the British political agent in Kuwait, Harold Dickson, offers a vivid description of the shanty towns that have sprouted near the areas of Jilib al-Shuyukh, Jahra and al-Ahmadi. She writes:

> Some Europeans assume that the population of these shanty-towns must be of a degenerate type, living, as I have heard it said 'no better than dogs'. But the only fault of these hut-dwellers is poverty. They are the ones who have fallen through the sieve of the welfare state .... If their menfolk are employed, it is the lowest-paid jobs, or else they are some of the unfortunate hundreds from the deserts outside Kuwait who have not yet acquired that desirable piece of paper, a *jinsiya*, or certificate of nationality, enabling them to find better-paid work.
>
> (Freeth 1972:175)

These shantytowns consisting mainly of wooden huts were 'the first humblest form of permanent residence of the badawin who has abandoned his tent'. (175). In Jahra, these huts have 'an air of depressing squalor' whereas near the Ahmadi oil fields, another shanty town was 'allocated an area with a high wire perimeter fence, and the settlement had the rather forbidding aspect of a concentration camp' (147). This solemn description of the precarious conditions of the shantytowns was exacerbated by the lack of citizenship of many of its dwellers.

In 1975, the Department Concerned with Illegal Dwellings was established by the Kuwaiti government to deal with the uncontrolled rise of the shanty dwellers. Many of the shanty towns were demolished as a result and their dwellers relocated to three controlled shanty areas (Al-Moosa 66). As Freeth put it, 'Kuwait was ashamed of its poor' (Freeth 1972:175), as the disordered sight of the shanty towns did not suit the city's modern image.

Yet the Kuwaiti government did not necessarily recognize many of these shanty dwellers as one of 'its poor'. In 1962, Yusuf al-Mukhlid, a member of the Constituent Assembly, criticized the government's neglect of *'sukkan al-ʾIshash'* (shanty dwellers) and their continual uprooting from one site to another. The *ʾIsha* dweller 'has become like the *Kawli* (a derogatory label to describe the gypsy population of Iraq) in a new location everyday'. In defence of the government's policy, the minister-in-charge Muhammad al-Nusif addressed the parliament saying:

> As to the issue of the *Ishash* (shanty towns), I believe that all bona fide Kuwaitis or Kuwaitis who have been sedentarized (*tahadaru*) have already resided in houses. As to those … in the *Ishash*, they are all Bedouins from the desert who have not been *sedentarized* and will not be before a year or two, some of them do not hold citizenship.
>
> (Minutes of the Constituent Assembly 1962)

This exchange highlights the differing conceptions of belonging in the nascent stages of the development of the nation state as well as the associations between the notions of citizenship and sedentarization. To the government official, 'unsedentarized Bedouins', many who have long lived within the geographical borders of Kuwait, remain outside of the nation's geographic imaginary.

To deal with the issue of increased number of shanty dwellers, the government set up temporary housing, commonly referred to as *al-Masakin al-Shaʿbiyya* (popular housing). Those who gained Kuwaiti citizenship were later rehoused to Low Income Housing (LIH) projects while 'non-Kuwaiti Bedouins', that is, the *Bidun*, resettled in popular housing mostly in Tayma, Sulaybiyya and Ahmadi where many still reside (al-Moosa 1976:300; al-Nakib 2014:19: Beaugrand 2017:98). The majority of *Bidun* writers, particularly the first or second generation *Biduns*, discussed in this book have experienced life in the *ʿAshish* including Sulayman al-Flayyiḥ, Dikhil Khalifa, Muhammad al-Nabhan and Nasir al-Ẓafiri whose aesthetic treatment of the *ʿAshish* is the major interest of this chapter.

The literary *ʿAshish*

The historical and symbolic significance of the *ʿAshish* carries some semblance with Hoda al-Saddah's analysis of the *'Ashwaʾiyyat* in the context of the modern Egyptian novel. The *'Ashwaʾiyyat* are 'new informal urban spaces that sprang up with minimal or no links with the nation-state apparatuses and structures' inhabited by 'marginalized subjects that have never been integrated in the national imaginary or progress of building a modern nation' (al-Saddah 2012:204). The sprouting of 'chaotic, unplanned, nonconformist, unruly' dwellings is 'a characteristic feature of the modern postcolonial city' (212). More importantly, the *'Ashwa'iyyat* are metaphorically read as a 'liminal space at the threshold of cities, narratives, identities' that 'is not exclusive to the inhabitants of the physical *'Ashwa'iyyat*' (212).

Similarly, the space of the *'Ashish* is often deployed by novelists, *Bidun* or otherwise, as a consistent spatial metaphor for a unique and fractured space of marginalization. This is following Ania Loomba, who in her critique of the emphasis on diaspora and exile in the 'postcolonial subjects', comments that 'large numbers of people in the third world have not physically moved and have to speak from "where they are", which is also often an equally ideologically or politically or emotionally fractured space' (Loomba 1998:180). An exploration of the *'Ashish* aims to explore the multitude of meanings embodied in that fractured space that Loomba hints at, a space that is embodied with different inflections by the novels that will be discussed.

On his lived experience of *'Ashish* in Aljahra, the *Bidun* novelist Nasir al-Ẓafiri reflects:

> My consciousness of the *Bidun* issue was linked with the poverty that was associated with the marginalised space. This space created the marginalised human who was cast far from the rapid development of a country witnessing an oil boom. Al-Jahra was one of those neglected areas inhabited by different groups of *Badu* (Bedouins) who settled far from the drought and famine of the desert. The possible jobs available for them included work in the army, police and in light labour that these fatigued and unlettered people were able to do. I was the son of one of those families who shared this difficult life. At first, it did not discriminate between us because of citizenship. Later, as a result of the unjust and selective naturalisation process, the area [al-Jahra] comprised of two groups: the *Bidun* and Kuwaitis. I was a member of the former.
>
> (Majjalat al-Ṭali'a 2016)

This account, presented in a newspaper interview, offers a descriptive rather than the aesthetic fictionalized narrative of the *'Ashish* that al-Ẓafiri presents in his novels. The *ʿAshish* is a space with a unique history of migration related to wider demographic shifts in the region; a marginalized space left out the nation's political, economic and social progress. Al-Ẓafiri depicts the statelessness of its dwellers as a process that arbitrarily discriminated between the *ʿAshish's* already marginalized inhabitants.

As the *ʿAshish* fell outside of the national state structures and economic development, it also remains a neglected space in the national literary imaginary. For example, a study titled *Al-Makan fi-l-Qiṣṣa al-Kuwaitiyya* (Space in the Kuwaiti Story) (2003) by Salaḥ Saliḥ designates five common reoccurring spaces in Kuwaiti fiction. The most common spaces are the sea and the old Kuwaiti quarters of mud houses. Both spaces are emblematic of a nostalgia for a lost social cohesion and values of the pre-oil era. The less prevalent spaces include the modern urban setting of the city, the space of the desert and other transnational spaces outside of the Kuwaiti geography such as European cities (Saliḥ 2003). In his comprehensive analysis, and in the critical responses to Saliḥ's study, the *ʿAshish* remains wholly outside of the commonly perceived Kuwaiti literary spatial imaginary. Despite this omission, recent times have seen a surge in representation of the *ʿAshish* in Kuwaiti fiction.

The rise of the '*Bidun* character' and the critical reception

Between 1995 and 2011, only two novels featured *Bidun* characters, whether by *Bidun* authors or otherwise: *Upturned Sky* (1995) by the *Bidun* novelist Nasir al-Ẓafiri and *An Unheard Collision* (2005) by the Kuwaiti writer Buthayna al-ʿIsa. Since then, novels dealing directly with *Bidun* characters have seen a significant rise in number, visibility and circulation. Since 2011, an increased presence of the '*Bidun* character' in novels written within the national context is highly noticeable. At least twelve novels and novellas have been published featuring *Bidun* characters (both as central or peripheral characters) including Fawziyya al-Salim's *Staircases of Day* (2011), Saud al-Sanʿusi *The Bamboo Stalk* (2012), Ismail Fahad's *In the Presence of the Phoenix and the Loyal Friend* (hitherto referred to as *IPPLF*) (2013), Nasir al-Ẓafiri's *Scorched Heat* (2013), a new edition of *Upturned Sky* (2013), *Kaliska* (2015), *Al-Maṣtar* (2017), Basma al-ʿInizi *A Black Shoe on the Pavement* (2013), Abdullah al-Buṣayyiṣ's *Stray Memories* (2014), Moudhi Rahhal's *Mghaisil* (2014), Hanadi al-Shimmiri's novella *A House Made of Tin* (2015) and Khalid Turki's *The Tale of Three Northerners* (2017). In addition, a number of short story collections included *Bidun* characters such as Abdullah al-ʿUtaybi's *ʾIkʿaybar* and Muna al-Shimmiri's *The Rain Falls, the Princess Dies*.

It is worth noting that a number of these novels have been widely circulated within local, Arab and global readership. In particular al-Sanʿusi's *The Bamboo Stalk*, which features a peripheral *Bidun* character, stands out as the most widely circulated novel. The novel was the recipient of the much-celebrated International Prize for Arabic Fiction in 2013. Since then, it has received increased attention by local and Arab audiences.[1] The novel introduced Arab readers to issues of otherness, the status of migrant workers and the *Bidun* in Kuwait. The novel also enjoyed wider popular circulation when it was turned into a TV drama series broadcasted in the holy month of Ramadan (June–July) in 2016. As a TV drama, the novel's peripheral *Bidun* character was turned into a central character. More globally, *The Bamboo Stalk* has been translated to English by Jonathan Wright and is currently the only novel in English featuring a *Bidun* character. Ismail Fahad's *IPPLF* has also been widely circulated within an Arab readership as it was long-listed for the International Prize for Arabic Fiction in 2014. Interestingly, al-Ẓafiri has consistently asked his publisher, Dar Masʿa, not to nominate any of his novels to the prize because of the prize board's lack of 'awareness of the form of the novel' (Majjalat al-Ṭaliʿa 2016). Al-Ẓafiri's novel *Scorched Heat* was banned by the censors in the Ministry of Information from circulation in Kuwait.

With the exception of novels by Nasir al-Ẓafiri and Hanadi al-Shimmiri, most novels depicting *Bidun* characters are written by non-*Bidun* novelists. One can read this surge of interest in the *Bidun* character within national literature in a number of ways. First, it can be read as consequence of the undeniable presence and increased visibility of the *Bidun* community on the social, political and cultural levels. Secondly, and at the level of the national novel, and perhaps the Arabic novel more broadly, questions of national identity, difference and otherness have recently become dominant themes. For many national writers, the ambience and marginality of the *Bidun* space have become an attractive position from which to explore that otherness and reflect on national identity. As Saʿdiyya Mufarriḥ notes in relation to the proliferation of the *Bidun* character in contemporary fiction, the creative impulse often comes at its subject matter from the marginal space (Mufarriḥ 2014). One can also argue that representing the *Bidun* character is a form of appropriation of the marginal voice and space by writers outside of the *Bidun* community.

This surge in interest in the '*Bidun* character' has, unsurprisingly, caught the attention of *Bidun* writers themselves, who have offered their critical insight into the representations of the *Bidun* in these novels. Both Saʿdiyya Mufarriḥ and Nasir al-Ẓafiri have surveyed the representations of *Bidun* characters in novels written by Kuwaiti writers, and both have expressed certain anxieties related to the problematic depictions of *Bidun* characters and the community at large. What is mostly emphasized in their critique is the creation and reiteration of a *Bidun* archetype who stands as the national's 'other' and whose individuality is constantly threatened by collective and reductionist representations.

In his paper titled 'The Representations of the *Bidun* in the Kuwaiti Novel'[2] Nasir al-Ẓafiri's focuses on three novels*: An Unheard Collision* by Buthayna al-ʿIsa, *The Bamboo Stalk* by Saud alSanʿusi and *IPPLF* by Ismail Fahad. In the three novels, al-Ẓafiri identifies a reoccurring trope of the *Bidun* male character pursing a Kuwaiti female character. In this pursuit of the Kuwaiti national female, the *Bidun* male ultimately strives to attain a form of self-realization, material gain and upward social mobility through citizenship. This representation, al-Ẓafiri argues, cements an archetype of the *Bidun* as an opportunist 'other'. At the same time, the novels fail to articulate the *Bidun* character's sentiments and life story outside of that pursuit of citizenship.

In Saʿdiyya Mufarriḥ's paper titled 'the Novels of Marginalisation' (*rewayat al-tahmish*), she offers a critical reading of five novels. Starting with Nasir al-Ẓafiri's *Upturned Sky* (1995), she argues that while establishing a beginning for the *Bidun* in the history of Kuwaiti fiction, the novel 'doesn't call things by their real names'. The novel, as will be discussed later in the chapter, is implicit in dealing with the *Bidun* issue as the word '*Bidun*' itself throughout the novel remains unmentioned. Buthayna al-ʿIsa's *An Unheard Collision* (2004) wasn't able to offer any depth into the *Bidun* character. Saud al-Sanʿusi's *The Bamboo Stalk* comes closest to the understanding of the *Bidun*'s position in society as it represents the *Bidun* character as constitutive of the national cultural milieu while Ismail Fahad's *IPPLF* presents the most nuanced representation of the environment of the marginal space. Finally, in *Scorched Heat* (2015) by al-Ẓafiri, Mufarriḥ points to how the author's own lived experience as a *Bidun* allowed for a proximate representation of the *Bidun*. It is worth mentioning that both al-Ẓafiri and Mufarriḥ totally dismiss Fawziyya al-Salim's *Staircases of Day* (2011) because of its unfavourable portrayal of the *Bidun* community.

Representations of the ʿ*Ashish* between the ontological and the relational

The analysis of the depictions of the ʿ*Ashish* in this chapter will follow and reorganize the critical impulses of both al-Ẓafiri and Mufarriḥ. The depictions of the ʿ*Ashish*, as a unique space of *Bidun* exclusion, can be understood in two main approaches. On the one hand, the ʿ*Ashish* is approached as an ineluctable ontological space of exclusion where notions of *Bidun* identity are confined to expressions of lack. On the other hand, the ʿ*Ashish* is depicted relationally as a potential site where counter-narratives are exposed, liminal identities are performed and where ontological representations are disrupted and problematized. The difference between ontological and relational depictions is between those characters who are ultimately defined and confined by their statelessness as an *a priori* ontological condition and those whose statelessness is historical, contingent and bounded by context.

On one side of the analysis is Buthayna al-ʿIsa's *Unheard Collision*, Fawziyya al-Salim's *Staircases of Day*, and Ismail Fahad's *IPPLF*. These three novels, all incidentally written by Kuwaiti novelists, represent the ʿ*Ashish*, as I will argue, in ontological terms. The ʿ*Ashish* becomes the ultimate embodiment of the ontological space of exclusion. In the ontological representations of the ʿ*Ashish*, the *Bidun*'s unique space of exclusion is often constituted in terms of difference to the national space. The agency of *Bidun* characters is often restricted to the instrumental role of self-reflection as the national's 'other'. The ʿ*Ashish* is largely defined in terms of lack: of citizenship rights, and as a corollary of agency, of visibility, and of an intrinsic expression of identity. Any sense of identity beyond the quest for citizenship rights is limited. This is demonstrated in the *Bidun* character's often-unchallenged self-identification with extrinsic imposed labels while internalizing stereotypical depictions of the community. At the same time, the ontological ʿ*Ashish* often positions the *Bidun* synchronically, described voyeuristically from afar in a specific historical moment. As a corollary, the *ʿAshish* is often devoid a historicized positionality. When the particular *Bidun* experience is narrated diachronically, as in the *IPPLF*, the *Bidun*'s particular historical narrative is often subsumed and overpowered by a national narrative.

Novels such as Buthayna al-ʿIsa's *Unheard Collision* and Ismail Fahad's *IPPLF*, which can be categorized as sympathetic, or even committed, towards the *Bidun* community's plight tend to offer a positive image of *Bidun* characters. Fawziyya al-Salim's *Staircases of Day*, on the other hand, is more hostile in its representation of the community. Yet both approaches risk reducing *Bidun* characters to repetitive archetypes. On one hand, the *Bidun* character is portrayed as the archetypical victim who is often also an ever-loyal and patient 'citizen' barred from his or her rights. On the other hand is the archetype of the undeserving, opportunist interloper.

On the other side of the analysis is Nasir al-Ẓafiri's novel *Scorched Heat*, the first of the al-Jahra Trilogy which presents the *ʿAshish* in more relational terms. The relational *ʿAshish* is a permeable space of presence, agency and visibility. A sense of exclusion is realized from a subjective experience and an interaction within the space rather than preconditioned imperative. The *ʿAshish* is not necessarily constituted in opposition to the national space, but as a space laden with childhood memories, memories of certain particular events and a personal and collective memory that is not restricted to expressions of lack and narratives of victimization. The agency of *Bidun* characters is most evident in their ability to negotiate their positionality in claiming, rejecting or going beyond the *ʿAshish*. As well as actively interacting and negotiating a presence within the national space, a relational approach is concerned with pre-national spaces such as the desert as an alternative space of beginnings and postnational exilic and diasporic spaces.

At the same time, the relational *ʿAshish* is context bound and understood historically. The interplay between history, fiction and narrative highlights the contingency and interconnectedness of both the national narrative and the *ʿAshish*'s particular narrative. An overpowering national narrative does not necessarily subsume the historical particularity of the *Bidun* community's experiences. The particular choice of novels selected is guided by the relevant themes of the chapter: the manifestations of agency, identification and visibility in the spatial and temporal representations of the *ʿAshish*. From the Al-Ẓafiri's al-Jahra trilogy, I have opted to analyse the first novel *Scorched Heat* as representative of his work.

Buthayna al-ʿIsa's *An Unheard Collision*: The *Bidun* as balconies of self-reflection

Published in 2004, *An Unheard Collision* is the first novel by Buthayna al-ʿIsa (b.1987). The novel was originally conceived as a short story published in the online cultural forum *Jasad al-Thaqafa* (http://jsad.net/) in 2002. The general plot of the novel doesn't differ much from the original short story. The main difference between the two is in the way Dhari, the main character, is depicted as a *Bidun*. While the short story does not explicitly mention Dhari's *Bidun* status, the novel directly elucidates the condition for its readers. This difference is perhaps due to the nature of the readership between the online forum *Jasad al-Thaqafa* and the novel published by Dar al-Mada in Damascus. The readership of the online cultural forum *Jasad al-Thaqafa* is more familiar with the background and history of the *Bidun* issue as it was one of the main platforms from which *Bidun* writers gained literary exposure online (Khalifa 2013). *Jasad al-Thaqafa*'s readership is able to make sense of Dhari's Bedouin accent, his Swedish citizenship and his *Bidun* upbringing without explicit explanation. The novel's wider Arab readership and circulation, however, necessitated a more descriptive approach of the *Bidun*'s situation for the uninitiated reader.

The short story was published under the title *Wa Khanat al-Awṭan Fih* (And the Homelands Have Betrayed Him) which is a direct quote taken from a poem by the *Bidun* poet Fahad Duhan. Excerpts from Fahad Duhan are also embedded within the text itself. This contextual note can give some insight into al-ʿIsa's links to and solidarity with the *Bidun* literary community. The sympathetic impulse entailed in the story demonstrates how the author aligns herself with the plight of the community by projecting a positive image of the *Bidun*. Yet, in that attempt to positively image the *Bidun*, the novel, as will be argued, restricts the *Bidun*'s agency to a tool for self-reflection on the national.

An Unheard Collision is narrated by Farah, an 18-year-old Kuwaiti student, who travels to Sweden to represent her country in an international biology competition. There, she encounters Dhari who is sent by the Kuwaiti embassy as an interpreter. Dhari, a Swedish citizen with a Kuwaiti Bedouin accent, remains ambiguous to Farah throughout the first part of the novel. Later, she comes to realize that because of his *Bidun* status, Dhari left Kuwait for Sweden as a teenager to seek citizenship. The narrative throughout primarily revolves around Farah and Dhari's relationship and their insightful discussions about love, homeland and belonging. After seven days in Sweden, Farah returns to Kuwait with new feelings towards Dhari and a new revised national consciousness.

The *Bidun* status of Dhari is central to the narrative. The novel is written in two main parts divided by the moment of Farah's realization of Dhari's *Bidun* status. Throughout the first part of the novel, Dhari's *Bidun* status is only hinted at. When Farah first encounters Dhari, she is taken aback because of his use of an informal greeting in Kuwaiti dialect '*guwwa*' (al-ʿIsa 2004:17).

This first encounter instigates Farah to ask: 'Are you Kuwaiti?' (19) Dhari replies with a smile that 'eludes any identity' (19) simply saying 'I am Dhari'. (19). He continues to resist any explicit mention of his previous *Bidun* status. When asked why he left Kuwait for Sweden, he replies, 'let us just say that Sweden is better than Kuwait' (25). After further interrogations by Farah, the first part of the novel ends with Dhari's confession that he left Kuwait because it had refused to give him citizenship.

During the first part of the novel, Dhari's elusiveness puts him in a position beyond national definition giving him an epistemic edge over Farah's 'naïve' national tendencies. He asks her, '[W]hy should I tire myself in being on one land and not another and call it – with all the world's naivety – a homeland'. He goes on, 'I … want nothing. (44). You are the one in need'. Yet, in the second part, Dhari's multidimensional awareness is suddenly halted with Farah's realization of his *Bidun* status.

In a climactic scene Farah asks Dhari, '[A]re you *Bidun*?' adding 'I ask you while tears fill my eyes, my limbs shake. I fall tired while you drag your sad steps towards the car with your head lowered, noble one, for the first time' (73).

After Farah's realisation, she contemplates on the word *Bidun*:

> That is what they name you there. It means that you live without any formal papers confirming your existence … it means that you see the world, while it does not see you. It means that you are always in need of a hell called 'others' to have a life, job, education … it means that you are supposed to conceal your existence because you are an illegal resident in a place you call home. It means that you are deprived of marriage and divorce because the government records do not bless your statelessness.
>
> (73)

After enjoying a 'worldly' self-sufficiency and an upper hand earlier, Dhari is left powerless and in need of sympathy as a wronged *Bidun*. It is a scene where Dhari is described from afar and reduced to an archetypical victim of his condition most explicitly.

This archetypical depiction is then affirmed in Dhari's own recollections of his particular experiences of living as a *Bidun* in Kuwait. He tells Farah: '[A]dd to my CV, a previous felon in the juvenile detention center, a tissue box seller in traffic lights around Damascus street under the *ʿUdailiyya* bridge, and finally … a fugitive from the homeland of no-future' (81). Dhari goes on:

> Imagine living without a future, without guarantee. Imagine depending on others all your life, or become a trader in the black market chased by the authorities …. Imagine loving someone who doesn't love you. I was that person and Kuwait was my love.
>
> (81)

Dhari identifies with stereotypical images of the *Bidun* community in the national imaginary as hawkers and hucksters, which reoccur in many of the works depicting *Bidun* characters.

The allegorical implications in the novel are not implicit. Farah and Dhari's tumultuous relationship, or 'an unheard collision', suggests a mirroring of the wider relationship between Kuwait and the *Bidun*. In one scene, Dhari puts it explicitly: '[F]or some time I had a feeling that Kuwait will visit me one day' (78). He continues: '[Y]ou are Kuwait in all its sumptuous details in the shape of a female' (78). Similarly at the opposite end, Dhari is a 'balcony' from which Farah can view Kuwait (41). He offers her a fresh outsider's perspective and a way to reflect on her previously unquestioned sense of nationalism. Through Dhari, Farah's conception of national belonging is interrogated.

Farah asks him: 'I want to see Kuwait through your eyes' (77). Throughout, Dhari provokes and unsettles her sense of unquestioned nationalism. He later explains that his provocative stance is a form of revenge from a country that had previously rejected him.

What is significant in the allegorical framing of Dhari is how he also seems to serve a purpose for the narrator, namely, as 'a balcony' for the national embodied in Farah to self-reflect. The *ʿAshish* in *An Unheard Collision* seems to represent a space restricted to utterances of victimization and pain. In the attempt to draw a positive image of the *Bidun*, the novel reduces the agency of the *Bidun* to instruments of self-reflection whose lives are not comprehended beyond the national gaze.

Fawziyya al-Salim's *Staircases of Day* (2011): Nothing beyond the national gaze

Unlike al-ʿIsa's *An Unheard Collision* which arose out of a position of solidarity with the *Bidun*, al-Salim's *Staircases of Day* is perceived to represent the *Bidun* in an uninformed and hostile manner. In both Saʿdiyya Mufarriḥ and Nasir al-Ẓafiri's critical reception of novels representing the *Bidun*, this novel has been totally neglected. In an online review, Mona Kareem writes:

> Setting aside its mediocre language, the novel is a good example of how the aristocracy (*al- ṭabaqa al-aristuqraṭiyya*) does not understand a thing about the social structure except that which concerns them …
>
> The writer expresses a number of racist myths created by her social class that depict the *Bidun* as mercenaries, opportunists and even prostitutes …
>
> The writer is surely unaware of the forms of legal exclusion practiced against the *Bidun*. Neither is she aware of the *Bidun* community's general conservative make-up. The characters do not emerge from any real context. (Kareem 2014a)

Similarly, Buthayna al-ʿIsa criticized the inimical representation of the *Bidun* in *Staircases of Day*:

> I didn't like the way the writer depicted the *Bidun* in Kuwait as a locus of illegal, psychopathic and immoral dealings: as drug dealers, human

> traffickers, and pimps. The likes of her know well the cultural richness of this community as they constitute a large component of writers and artists in Kuwait.
>
> (al-ʿIsa 2011)

On the other hand, the novel's author al-Salim believes that *Staircases of Day* aimed to reflect an accurate reality of *Bidun* life in Kuwait:

> In the time of writing the novel in 2011, they [the *Bidun*] had much less rights. Thankfully, much progress has been achieved since then such as issuance of marriage and birth certificates and civil ID cards. Now, the government has given them even more rights than legal expatriates.
>
> (Layali Programme 2016)

Al-Salim frames her novel within an uncritical aesthetic of realism. Her novel attempts to accurately represent the social reality of the *Bidun*. What is at stake here between al-Salim's attempt at accurate representation and the hostile reception of her novel is the understanding of the *ʿAshish* between the ontological and the relational. The *ʿAshish* in the novel is purely constituted in opposition to the national space as the ultimate embodiment of an ontological space of exclusion.

Fahda, the female *Bidun* protagonist, recounts her material and spiritual life journey from a life of poverty in the *ʿAshish* to a life of affluence outside of it after marrying her Kuwaiti husband Dhari. Fahda and Dhari first meet in a private party held by affluent Kuwaitis where Fahda and her sisters were hired as call girls. After noticing her lustfully dancing along with 'prostitutes, homosexuals ... and the elite of Kuwaiti society (*ʿilyat al-qawm*)', Dhari proposes to her. Much to her chagrin, Fahda's marriage is kept secret from Dhari's family. Before the birth of their first son, Dhari passes away.

The novel understands society in simple binary terms between those who have Kuwaiti citizenship and those who do not. The transparency through which the novel presents these stable binaries makes it an unchallenging read, one that continually affirms the binaries rather than troubling them with the complexity of lived experience. Spatially, the novel distinguishes between two clearly delineated spaces, what Fahda calls 'their streets', or the national space, and 'our streets', a non-national space to which she belongs. The former is defined by presence; a space where characters can be seen in action and the latter defined by absence and mystery. 'Our streets' is a marginal space; a hybrid melting pot of nationalities:

> In our streets, the smells and tastes effused from the frying pans in the alleyways and street corners mix … Indian, Chinese, Bengali, Korean, Pakistani, Filipino, Iranian, Thai, Somali, Abyssinian, Egyptian, and Kurdish traditions and odours rise upwards and define our identity … Muslims (Shiites and Sunnis), Christians, Buddhists, Hindus, Baha'is and Sikhs, all melt and mix in our streets. A new unique language is created and understood by everyone … a unique hybrid identity is born out of our streets which produces all that is strange, peculiar and distinct.
>
> (23–24)

Implicit in this description of hybridity and peculiarity is the national's space stable and reliable sense of identity. The general lack of 'our streets' is compared to the plenitude and sufficiency of 'their streets'. She goes on:

> Their streets and neighbourhoods are filled with an aura of gentle tranquillity …. Nothing we have corresponds to what they have. Every element of grandeur and beauty is unknown to us. All these sport, health, educational, cultural and entertainment centres are unheard of here …. Every stone in the pavement is left in its place, every flower is not yet picked, every manhole cover has not yet been melted and sold, every street lamp is intact, every pigeon, *bulbul* or bird hasn't been shot at yet, every car passes by without a scream from its horn.
>
> (35–36)

The national space is identifiable by a sense of order, stability, normalcy and by certain institutional markers (sports, health and educational centres) while the non-national is defined simply by the lack of the above.

Non-nationals are only made visible when they are within the national's scope of vision. Anything outside is an illegible 'non-place'; empty and silent. During the hot time of *thahira* when 'everyone' in the suburbs is asleep under air-conditioned roofs, a 'society of noon' bursts into action. Baṭṭaḥ, Fahda's *Bidun* uncle, Abu-l-Kalam the Bengali, Abu Kiroz the Kurd, Abu Daghfas the Afghan and Ayman the Egyptian *Shaṭir* are all part of an underground industry illegally manufacturing recycled waste. They are most visible at noon in the suburbs and become less visible as they move back to their own space: 'after a long journey they arrive at their destiny in the non-place … they go off the grid … in an emptiness shaded by silence' (46).

Non-nationals, particularly the *Bidun*, are subject to a totalizing subsuming national gaze. Fahda continually self-identifies with unchallenged stereotypes limited to what the national gaze permits. Her family profile is described in a strikingly archetypical manner. Fahda's father, a soldier in the army, was denied his previously enjoyed housing because of his *Bidun* status. Uncle ʿAwwad helps keep Fahda and her sisters safe while they work as call girls. Uncle Baṭṭaḥ, a taxi driver and pimp, deals in underground activities. Uncle Mirdas and uncle Sager are both involved in drug trafficking. This description of Fahda's *Bidun* family is not too far from the prevalent demonizing discourses in local media.

In another passage, Fahda lists all the typical 'jobs' that are available for *Bidun* women like her: assembling spray perfumes to sell by the traffic lights, making *ruqaq* bread for weddings, restoring the muscles of the uterus, holding Zar nights to exorcise people from Jinns, witchcraft, Tasseography, black magic and practising traditional medicine among others (25–26).

As to *Bidun* adolescents, they mostly work in selling spray perfumes by the traffic lights in the suburbs of Kuwait. This image has been previously encountered in *An Unheard Collision* and is perhaps the most stereotypical and accessible image for the national gaze. A chapter under the title of *Rushush* (spray perfumes) is dedicated to describing the process of assembling and selling these spray perfumes. Fahda's mother concocts the bottles while her brother Baṭṭaḥ steals some bottles to get drunk. What remains is later sold by young *Bidun* boys.

More importantly, Fahda unchallengedly internalizes the label *Bidun* as a legal identifier:

> We are not expatriates, nor are we residents. We did not arrive with contracts or official agreements. We are 'the withouts'; without protection or shelter. We are an abandoned nakedness of withoutness.
>
> (36)

The term *Bidun* is presented as a legal status contrasted with expatriates and residents, who've arrived through legal means. Fahda internalizes the label, in its legal connotations, without any form of resistance or an attempt to claim, interrogate or problematize it. The internalization of the label and the affirmation of stereotypical images are markers of how the representation of the *ʿAshish* is totally subject to a centralizing national gaze.

In *Staircases of Day*, being *Bidun* is not depicted as a condition brought about or understood by the unfolding of events within a particular lived space. Rather, it is an *a priori* condition that delineates Fahda and the *Bidun* community's agency in that space. The *Bidun* become entirely visible and easily identifiable by reductive stereotypical representations.

While the analysis of the *An Unheard Collision* and *Staircases of Day* emphasized the spatial dimensions of the ontological *ʿAshish*, the third novel in the analysis, Ismail Fahad's *IPPLF*, looks into the diachronic representations of the *ʿAshish* and its relation to an overpowering national historical narrative.

Ismail Fahad's *In Presence of the Phoenix and the Loyal Friend* (2013): The *Bidun* in the national memory

Within the local scene, Ismail Fahad has consistently shown an affinity to *Bidun* writers. He had been one of the main sponsors of the Tuesday Gathering since its establishment in 1995, which for a period of time held its meeting in his private office. Ismail Fahad's long-established cultural connections also assisted the publication of Mona Kareem's first poetry collection *Absence with Severed Fingers* (2004) in Cairo (Kareem 2014b). Along with Saʿdiyya Mufarriḥ and Dikhil Khalifa, Ismail Fahad is also one of the dedicatees of Nasir al-Ẓafiri's novel *Scorched Heat*. In addition, the introduction of *IPPLF* is written by Saʿdiyya Mufarriḥ. In an interview, Ismail Fahad mentions that the main impulse behind writing the novel was the 'duties of citizenship' (*wajib al-muwaṭana*), to tell the nation of historical injustices practised against the *Bidun* (Hussain 2014).

Ismail Fahad's positive stance towards the *Bidun* community was reflected in the novel's favourable reception. Even though the novel was published many years after al-Ẓafiri's *Upturned Sky* (1995), al-ʿIsa's *An Unheard Collision* (2004) and al-Salim's *Staircases of Day* (2011), the literary critic, Suʿad al-ʿInizi, writes that the novel 'deserves to be the first foundational novel; a "god-text" for any future work on the subject' (al-ʿInizi 2013). While in her introduction Saʿdiyya Mufarriḥ writes:

> *IPPLF* attempts to delve into the psychological core of this group of people through a single being which is not viewed as an archetype, but a unique case. Perhaps this highlights that every single individual in the overall group is a unique case in a humane context and not simply a number in the collective context.
>
> (Fahad 2013:7)

IPPLF characterization of the 'the single being' protagonist Mansi ibn Abih (literally the forgotten one, son of his father) is seen as a departure from collective reductionism.

Notwithstanding the favourable reception, Mansi's individuality, as will be argued, is constantly sabotaged by a passive self-identification with an overpowering collective condition of being *Bidun*. Being *Bidun*, in the legal or administrative sense, seems to be his main identifier. He is not necessarily depicted as Mansi who happens to be *Bidun*. Rather, he is the *Bidun* who happens to carry the name Mansi. More importantly, in his recollection of his 'singular' life story, an overpowering national narrative subsumes the particular historical experience of the individual *Bidun*.

IPPLF is written in the form of a long personal letter written by the *Bidun* narrator Mansi ibn Abih directed to his daughter Zaynab, who stands as a signifier for a national memory that has dropped Mansi's life story and the *Bidun*'s particular historical experience altogether. In his letter, Mansi attempts to justify, through recollecting his life story, his enforced absence.

Mansi, unlike Fahda in *Staircases of Day*, does not reside within the specific geographical space of the *ʿAshish* with other *Bidun* members. Along with his mother, Mansi resides in an attached room in al-Nugra, a residential area well known for its Arab expatriate community, especially the Palestinian community. Throughout the novel, his relations and interactions are mostly with Kuwaiti nationals or other expatriates. Mansi is severed from any *Bidun* communal links. Along with his mother, they are the only *Bidun* characters present in the novel.

Unlike the previously discussed novels, the novel engages deeply with questions of historicization of the *Bidun* issue. The development of the *Bidun* issue is approached through the individual story of Mansi. The narration of his life story is set chronologically in accordance with critical junctures in national history. The timeline of the novel follows three main periods: pre-Iraqi invasion, the invasion and post-liberation Kuwait.

The novel reflects how the *Bidun* have been treated differently in each period in accordance with shifts in official policy. In the pre-invasion period, the Kuwaiti scene is depicted in its Arab nationalist state of mind where Kuwaitis, Arab expatriates and *Bidun*s interact in the political, social and cultural spheres. Mansi is frequently visited by his neighbour Naji al-Ali, the well-known Palestinian caricaturist, who gives Mansi the label of *Hanḍalat* al-*Bidun*. At the same time, Mansi along with the theatre troupe travel to Damascus to perform one of the Syrian playwright Saʿdallah Wannus' plays. However, this Arab nationalist spirit is entirely ruptured with the Iraqi invasion of Kuwait. The 'other' simply starts to take the form of the non-Kuwaiti. 'Uhud, Mansi's Kuwaiti wife, questions her husband's loyalty to the nation and later totally rejects him. In the post-liberation period, Mansi is only remembered for his forced participation with the occupying forces while his involvement with the Kuwaiti resistance is deliberately ignored. His imprisonment as a result reflects the official governmental stance characterized by rejection and accusation of the *Bidun*.

What is significant in the above timeline is how Mansi is treated as a lens from which one can understand the development of the *Bidun* issue in Kuwait. If one would substitute the character's name with the word *Bidun*, the novel perhaps would not be read differently. It would probably be read as different episodes in the life of a *Bidun* character in Kuwait during those different historical markers of national history narrativized to highlight the psychological weight of such episodes on the character.

The main subject of enquiry in the novel is not the *Bidun per se*, but the nation at large. Mansi and the *Bidun*'s particular history serve as a function of national history. It is a way of narrating the national through the experiences of the *Bidun* and narrating the *Bidun*'s history solely through the experiences of the national. While the history of the *Bidun* is inextricable from national history, the *Bidun*'s particular memory is presented as nothing other than the history of official exclusion.

In an attempt to incorporate the *Bidun* within the nation as deserving citizens, the novel limits an understanding of the historical process and contingency of both the national and the overall condition of being *Bidun*. In the act of narrating his life as a *Bidun* facing legal, political, social and psychological exclusion, Mansi is unable to escape the ontological *ʿAshish*.

Nasir al-Ẓafiri's *Scorched Heat*: The novelization of historiography

Nasir al-Ẓafiri (1960–2019) cannot be easily situated within established national literary categorization. Having grown up stateless in the *ʿAshish* of al-Jahra, he then left Kuwait in the mid-1990s to Ottawa, Canada where he gained Canadian citizen. In her introduction to his novel *Upturned Sky*, Mufarriḥ he is not introduced as a Kuwaiti writer, a Canadian writer, or even a *Bidun* writer. Al-Ẓafiri is carefully placed as 'an important writer of the nineties decade in Kuwait' emphasizing the emotive and contributive aspects of belonging. To al-Ẓafiri, gaining official Canadian citizenship is not necessarily equated with a cultural sphere of belonging and engagement. As he puts it:

> I was one of those who preferred to migrate to Canada in search for a wider margin of freedom of movement … yet, the belief in my right to my homeland has never waned. I still believe that I am a Kuwaiti writer. I will not become a writer belonging to any other country.
>
> (Majjalat al-Ṭaliʿa 2016)

As al-Ẓafiri puts it 'the *Bidun* is my concern since I was born and until the day I die' (Fajr 2014). This self-proclaimed concern is the main theme of his literary oeuvre. Informed by his upbringing in the *ʿAshish* of al-Jahra, all of al-Ẓafiri's novels, with the exception of his first novel *Snow Lover* (1992), are mainly concerned with the depictions of the marginalized space of the *ʿAshish* and the untold histories of its characters. Of his experience of al-Jahra, al-Ẓafiri comments, 'I lived the people's hardships and miseries …. As a writer, I am enamoured with their characters, their madness, and their fervor of life' (Majjalat al-Ṭaliʿa 2016).

Al-Ẓafiri's second novel, *An Upturned Sky* (1995), which narrates the tumultuous upbringing of the *Bidun* adolescent Sulayman Abdullah, is the first novel ever to capture the ambience of the *ʿAshish* in al-Jahra. His third novel *The Gullible Ones* (2008) is his most experimental novel as it is spatially and temporally ambiguous. Yet the story of a brother's revenge, unchecked crime and scandalous sexual encounters carries traces of an abandoned marginalized space as in *An Upturned Sky*. In 2013, al-Ẓafiri published his fourth novel, *Scorched Heat*, the first of his 'al-Jahra Trilogy'. The novel is very explicit in its dealing with the historical origins of the Bedouin patriarch Shuman and subsequent exile and return of his *Bidun* son Ali to Canada. The second and third novels of the trilogy *Kaliska* (2015) and *Al-Maṣtar* (2018) further narrate the multitude of untold stories of the wronged generations of *Bidun* in Kuwait and in the diaspora. In addition, al-Ẓafiri published three short story collections: *Feast of the Moon* (1990), *First Blood* (1993) and *A Brutalized Whiteness* (2017).

As a novelist who is concerned with the *Bidun* cause, al-Ẓafiri is very careful in distancing himself from any autobiographical imprints or claims of authentic realistic communal representations of the *ʿAshish*. He is aware of the fine line between the realistic and the aesthetic impulses. He writes, 'I don't write articles or political manifestos on the *Bidun*. I am a novelist and that is all. I am not concerned with matching characters with real life' (Fajr 2014). As opposed to producing sociological or political statements, al-Ẓafiri prioritizes the imaginative aesthetic act as a potent form of agency. The fictionalized narrative of the *ʿAshish* allows for an agency of individual voice that disrupts hegemonic collective modes of representation, which often reproduce ontological notions of fixed identities and schematic belonging. The analysis of al-Ẓafiri's relational depictions of the *ʿAshish* will focus on *Scorched Heat* (2013), which he considers to be his 'most important novel' (Fajr 2014). The novel, in its comprehensive attempt to historicize the *Bidun* issue, complicates the existing depictions of this space.

Scorched Heat (2013), published at a time when the *Bidun* issue became perceived within Kuwait and the region, as an undeniable everyday reality, is the first of al-Ẓafiri's novels that deal with the issue in an explicit manner. In *An Upturned Sky* (1995), when debates on the *Bidun* issue were highly sensitive and monopolized by state discourse, the term *Bidun*, throughout the novel, is left unmentioned.

The inauguration of *Bidun* street protests in February 2011 at the wake of the 'Arab Spring' created a paradigm shift in the political modes of representation of the *Bidun* as highlighted in Chapter 1. On the literary front, the rise of the '*Bidun* novel' and the contested representations of the community necessitated a more direct dialogical approach to the *Bidun* issue. *Scorched Heat* directly confronts the underlying problematic of ahistoricity which enables the ontological representations analysed earlier.

In an interview, al-Ẓafiri mentions that the novel's main impulse is 'to demonstrate to the people in Kuwait that those labels that separate Kuwaitis are nothing but myths, which have been behind the enforced exile of many, myself included, from Kuwait' (Ahmad 2013). The way these myths are exposed is through an 'understanding of the historical process behind the creation of the *Bidun* issue in Kuwait' (Fajr 2014). This historicizing impulse is reflected in the two-part structure of the novel. The first part is titled *Taʾrikh* (historiography) that aims to rewrite 'a historiography of Kuwaiti society that is inclusive of the *Bidun*' (Fajr 2014). The second part, titled *riwaya* (the novel), is 'purely novelistic in terms of language, stylistics and entangled narrative lines' (Fajr 2014). Through this dichotomy of historiographic narrative and fictional narrative, al-Ẓafiri aims to 'transform history into a novel and the novel into a history' (Majjalat al-Ṭaliʿa 2016).

The structure of the novel, between historiography and novelization, lends the tools of analysis. Al-Ẓafiri blurs the line between the putative objectivity of historiography and the subjectivity of mythical narratives. Historicizing the narrative enables the novelizing of history. In other words, historicizing the narrative reorders the historiography of the past to offer a critical perspective on the contingency and fictionality of present categories.

Historiography: Itineraries of arrival

The opening scene of the novel describes the mythical origins of Shuman, the Bedouin patriarch and the mythical moment of excommunication from his tribe. Shuman (translated to the doubly cursed one) emerges naked out of a pool of water interrupting a group of naked Bedouin women. As a result, he is summoned by the tribal Sheikh and is excommunicated from the tribe. The narrator describes how the story of Shuman travels throughout the desert:

> [T]he wind carried the story of the being … everyone treated the story as nothing but a myth. A myth, like any other, weaved by the wind, to tell of a certain age. The same wind then overturns the narrative with a substitute myth.
>
> (15)

The sacred moment of origin is treated by the desert dwellers as nothing but a necessary myth illustrating the inherent fragility of any moment of origin. This in turn opens up the space for the multitude of possible beginnings at the level of the *Bidun* community's displacement and the moments of genesis within national historiography.

The notion of historiography then turns from questions of mythical origins to historical beginnings. Unlike *IPPLF*'s narration of the history of the *Bidun* from a national perspective, *Scorched Heat* explores how the margins narrate the many moments of the nation's genesis. The nation is narrated through the multiple, decentred and fragmented historiographies of a generation of displaced characters who for different particular historical processes all converge in the *ʿAshish* of al-Jahra. These characters include the Bedouin patriarch Shuman, the Palestinian teacher Kamal al-Askalani, the Indian Ocean merchant Ibn Faḍl, the Iraqi Shiite scholar Sayyid Jassem and the Basran farmer Shakir. The itineraries of these characters are traced back from different pre-national and transnational spaces such as the desert between recently established national borders and the sea along the littoral zones of the Indian Ocean trade route. The displacement and eventual arrival of these characters is situated within wider narratives of displacement concomitant with new postcolonial political and economic realities. The first of these new realities is the demise of a sustained tribal mode of life in the desert compelling many tribes residing in-between recently established borders to settle at the outskirt of cities. The second is the shift in economic orientation from the Indian Ocean trade route to oil production that acted as a pull factor for new arrivals. The third relates to wider regional political upheavals such as the *Nakba* in Palestine and the 1958 military coup in Iraq and the consequent migration to the Gulf.

The first chapter in the first part of the novel is set in an undisclosed area in the desert between the recently formed borders of Kuwait and Iraq. The description of the desert is reminiscent of al-Flayyiḥ's apocalypse scene in Chapter 4. The narrator describes the influence of the harsh and abrupt end of the desert life on Shuman. To Shuman, with 'his mother Fiḍḍa, a camel or two, a steed, a *saluki* and a hunting rifle' the desert is a 'universe in itself' (19). Desert life is then transformed, 'the sky was barren like a dried-up udder, nothing sprung from the earth but heaps of sand, snakes, lizards, scorpions and desert plants that did not satisfy his lonely camel's hunger' (19). The narrator describes the arbitrariness of Shuman's life choices, 'he sat on a pasture land not far from the hills between Kuwait and Iraq … he used to tell his mother, if the camel dies in spring we'll enter Iraq, if it dies in summer we'll enter Kuwait' (18).

At that particular in-between desert space, the second major character, Ibn Faḍl, is introduced. After his car broke down in the desert, Ibn Faḍl finds Shuman's tent and asks him for a ride back to his estate in Basra. In a noble Bedouin gesture, and without asking him any questions, Shuman offers him a ride on his only camel. The narrator describes their journey: 'Shuman took a path that he knew well. He memorized its stones, hills, and plains, as if he was traveling on a paved road, eliding the eyes of the border control guards' (21). After their arrival at Basra, Shuman realizes that this man is Ibn Faḍl, one of the most influential merchants whose transnational business extends to Kuwait, Basra, Aden and Bombay.

Given Shuman's knowledge of the desert, Ibn Faḍl offers him work as a gold smuggler between Basra and Kuwait. Shuman's encounter with al-Jahra is incidental, 'on his way to his desert, al-Jahra appeared to him a village of mud houses, tents, and sheets of wood and metal' (37). Eventually, Shuman gets married and settles in al-Jahra. Shuman then returns to Basra to smuggle Ibn Faḍl and later his loyal Iraqi servant Shakir to Kuwait in the wake of the 1958 coup. All three characters, Shuman, Ibn Faḍl and Shakir along with their families, eventually settle in al-Jahra.

The second chapter in the first parted, titled 'The Mangrove Load', is set on a dhow owned by Ibn Faḍl, travelling through the different ports of the Indian Ocean trade route from Kuwait to East Africa. As with the Bedouin smugglers, the dhow's *nukhidha*, or sea captain smuggles goods along the way. In its constant movement between ports, Sayyid Jassem, an Iraqi Shiite scholar, asks the *nukhidha* for a ride back to Najaf. Prior to embarking in Aden, Sayyid

Jassem itinerary included travels around Shiite religious networks in Iraq, Iran, and Mecca. On their way back, Sayyid Jassem cures a fellow Bedouin seafarer who later promises him his daughter's hand. As a result, he marries the Bedouin's wife and moves to Iraq. Yet he is later executed because of his involvement with the Iraqi communist party. His wife and daughter Layal, who plays a major in the second part of the novel, end up stateless in Kuwait.

The third historiography of displacement is that of the Palestinian teacher Kamal al-ʿAskalani. Kamal's itinerary starts with his enforced departure from ʿAskalan in 1948 to Gaza. As a result of the 1967 Israeli occupation, he is again forced to leave to Cairo. From Cairo he travels to Buraydah, in Saudi Arabia to work as a teacher. Kamal finds Buraydah intolerable, mainly due to the prohibition of tobacco which encourages him to leave. Through the help of a Bedouin tobacco smuggler, Ibn Ghazzay, Kamal and his family are smuggled to Kuwait. Finally, Kamal arrives at al-Jahra where the influential Ibn Faḍl offers him work as a teacher in the newly developed public school.

What is of interest in the above itineraries is the often-underplayed role of the pre-national and transnational spaces in national historiography. The symbols of the camel and the dhow in constant movement in-between established borders are legitimized as points of alternative historical beginnings where notions of the national were originally conceived. The desert and the sea symbolize a particular fluid subjectivity and problematize notions of belonging by contesting the rigid fixities imposed on these communities retrospectively. The desert and the sea here contain within them the alternative historical origins for the modern realities that the novel enters into in its second part.

Al-Jahra becomes the focal point where all the above characters converge and where another history begins. The new arrivals, including the *Bidun*, are positioned within the general condition of marginality under the scorching heat of al-Jahra. The historical process and arbitrariness of citizenship distribution are then highlighted as a critical juncture in national historiography shaping the future life of the sons and daughters of the generation.

The establishment of a centralized bureaucracy in al-Jahra is illustrated in the increasing powers of Ibn Faḍl, 'the government's close friend who holds to key of miracles' (86). He becomes the main link between al-Jahra's residents and the emerging bureaucracy in the capital. Ibn Faḍl asks Shuman to recruit Bedouins to work in the government, 'we will find them work in the army, police, guards, or the mounted police (*Hajjana*). We are building a modern country, don't you understand Shuman?' With time, Shuman realizes that he hasn't been offered 'papers that validate his belonging', an idea that seems strange to him. Ibn Faḍl becomes selective in documenting the town's people in the mid-1960s often excluding the Bedouins. Ibn Faḍl's Iraqi servant Shakir is offered citizenship while Shuman is left stateless as his 'time did not yet come' (88). Shuman reminds Shakir, '[Y]esterday I brought you here on my camel's back when you were terrified like an ostrich chick' (89). In a symbolic reply highlighting the gullibility of the noble Bedouin, Shakir responds, 'You always bear what you are incapable of valuing, ever since you used to carry gold around your waist like an ass' (89).

The first part of the novel works against the prevalent ahistorical depictions of the *Bidun* community. It offers a nuanced understanding of the historical process behind the creation of the *Bidun* as a stateless community and the arbitrariness of the naturalization process and contingency of citizenship. The historiography of the displacement of this generation of fathers informs the contingency of the present social and political categories in the second part of the novel.

The *Rewaya*: Itineraries of departure

The second part of the novel titled *Riwaya* (the novel) is mainly concerned with the 'novelisation of the histories' of the sons and daughters of the father's generation. While the first part was concerned with untold history of arrivals of the fathers' generation, the second part narrates the untold itineraries of departures and histories of displacement of the sons and daughters. Shuman's son Ali and Sayyid Jassem's daughter Layal end up *Bidun*. Kamal Askalani's daughter Rima is a stateless Palestinian who migrates to Canada. Ibn Faḍl's son Sherif works on expanding his father's wealth with the assistance of Qays the son of Shakir. What is of particular interest in the second part is the interplay between a *Bidun* particular memory and national historiography. While the *Bidun* characters' histories are entangled with key events in national history, a *Bidun* particular memory is not totally subsumed by an official national historiography.

The second part begins with the return of Ali, the son of Shuman, who is now a Canadian 'expatriate' working in Kuwait. In an encounter with a government officer Ali is asked mockingly, 'Are you Canadian?' (157). The complexity of answering such a question is tackled throughout the second part of the novel. As the first part is concerned with legitimizing transnational spaces as constitutive of national historiography, the second part works on historicizing and legitimizing spaces of exile and diaspora as integral extensions of national historiography. The camel and the dhow in the first part are replaced with scenes from airplanes, buses carrying asylum seekers between the borders of the United States and Canada and asylum shelters in Canada. The desert sands are replaced with snow. In other words, the answer to a seemingly simple questions such as 'Are you Canadian?' demands a novel, or even a trilogy, as an answer.

During his years as a student in Kuwait University, Ali continuously maintains an aloofness from key political events. He writes: 'It was the winter of 1989, I find myself lonely and isolated not knowing which side I should be on … both sides aren't concerned with my issue' (218). His aloofness comes as a result of his feeling of being totally cast out of the historical time of the nation. He goes on:

> I have never participated in a political union, nor have I participated in a leftist rally smearing the right, nor have I attended a rightist rally smearing the left. I have never participated in Earth Day. I do not participate in national day celebrations. I am in the place, but outside of its time. I await that moment when my space and time coincide. If I fail in this life, then I believe that I have fallen on the wrong land in the wrong time.
>
> (230–231)

Ali expresses a wilful distance from aligning himself within the existing structures and limiting binaries. Rather, he insists on legitimizing an existence outside of the historical time of the nation. The moment when 'space and time coincide' is perhaps only actualized in the act of writing, or 'novelising the history' of his untold exile.

Ali's wilful distance then is materialized in his migration to Canada. A great part of the second part is set between New York, New Jersey, Ohio, Ottawa and Montreal, and in spaces between the United States and Canadian Border. There, Ali meets his friend Fawaz, a fellow diasporic *Bidun*, who has married an American. Fawwaz assists Ali in the asylum seeking process. Similarly, Ali reconnects with Rima Askalani who is now studying in Canada. The novel offers insight into the *Bidun*'s particular history of internal marginalization, migration and exile that is often excluded from national historiography.

Multiple narration

The second part is also characterized by a plurality of spatial and temporal planes, narratives and voices. The chapters alternate between three main narrative lines, often interrupting each other. The first is set in the present and is narrated by Ali Bin Shuman who lives in Kuwait as a Canadian 'expatriate'. The second narrative line, also narrated by Ali, is set between 1989 and 1990 and describes his time in Kuwait University, his affair with Layal and love of Rima, and his subsequent migration and arrival in Canada. In the third narrative line, Ali reads the long letter addressed to him from Layal, which she wrote before committing suicide in prison.

The technique of narrative polyphony challenges hegemonic representations of the *Bidun*. The contending representations and multiple narratives and histories of *Bidun* character are played out. Differences in gender, social and political standing, and personal disposition are emphasized to highlight the diverse narratives and experiences of statelessness within the *Bidun* community. In addition, the overlapping fates of Palestinians and *Bidun* highlight how *Bidun* characters share a wider marginal memory of displacement.

While sharing a legal status, Ali and Layal substantially differ in their experiences of statelessness. Firstly, Layal is exposed to particular pressures due to her gender. In her letter, Layal discloses to Ali the sexual abuses she faced as a child from her stepfather. Later, she also becomes vulnerable to sexual abuse when she works as a secretary in Sherif's company. Ali is only made aware of these episodes through reading Layal's own words, which highlights the multiple untold narratives within the *Bidun* community.

Secondly, and at the political level, Ali is critical of Layal's non-contemplative political engagement. Whereas Layal is continuously active politically during the events of 1989, Shuman maintains a neutral stance. He tells her, '[Y]ou and I, no one will bother with us' (219). Ali is also critical of Layal's ignorance of his particular experiences in al-Jahra:

> Layal does not live her real condition. She does not acknowledge that she is *Bidun Jinsiyya* (without citizenship) and doesn't see the existential angst of the condition … she never lived amongst them and like most politicians, writers, and a great segment of the population, she never thought of visiting their homes or getting close to their public or private lives.
>
> (313)

Layal, another *Bidun*, is equated with the rest of the population in their lack of awareness of the intricate daily challenges of life as a *Bidun*. This disparate representation of two *Bidun* characters attests to the novel's problematization of a monolithic representation of the *Bidun* community's particular memory and experience.

The *Bidun* characters' statelessness is shared with the Palestinians living in Kuwait. Within life in al-Jahra, both Shuman's family and Kamal's family share a similar vulnerable position. This is made clear to Ali when his love of Rima is mocked by Qays: 'What would a Palestinian girl do with a young *Bidun* man?' (23). Eventually, both Ali and Rima find no real hope of establishing their lives in Kuwait and migrate to Canada in pursuit of college degrees and citizenship. The Iraqi invasion becomes a defining moment in Ali and Rima's relationship. Rima's nonchalant attitude towards the invasion enrages Ali: '[S]he doesn't know the meaning of homeland within me and wants it an occupied homeland. She doesn't understand that I've left my homeland not because I don't belong to it, but because I didn't want for it to leave me' (361). While Ali and Rima share the condition of statelessness marginalized position, Ali's distance from Rima further complicates the question of homogenous narratives of the marginalized by emphasizing the complexity of their experiences. The entangled narrative lines and multiple narration illustrate how a *Bidun* particular memory is always unique within the histories of marginalized communities and national historiography and heterogeneous within the community itself.

Conclusion

The novel as a commercial, mobile, translatable and adaptable (from a novel to a TV drama series) form has probably had more popular impact on the knowledge of the *Bidun* issue than human rights discourse or political activism. Yet the form of the novel invites both strands of representation of the *Bidun* experience, those that allegorize the *Bidun* experience synchronically in broad strokes as highlighted in novels of the 'ontological *'Ashish*' and those, such as Al-Ẓafiri's Trilogy, that offer a more nuanced representations. Interestingly, it is the former type of novels, mainly through prize winning and translation, that brought the *Bidun* issue to the forefront of cultural discussions on Kuwaiti society in the wider Arab and global English contexts. A prime example is *The Bamboo Stalk* by Saud al-Sanousi, which after winning the International Prize for Arabic Fiction was translated to English in 2015. It remains the only novel featuring a *Bidun* writer to be translated and circulated as 'world literature' beyond its culture of origin. If world literature offers as Damrosch puts it, 'multiple windows on the world', then *The Bamboo stalk* remains, the only window into the *Bidun* issue in the English language (Damrosch 2003:15).

In contrast, as mentioned earlier in the chapter, al-Ẓafiri has refused to participate or allow his publisher, Dar Masʿa, to nominate any of his novels to the International Prize for Arabic Fiction because of the prize board lacks an 'awareness of the form of the novel' and general incompetence in reading literary works (Majjalat Al-Ṭaliʿa 2016). Al-Ẓafiri criticized the impinging role of big publishers and the politics behind the nomination and selection processes. I would also argue that the nature of the prize elicits a particular preference for, what Jameson calls, 'Third-world literature' novels, which can be simply read as national allegories (Jameson 1986). This preference is mainly driven by the necessities and politics of translation to a global English readership.

In his critique of Jameson's postulate that all third world texts are to be read necessarily as national allegories, Aijaz Ahmad writes:

> I find it significant that first and second worlds are defined in terms of their production systems (capitalism and socialism, respectively), whereas

> the third category – the third world – is defined purely in terms of an "experience" of externally inserted phenomena.
>
> (6)

Ahmad's critique resonates with al-Ẓafiri relational depiction of the *Bidun* that similarly goes beyond the articulations of an external 'experience' of statelessness. Transposed globally, the ontological representations of the *Bidun* are but a reflection of a wider problem pertaining to the translation, circulation and modes of reading of 'third world texts'.

6

'Crossing borders': '*Sons of Kuwait*' in the diaspora

In 2009, the poet Muhammad al-Nabhan was invited to participate in the annual Nichita Stănescu international poetry festival in Romania to celebrate the Romanian translation of a selection of his poetry titled *Loneliness under the Shade of Palm Trees: Translations from Kuwaiti Poetry* (2009).[1] On the final day of the festival, al-Nabhan was awarded the festival's special prize and considered 'the most important contemporary Arab poet' (Maxim 2009). In addition to the Romanian translation of his poems, German, Spanish and English translations of his poems are available online. It was al-Nabhan's third participation in an international poetry festival. Previously, he had participated in the Sixteenth International Poetry Festival in Medellin, Columbia (2006) and in Curtea De Argeş Poetry Nights in Romania (2008) where he was introduced as a poet from Kuwait.

Yet news of al-Nabhan's award of an international prize barely received any attention in Kuwaiti media, which is never short of praise for citizens who achieve any kind of international award. A local online newspaper in a carefully worded headline wrote: 'the *son of Kuwait*, a world-acclaimed poet'. While al-Nabhan's accomplishment was overlooked in both his country of citizenship (Canada) and his country of birth (Kuwait), it was acknowledged and celebrated in Kuwait by an event organized by the 'Tuesday Gathering', which brought together the poet's friends and colleagues, many of whom due to their *Bidun* status, have regularly declined invitations to attend international cultural events.

Sa'diyya Mufarriḥ, for example, could not travel when invited, as a representative of Kuwait, to attend the 2012 edition of the Festival '*Voix vives*' in Sète, France. In 2012, she was also chosen as a representative of Kuwaiti poetry in the BBC and Scottish Poetry Library project titled *The Written World* in 2012, which broadcasted poems from different parts of the world daily during the London 2012 Olympic Games. The description of her translated poem *My Dreams Often Humble Themselves* read: 'This poem, representing Kuwait, is part of The Written World – our collaboration with BBC radio to broadcast a poem from every single nation competing in London 2012' (https://www.scottishpoetrylibrary.org.uk/poem/my-dreams-often-humble-themselves/).

Associating the celebration of international poetry with the Olympic Games is perhaps a telling example of the centrality of the nation state in current understandings of world literature. These 'world'-acclaimed poets, al-Nabhan and Mufarriḥ, are celebrated as representatives of nation states that do not officially recognize them in a global literary environment that often takes national belonging as a precondition of cultural recognition.

The unique position of *Bidun* writers existing within the interstices of established borders and national literatures necessitates an approach to the body of work that investigates wider contexts and categories that engage beyond national borders. From Goethe's 'universal possession of mankind' to Emily Apter's 'dispossessive collectivism', debates in world literature have continued to formulate theorizations of categories beyond national canons such as the global (Pratt 1995; Suassy 2006), the cosmopolitan (Dominguez 2012), the planetary (Spivak 2005), diasporic writings (Frydman 2012), the translational or the untranslatable (Apter 2013), the postcolonial (Bassnett 2003; Hassan and Saunders 2003; Young 2012) and the vernacular (Shankar 2012) among many others.

Al-Nabhan's peculiar position poses a question that is central to the literary and cultural production of stateless writers: What place in the world do stateless writers occupy in the 'Olympics' of literature? What are the possible modes of production and circulation for writers located outside of the dominant category of national literature? The chapter traces the physical and cultural journey of the diasporic *Bidun* poet Muhammad al-Nabhan as he travels in-between many borders from Kuwait to Canada and back and in his many attempts at forging literary networks and literary histories that attempt to 'cross borders'. While these attempts express an incessant desire to find affiliative spaces above and beyond official state categories, they nevertheless continuously negotiate their presence within the material considerations of officiality manifest in bureaucracy, the omnipresence of papers, border controls and geopolitical realities.

The poet and his papers

Born 1971 in Kuwait, Muhammad al-Nabhan traces the ultimate realization of his condition of statelessness to the early 1980s with the advent of the national card scheme.[2] The true beginning of the *Bidun* problem was when 'humans were reduced to digits'. Without an ID card and official paper, his generation were refused entry to higher education in Kuwait, and some other traditional jobs previously occupied by *Bidun*.

The absence of documentation was a physical manifestation of his exclusion. While denied official paper, al-Nabhan throughout his life enjoyed an intimate relationship with 'paper' in the widest sense of the word. Prior to the Iraqi invasion in 1990, he worked as a freelance calligrapher and designer. His skills in design during the invasion proved useful as he forged official documentation; ID cards for Kuwaiti military officers that were used to avoid persecution from the Iraqi army. A paperless person, denied documents throughout his life, was now able to forge and subvert state documents, in a time when the state papers lost their potency under the weight of occupation. Between 1992 and 1995, al-Nabhan created a graphic design studio and was continually being harassed, due to his *Bidun* status. This finally led him in 1995 to leave Kuwait to Canada to seek asylum.

While in Kuwait, al-Nabhan did not publish any of his poetry. His literary activity was restricted to intermittent contributions in local newspapers' cultural pages. Along with other *Bidun* poets, who were shunned by the state-sanctioned cultural institution, al-Nabhan participated in cultural networks operating outside the radar of the cultural institution such as the aforementioned Tuesday Gathering.

To live paperless is difficult, but to depart without them is practically impossible. In order to leave Kuwait, al-Nabhan was issued a passage ticket (*tadhkarat murur*) from the Kuwaiti government. This ticket is a one-way brown travel document issued for special purposes to the *Bidun*. On its face, it reads: Valid for one trip!! (followed by two exclamation marks, as al-Nabhan carefully emphasized when describing it). To obtain such a ticket, he had to sign another paper, a consent form assuring that the traveller would never return.

With these papers of expulsion, he began his itinerary arriving in Syria, where he spent a year. From Jordan, he travelled to Canada and applied for asylum. During this time, al-Nabhan recalls writing a poem titled *The Wind … and the Fear of the Runaway at Night*, which he had started in Kuwait and continued writing throughout his journey in Syria, Jordan, and finally completing it in Canada; a poem written on a piece of paper that literally 'crossed borders'.

In the poem, al-Nabhan describes this runaway travelling at night and his peculiar relationship with paper:

> You travel, carrying no burdens of a tradition
> No provisions gathered from the exhausting journey
> No papers identify you
> On the face of your dumb document
> The one who was once your father, now denounces you
> Your name no longer resembles you
> Not even your date of birth
> The blood test doesn't refer to you
> Without paper, you are everyone but yourself
> A name, easily *forged*
> A homeland, never arriving.

In order for this poem, in the poet's pocket, to literally 'cross borders', the asylum-seeking poet needed to manoeuvre his way through the grim realities of checkpoints, border controls, obtaining different travel documents and the many accompanying predicaments of a travelling refugee. Crossing borders here is contingent on an act of creative forgery that exposes the fragility of official paper and mocks its ability to affirm and deny presence. Between the two papers, the easily forged state document and the creatively forged poem, the poet highlights the unresolved tension between a literary presence and a state-sanctioned absence.

Al-Nabhan is seldom present in national literary histories and anthologies save for Sadiya Mufarriḥ's *Cameleers of Clouds and Estrangement* (2007) and Abbas al-Ḥaddad's *Arabic Poetry in the Gulf and the Arabian Peninsula* (2018). Yet al-Nabhan's own works and engagement in cultural production have constantly looked for cultural spaces and literary networks outside of the national's scope of vision. One such placement is Migrant Literature as he was a co-founder of Juzoor Cultural Foundation in 2005, an attempt to establish a network of Arab writers in North America.[3] Of premier importance is his pioneer status in Arab digital publishing as he worked on forging a paperless digital literary network of peripheral poets who have been marginalized in Kuwait and the Arab world more broadly by establishing the e-zine Ufouq.com.

Paperless digital horizons

As mentioned previously in the second chapter of the book, the shift from paper to digital publishing was a critical juncture in the Arab publishing scene, particularly for *Bidun* poets. In an article, Mufarriḥ recalls how the advent of digital publishing freed poets from the constraints of paper publishing: 'the internet ... was a refuge for the Arabic poem and a homeland for its poets that depends on actual creativity as its only precondition' (Ḥaddad 2006:90). Her poetry collection *Merely a Mirror Laying* (1999) is dedicated to 'Bill gates, and his days'. Kareem al-Hazza' also pays a tribute to Bill Gates in an article, saying: '[I]t is as if Bill Gates and his comrades created especially tailored wings for the *Bidun* allowing them to publish their works in online cultural forums' (al-Hazza' 2012). Al-Flayyiḥ found in digital publishing a new transgressive space for the *Sa'alik* of the twenty-first century. The *Sa'alik* of today, he writes in a 2008 article, have 'relocated from the earth to space' raiding virtual camp*sites*. He goes on:

> In the old times, their principle was to rebel against the tribe, resist injustice and discrimination … rebel against poetic norms, steal from the miser to give the poor of the desert. They are loyal to their friends, generous to those in need … those are the *Sa'alik* of yore and today. When they were stripped of their artillery by the new world order, they drew their pens.
>
> (al-Flayyiḥ 2008c)

The shift from paper to digital publishing was initiated with the establishment of online literary magazines in the latter part of the 1990s and into the early 2000s. The 'Born digital'[4] literary magazines were mainly founded by Arab poets concerned with the publication and circulation of contemporary Arabic poetry, mostly the prose poem (qasidat al-nathr), and world literature in translation. The most notable sites included *Jihat al-Shi'r* (The Direction of Poetry) (www.Jehat.com), founded by the Bahraini poet Qassim Ḥaddad in 1996, *Kikah* (www.Kikah.com) founded by the London-based Iraqi poet Samuel Shimon in 2001 and *Ufouq* (Horizons) (www.Ufouq.com) founded in 2000 by the *Bidun* writers Muhammad al-Nabhan in Canada and Saleh al-Nabhan and Karim Al-Hazza' in Kuwait. These magazines offered new 'read-only' publishing opportunities for Arab poets, which later evolved into more interactive interfaces with the advent of web 2.0.[5, 6]

With the fervour of new converts, the founders of these magazines espoused an optimistic enthusiasm towards a new digital age. In their editorials, the founders called for a literature that distances itself from parochial, local, regional and nationalistic outlooks towards a more universalist or cosmopolitan horizons. This digital horizon was synonymous with progress, advancement, freedom, humanism, civilizational dialogue, future promises and new beginnings.[7] In a manifesto-like statement stating Jehat.com's goals, Ḥaddad writes: '[T]o begin with, as a point of departure, a universal horizon (*ufuq kawni*) and transcend the illusions and constraints of locality and regionality that do not suit the age of the internet. There is a need to advance self-assured with our creative spirit to share the discovery of the future with the world' (Ḥaddad 2008:10–11). In the first online edition of *Kikah*, Samuel Shimon outlines the ambitions of his magazine:

> We are in need for a literature that derives its value from its aesthetic and humanistic qualities. A literature that is based on art and beauty, believes in

> multiculturalism, calls for tolerance and dialogue with people without regard to race, color and religion. Our literature should be part of the universal human literature (*aladab al-insani al-alami*) … true literature belongs to all religions, colors and races.
>
> (Shimon 2003)

Ufouq.com's publishers used a more tropological language in their editorials. Ufouq is 'a lung to breath in a special kind of air under a horizon that allows everyone to have a dialogue … far from the monotony of institutional work' (al-Tariq al-Mufdhi ila al-Yunbu' 2000).

Ḥaddad, in particular, has long been interested in theorizing the new possibilities offered by digital publishing. To him the idea of the internet itself, in its abstraction and association with the future, freedom and beauty, is a form of poetry. Ḥaddad writes, '[W]hen uploading Arabic poetry on the web, I felt I was putting poetry in its true place. In this mysterious intersection of text, light, sound, and image' (Wazin 2001).

The new place for poetry is defined as one related to a *kawni* horizon. The use of the term, which translates from Arabic to 'relating to the cosmos or the universe', is ubiquitous in Ḥaddad's early theorizations of the new digital cultural sphere. In an article, Ḥaddad highlights how the Arab world is facing a '*Kawni* challenge' in a new '*kawni* cultural scene' defined by '*kawni* texts' directed to '*kawni* readers'. To engage in a '*kawni* dialogue' with the world, 'Arabs need to understand the true meaning of culture not as confrontation but an act of love'. The cultural forum section of Jehat.com that brought poets together in real time is aptly named *Al-Ghurfa Al-Kawniyya* (A Universe in a Room) (Ḥaddad 2005).

It is important to unpack Ḥaddad's use of the term *Kawni* to better understand early theorizations of Arab digital publishing. Translating the term to 'universal' or 'cosmopolitan' or 'world' literature risks carrying the respective connotative weight in which these terms have developed within literary studies. The term *kawni*, in Ḥaddad's usage, in the nascent stages of digital publishing, is a much broader nomenclature that emphasizes a horizon of possibility of greater inclusiveness rather than an association with an already existing category. Yet the term along with kikah.com's *aladab al-insani al-alami* (universal or world human literature) carries romantic humanistic undertones that seem closer to idealist notions of world literature as cosmopolitan, aesthetic and non-commercialized. In the early stages of Arab digital publishing, the promised *Kawni* horizon was more of a declaration of intent than practice. This is in opposition to Pollock's discussion of cosmopolitanism and the vernacular, which are understood as 'action rather than idea, as something people do rather than something they declare, as practice rather than proposition' (Pollock 2000:593). With time, as will be discussed in the case of al-Nabhan's *Ufouq.com*, promises of a borderless paperless digital horizon were continually being tested in practice.

Ufouq.com

In 2000, when in Ontario, Canada, al-Nabhan founded the online literary magazine *Ufouq.com* along with his brother Saliḥ and Karim al-Hazza' both based in Kuwait. Through *Ufouq.com*, al-Nabhan was able to retain a nascent literary network already established in Kuwait of *Bidun* and Arab poets gathering in coffee houses, private homes and other cultural spaces. In an article, al-Nabhan writes that 'these spaces were our *Rabita* … where we were planning our daring project of Ufouq.com' (al-Nabhan 2001). This new paperless online space allowed for the development a literary network including 'the *Biduns* of the Arab world in a wider sense' as al-Nabhan describes it.

In the early volumes of *Ufouq* from 2000 to June 2002, contributors from the Arab world were described by national belonging while *Bidun* contributors were described only by name. However, after 2002, a shift in the editorial policy was implemented where national belonging of all contributors was unmentioned. Entering this new digital terrain, the paperless existence of *Ufouq* was constantly debated. The editors of *Ufouq* originally expressed an incessant urge to see their e-zine in paper form; an urge perhaps reflecting an apprehension of materially establishing a literary presence, a literary history and a canon. A year later, an editorial read: '[I]t has been fourteen months of aspiration, challenges, and distress awaiting the publication of our first paper copy, but how?' (al-Nabhan 2001). After completing two paperless years, the editors ask again: '[H]ow effective is this digital experiment? Has it achieved any of our aspirations? What is the next step? Is digital publishing a real alternative to paper?' (al-Nabhan 2002).

The question posed by the publishers (how?) relates to the materiality of putting into print a paperless literature and a network including *Bidun* writers between Kuwait, Canada, the United States and other writers from the Arab world. How and where will this printed *Ufouq* be published and how will it circulate? These unresolved questions caused the editorial board to abandon their desire of seeing *Ufouq* in paper form altogether:

> Perhaps our first concern was to turn this publication into paper form. Yet, this concern slowly receded as every new volume opened broad horizons of new worlds that transcend time and space.
>
> (al-Nabhan 2002)

Ufouq remained a strictly paperless publication until 2005 when al-Nabhan abandoned digital publishing altogether.

With the realization of the ephemerality of digital publishing, the UNESCO adopted in 2003, the 'Charter on the preservation of the digital heritage'. Digital heritage or 'resources of information and creative expression … increasingly produced, distributed, accessed and maintained in digital form' were under a real threat of being lost to posterity. The charter specified the contributing factors to this loss as (1) the obsolescence of hardware and software, (2) uncertainties about resources, (3) responsibility and methods for maintenance and preservation and (4) the lack of supportive legislation. The onus of persevering the digital heritage was on the member states of the UNESCO who needed to develop a 'national preservation policy'. 'Born digital', materials should be given priority in preservation as they do not exist in any other non-digital form (UNESCO 2003).

All contributing factors to the loss of digital heritage apply to the three aforementioned 'born digital' pioneering literary magazines. The enthusiasm towards digital publishing was replaced by a more sceptic and pessimistic tone. At some point in the mid-2010s Ufouq.com could not be found on the server, and only some traces of its existence could be found in archive recovery software. Kikah.com and its archive have similarly disappeared from the internet. In 2013, Samuel Shimon switched back to paper publishing. Digital publishing, he writes in 2013, has lost its potency and is now a symbol of the 'era of chaos' (*zaman al-Fawdha*) (Shimon 2013) where the publishers lack any codes of preserving copyrights online. Jehat.com has not been updated since March 2018 yet is still online as an archive for browsing, research and recollection. In a statement to Jehat.com's visitors, Ḥaddad announced the closure of Jehat.com due to the lack of financial resources and expressed a 'deep despair' in the Arab World's institutional lack of support of 'serious cultural endeavors' (Ḥaddad 2018).

The digital aspirations of *Kawniyya* needed to continuously negotiate its promises within the material realities of digital publishing. Most of the 'born digital' archive of *kawniyya* is non-existent today and a UNESCO charter formulated along 'national preservation policies' is far from any attempt to restore it. However, digital publishing remapped the Arab publishing scene and allowed many of previously marginalized poets such as al-Nabhan to maintain and establish transnational literary networks that later manifested in paper publishing.

Back to paper

In 2004, al-Nabhan was able to publish his first poetry collection *Another Estrangement* with the Iraqi-based publisher *Dar al-Mada*. While still in Canada, in 2005, al-Nabhan along with Fadi Saʿad, a Syrian writer residing in the United States and Jackleen Sallam, a Syrian writer residing in Canada, established Juzoor Cultural Foundation. Juzoor was a short-lived publishing outlet for Arab migrant writers in North America that was intended to revive the spirit of the early twentieth-century *al-Rabiṭa al-Qalamiyya* (The Pen Bond), which included the likes of Khalil Gibran and Mikhail Naʿima. Through Juzoor, he published his long prose poem *My Heart Is Stone at Your Still Door* (2005) in the United States. The poem likens the singular story of the *Bidun* poet to Joseph in the Quranic tale. The *Bidun* poet, the 'son of Kuwait', is dropped and abandoned in a dark well unrecognized and overlooked by his own blood brothers. Yet as mentioned by Muhsin al-Ramli in the introduction, the poem was not 'faithful' to the Quranic tale as much as it was faithful to the poet's own life story. As a result, the collection was deemed offensive to religious belief and banned from circulation in Kuwait by the censors of the Ministry of Information. The blasphemous reworking and appropriation of the Quranic tale are but a continuation of his cultural forging activities.

This shift back to paper publishing put al-Nabhan in a direct confrontation with the state's hegemony over what books are allowed to cross into and circulate in its borders. Yet, al-Nabhan, in another act of creative forgery published, in Cairo, 'a selection of his works' titled *Between Two Cities* (2011), which included, not a selection of, but *all* of his previously banned poetry collection.

In 2008, and now as a Canadian 'expatriate' in Kuwait, al-Nabhan established the publication house *Dar Masʿa*. His moment of arrival as an 'expatriate' is described in *My Heart Is Stone at Your Still Door*:

I couldn't remember who I am anymore.
I entered my country with my other name
My other papers
My other estrangement
A visa of misery
Another person now carries me on his shoulders
And takes me to every direction.
Except to death

(al-Nabhan 2005:128)

The publication house then moved to Bahrain were barriers to enter the publishing industry (i.e. access to publishing paper) were less than Kuwait. Like *Ufouq*, *Dar Masʿa* provided access especially for young local *Bidun* writers to publish their works. Yet, this time, this publishing project was based within a context that is subject to government censors and the demands of local and Arab literary markets, festivals and book fairs. In 2018, al-Nabhan re-established Masʿa as a Canadian publishing house based in Ottawa, which allowed them more freedom in publishing and distribution. *Dar Masʿa* has continued to form a visible and substantial canon of works which could be found in annual book fairs, bookshops, online scanned copies and library catalogues while *Ufouq.com* has disappeared altogether from the internet and with it an archive of more than six years of paperless publishing.

His last publication, a poem titled the *Tale of the Old Man* (2013), was published by Masʿa. In an interview, he describes the poem as an attempt to poetically probe into the very foundations of identity, subjectivity and otherness as universal themes. To him, the central issue of the poem is not that of lack of citizenship, but the question of identity. The semi-autobiographic poem is driven by an urge to transcend the particularity of the *ʿAshish* or the experience of statelessness, to the universality of the notion of otherness and identity. However, the poem is crowded with images of everyday administrative violence and a bureaucratic vocabulary of checkpoints, border control, police interrogations, forged ID cards and passports.

In an interview, al-Nabhan recalls how scenes of protests and military checkpoints in his country of residence Bahrain during the Arab Spring invoked in him the memory of the Iraqi Invasion of Kuwait and triggered him to write the poem. Checkpoints, border controls and police interrogations play an important role in organizing the poem and are constitutive of the poet's literal and metaphorical itinerary. To cross borders and checkpoints, the old man, al-Nabhan, is continuously referred to as a forger (*Muzawir*), a swift-handed person (*sahib al-yad alkhafifa*), an eternal counterfeit (*al-muzayyaf al-abadi*), an imposter (*muntahil*), a plagiarist (*al-Sariq*) who engages in deceit (*ihtiyal*). The metaphor of forgery is utilized as an act of creative defiance allowing the poet to both navigate physical borders and undermine the verifiability of official paper.

The poem is thus a testament to the ways that the materiality of border regimes impedes not simply just a poet's travel, but works to structure the very form of poetic expression. As the poem vacillates between the universality of identity and the particularity of the *Bidun experience*, the prevalence of the checkpoint serves as constant reminder of the *Bidun* poet's 'quintessential experience'. In his characterization of the exilic Palestinian experience, Walid Khalidi's writes: '[T]he quintessential Palestinian experience, which illustrates some of the most basic issues raised by Palestinian identity, takes place at a border, an airport, a checkpoint: in short, at any one of those many modern barriers where identities are checked and verified' (Khalidi 2010:1). The case of Muhammad al-Nabhan, and his journey from Kuwait to Canada and back, and from paper to digital publishing and back, highlights the materialities, everyday obstacles involved in the attempts to cross borders whether literally or metaphorically. As al-Nabhan's case demonstrates, the affiliative networks forged by *Bidun* writers are continuously negotiated in light of the everyday inescapable authority of paper.

In his discussion of exile, Edward Said mentions how the experience of exile makes possible an originality and plurality of vision. Exiles maintain a reflective distance from their setting and cultures that gives rise to an awareness of at least two simultaneous dimensions. At the same time, an exilic subjectivity becomes aware of the contingency of homes and borders and allows an exile to 'cross borders, break barriers of thought and experience'. The ability to cross, transcend or reject such borders and barriers is however also contingent on a process of detachment. This paradox is best delineated in Said's commentary on St Victor of Hugo's quote on achieving perfection through seeing 'the entire world ... as a foreign land'. As Said puts it, 'the "strong" or "perfect" man achieves independence and detachment by *working through* attachments, not by rejecting them. Exile is predicated on the existence of, love for, and a real body with one's native place' (148 Reflections).

Similarly, in the case of *Bidun* writers, the ability to transcend or reject notions of homeland or national belonging is always inextricably link to an experience of it. *Paper, in the wider sense of the word, is still very relevant.* The *Bidun* community are still, even more intensely at the time of publication, facing a unique and systematic type of violence and exclusion at the level of everyday life due to their lack of official papers. With no birth certificates, death certificates, passports, demeaning ways of obtaining marriage licenses, minimal access to public education, healthcare and employment opportunities, the *Bidun* continue to live with temporary cards labelling them as illegal residents in what they consider their own homeland.

Yet in light of all this, *Bidun* writers continue to resist and articulate a presence outside of official recognition. In a review of Nasser al-Ẓafiri's works, Hanadi al-Shammiri, a *Bidun* short story writer, writes: 'If one day government officials succeeded in erasing all records pointing to the existence of the *Bidun* in Kuwait ... Nasser al-Ẓafiri's novels will save us' (al-Shimmiri 2017).

Conclusion

The analysis of the body of works and varied collection of poets and writers in this book, albeit limited in scope, is an attempt to foreground this significant, yet overlooked, literary phenomenon in contemporary Arab and world literatures. We have seen in previous chapters how a literary critical approach allows for a widening of the categories of representation for *Bidun* writers. A study of a highly politicized 'stateless literature' has demonstrated the dangers and limitations of approaching literature as a mere reflection of a condition or an experience. The works of *Bidun* writers go beyond immediate political, anthropological and activistic concerns.

This book has presented *Bidun* literature as a struggle for intrinsic articulations of belonging, presence and representation through complex modes of affiliation, beyond official acts of absencing, labelling and ontological representations. Every chapter aimed to play out an aspect of this struggle. The first chapter highlighted the necessity of engaging critically with the cultural production of *Bidun* writers beyond the limitations of descriptive accounts. Chapter 2 highlighted the ways in which *Bidun* writers actively create their own affiliative cultural networks and spaces of representation beyond the exclusionary forces of the cultural institution. The third chapter explored the articulations of belonging to an unofficial national literary history. Chapter 4 analysed how the works of Sulayman al-Flayyiḥ contest romanticized ahistoric representations of the desert depicting it as a site of alternate historical beginnings. In Chapter 5, the works of Nasir al-Ẓafiri contest the reductive depictions of the *Bidun* identity in novels written by Kuwaiti writers offering a more fluid, nuanced and relational understanding of identity. The final chapter highlighted the often-forgotten 'sons of Kuwait' in exile who continue to assert a transnational literary presence despite being disowned by their kin.

Through literary expression, *Bidun* writers have consistently refused to be contained by a totalizing force that aims to define their presence in limiting terms. *Bidun* writers have contested hegemonic representations whether it be an 'adjacent' phenomenon cast outside of national literature, a passive group belonging to an ahistoric desert of authenticity or caged in an ontological statelessness of the *ʿAshish*, or an invisible unrecognized exile severed from any belonging to the homeland.

In her discussion of statelessness, Hannah Arendt maintains that lacking citizenship rights, and the all-encompassing 'right to have rights', does not only leave a person stateless, but also placeless. The stateless are in a condition of political void and 'deprivation of a place in the world, which makes opinions significant and actions effective' (Arendt 2004:296). A 'place in the world' is a corollary of official belonging to some kind of organized political community. The stateless are ultimately 'deprived, not of the right to freedom, but of the right to action; not of the right to think whatever they please, but of the right to opinion' (296). Arendt goes further to say that a 'life without voice and without action' outside of political responsibility 'is literally dead to the world' (Arendt 1998:176). In critique of Arendt's view, Etienne Balibar writes:

> Arendt's idea is not that only institutions create rights, whereas, apart from institutions, humans do not have specific rights, only natural qualities. Her idea is that, apart from the institution of community … there simply are no humans …. Humans simply are their rights.
>
> (Balibar 2007:733)

Similarly, other approaches that pin down the Bidun back to their anthropological, sociological or legal grids fix the Bidun into ontological categories and limit the understanding of the complexity of the humans behind these categories. Through engaging with the literary and cultural production of the Bidun, one can invert Arendt's earlier proposition that the stateless are 'literally dead to the world' by saying they are '*literalily* alive in the world'.

An investigation into the cultural and literary articulations of a marginalized community offers critical insight into how notions of belonging, resistance and agency can be analysed beyond the logic of conventional descriptive, sociological and anthropological methodologies. Approaching and understanding this literary phenomenon by engaging with the subjective language in which it is expressed allows for a more complex understanding of the people involved. In understanding how *Bidun* writers articulate a presence beyond official categories, I hope that this book, and some of the tools it proposes, will be useful to understanding how a different type of knowledge on the 'people of the Gulf' can be produced.

This book barely scratches the surface of *Bidun* literature and its interconnections. There are many more potential sites of further investigation. One important aspect is an emphasis on a new generation of writers in the diaspora publishing in both Arabic and English.[1] Another way in which the subject can be taken forward is by reading this body of literature in conjunction with literatures of other marginalized communities both regionally and globally. A comparative study of *Bidun* and Palestinian writers is especially relevant. The powerful *Bidun*-Palestinian cultural connection, as highlighted in the Introduction, and the modes of identification, can offer insight into new ways of conceiving questions of literary history in contemporary Arabic literature and marginalized literatures more broadly.

Notes

Introduction

1 See The Economists Intelligence units piece titled '"Jihadi John" Case Raises Issue of Bidoon's Status Again'. Available from: http://country.eiu.com/article.aspx?articleid=1262951310, Murphy, Brian. 2015. 'Jihadi John Belongs to a Forgotten Stateless People'. *The Washington Posts.* March 3. Available fromhttps://www.washingtonpost.com/news/worldviews/wp/2015/03/03/jihadi-john-belongs-to-a-forgotten-stateless-people/, and Mcauliffe, Anneliese. 2015. 'Kuwait's disenfranchisement of *Bidun* leads to growing ISIS threat' *The Interpreter*. 7 July. Available from https://www.lowyinstitute.org/the-interpreter/kuwaits-disenfranchisement-*Bidun*-leads-growing-isis-threat.

Chapter 1

1 Beaugrand, highlights the difficulty 'to establish a typology of *Bidun*s' as the reasons behind the group's statelessness vary. One group is composed of the children of Kuwaiti mothers married to *Bidun*s who have been denied citizenship as per the 1959 Nationality Law. Another group are those who have refused second degree of nationality because they felt entitled to the first degree. Others have never registered with nationality committees while others' files have been rejected. Another group consists of army recruits from neighbouring countries, some who may carry existing nationalities. Finally, there are those, arriving in the 1980s, who took advantage of the stalemate surrounding the issue (Beaugrand 2017:112).

2 *Badu* is the term commonly used to denote Kuwaiti citizens from Bedouin origins mostly living outside the 1920 town wall, and Hadar denotes the townspeople residing within the wall.

3 Refer to Refugees International report entitled 'About Being without: Stories of Stateless in Kuwait' for more on the day-to-day hardships that the *Bidun*

experience. Available at: http://www.refugeesinternational.org/policy/in-depth-report/about-being-without-stories-stateless-kuwait.

Chapter 2

1 See Adam Yusif's *Qaṣidat al-Tafaṣil al-Yawmiyya fi al-Shi'r al-Khaliji al-Mu'aṣir.* (The Poem of the Everyday in Contemporary Gulf Poetry) (2009).

2 See Sa'ad al-Juwayyir's *Bawṣalat al-Jihat al- 'Ashr al-Mashhad al-Shi'ri fi al-Kuwait: al-tis'inat namudhajan.* (A Compass of the Ten Directions, the Poetic Scene in Kuwait: The Case of the 90s) (2006).

3 I have received the original article from al-Hazza' in a personal email after *al-Waṣat* newspaper was shut down along with its online archive. A copy of the original article is available here: http://Bidunliterature.blogspot.co.uk/2013/04/blog-post_2133.html.

4 These publications include Muhammad al-Nabhan's *Imra'a min Aqsa al-Madina* (A Women from the Limit of the City) (2011) and *Ḥikayat al-Rajul al- 'Ajuz* (The Old Man's Tale) (2013), Sa'diyya Mufarrih's *Layl Mashghul bi-l-Fitna* (A Night Busy with Temptation) (2008), *Hawamish 'Ala Shahwat al-Sard* (Comments on the Lust of Narration*)* (2009), *Mashiat al-Iwizza* (The Stride of the Swan) (2010), Dikhil Khalifa's *Ṣa'idan 'Asfal al-Bi'r* (Ascending from the Pit of the Well) (2014), and Nasir al-Ẓafiri's *Aghrar* (2008), *Sama' Maqluba* (Upturned Sky) (2014), *al-Ṣahd* (Scorched Heat) (2014), Hanadi al-Shimmiri's *Safiḥ* (A House Made of Tin) (2015) and Shahad al-Faḍli's *Faṣila Manquṭa* (Semicolon) (2015).

5 National anthologies that exclude *Bidun* writers include the following publications: *Mukhtarat min al-Shi'r al- 'Arabi al-Ḥadith fi-l-Khalij wa-l-Jazira al- 'Arabiyya* (Selections of Modern Arabic Poetry in the Gulf and the Arabian Peninsula) (al-Babtain 1996), *Mukhtarat min al-Shi'r al- 'Arabi fi-l-Qarn al-'Ishrin* (Selections of Arabic Poetry in the twentieth Century) (al-Babtain 2001) and *The Echo of Kuwaiti Creativity: A Collection of Translated Kuwaiti Poetry* published by the Centre for Research and Studies on Kuwait (al-Sanousi 2001). Anthologies and general studies on national literature that include *Bidun* writers include the following publications: *Diwan al-Shi'r al- 'Arabi fi al-Rub' al-Akhir min al-Qarn al- 'Ishrin: al-Khalij al- 'Arabi- al-Kuwait wa-l-Bahrain (Arabic Poetry in the Last Quarter of the twentieth Century: the Arabian Gulf-Kuwait and Bahrain)* (Mufarrih and al-Ajmi 2008), *Dalil al-Udaba' al-Mu'aṣirin fi-l-Kuwait: al-Shi'r -al-nathr (The Guide to Contemporary Writers in Kuwait: poetry-prose)*

(al-Utaybi et al. 2012), *Ḥudat al-Ghaym wa-l-Wiḥsha* (The Cameleers of Clouds and Estrangement) (Mufarrih 2007), *ʿAlam al-Shiʿr fi-l-Kuwait* (Notable Poets in Kuwait) (Abd al-Fattah 1996), Mirsal al-Ajmi's *al-Baḥth ʿan Ufuq ʾArḥab: mukhtarat min al-qiṣaṣ al-Kuwaitiyya al-muʿaṣira* (A Search for Broader Horizons: a selection of Kuwaiti contemporary short stories) (al-Ajmi 2013), *al-ʾAjniḥa wa-l-Shams* (The Wings and the Sun) (Idris 1998), *Qaṣidat al-Tafasil al-Yawmiyya fi-l-Shiʿr al-Khaliji al-Muʿaṣir* (The Poem of Everyday Detail in Contemporary Gulf Poetry) (Yusuf 2009), and *Bawṣalat al-Jihat al-ʾAshr al-Mashhad al-Shiʿr i fi-l-Kuwait: al-tisʿinat namudhajan* (A Compass of the Ten Directions, the Poetic Scene in Kuwait: The Case of the 90s) (al-Juwayyir 2006), *Al-Shiʿr al-ʿArabi al-Ḥadith fi-l-Khalij wa-l-Jazira al-ʿArabiyya* (Modern Arabic Poetry in the Gulf and the Arabian Peninsula) (Al-Ḥaddad 2018).

6 Refer to Abdulla and al-Rumaidhi's *Fihris Kuttab Majallat al-Bayan* (The Index of Writers in al-Bayan Magazine) (2013) for a list of contributions by *Bidun* poets.

Chapter 3

1 Born in Kuwait, the poet and musician Abdullah al-Faraj moved to Bombay at a young age where he was educated. He later lived between Basra and Kuwait (al-Zaid 1967:58; al-Faraj 2002:16–17).

Chapter 4

1 The poem was originally published in *Majallat al-Bayan* in June 1975. The original title of the poem was *The Apprehensions of the Lakhmid Knight in Corrupt Times*.

2 For more on the theme of rebirth and the nation within the context of poetry in the Arabian Peninsula, refer to Al-Bazei's *Desert Culture* (1991), pp. 65–80.

3 In Edward Lane's the *Arabic-English Lexicon*, the *khaliʿ* is an excommunicated individual from the tribe due to continual unwarranted aggression. Cast off repudiated or renounced by his family (Lane 1863:700).

4 In Edward Lane's *Arabic-English Lexicon*, the *fatik* is 'one who comes upon another suddenly, with some evil, or hateful act, or [more commonly] slaughter … one who when he proposes a thing, does it … any one who attempts to

venture upon, great, or formidable affairs ... bold or daring, courageous' (Lane 1863:2333).

5 In Edward Lane's *Arabic-English Lexicon*, the *shaṭir* 'one who withdraws far away from his family ... any clever or cunning person' (Lane 1863:1551).

6 For more on Shlaiwiḥ al-'Atawi, refer to the work of Marcel Kurpershoek *The Story of a Desert Knight: The Legend of Shlaiwiḥ al-'Atawi and Other `Utaybah Heroes* (1995).

Chapter 5

1 The novel is currently in its twenty-seventh edition.

2 This paper was presented by Nasir al-Ẓafiri as part of the weekly cultural activities of the Tuesday Gathering on the 11th of February 2014. The hand written excerpt of the lecture was made available to the author through the event's organizer Dikhil Khalifa.

Chapter 6

1 The original title of the translation is *Singurătatea din Umbra Palmierului: traduceri din poezia kuweitiană* (2009) translated and introduced by Dumitru Chican.

2 The discussion of Muhammad al-Nabhan's journey is informed mainly by an interview conducted with him in the summer of 2013 in Bahrain (al-Nabhan 2013a).

3 Al-Nabhan can be found in Lutfi Ḥaddad's *Anthology of Contemporary Arabic Migrant Literature* (2004).

4 A term coined by the Charter on the Preservation of Digital Heritage (Oct 2003) to refer to resources that exist only as digital objects with no corresponding analogue formats.

5 For more on the development of online publishing in the Arab, see Teresa Pepe's *Blogging from Egypt:Digital Literature: 2005–2016* (2018), pp. 30–3.

6 Other websites on Arabic literature existed at the time, but were mostly encyclopaedias concerned with archiving the Arabic literary tradition online such as: adab.com (2001), al-Mawsuʿa al-Shiʿriyya first established in 1998 https://poetry.dctabudhabi.ae/.

7 Early digitization in the Arab world was also driven by other less inclusive forces. Websites particularly concerned with the dissemination and digitization of religious texts 'served as a means of articulating and demarking communal identities'. See Travis Zadeh's 'Uncertainty of the Archive', in *The Digital Humanities and Islamic Middle East* (2016) edited by Elias Muhanna.

Conclusion

1 See: Alshammiry, A. 2020. 'Writing in Exile: Bidoon Resistance and Speaking Truth to Power'. *Cultural and Pedagogical Inquiry*, 12(1), pp. 149–64.

Bibliography

Abdulfattaḥ, ʿAli. 1996.ʾ *ʿAlam al-Shiʿr fi al-Kuwait* (Notable Poets in Kuwait). Kuwait: Maktabat ibn Qutayba.

Abdulhalim, Adam. 2014. 'Fi Nadwa Aqamaha al-Minbar al-Dimuqraṭi ʿan katatib al-Bidun: ḥirman al-ṭullab min al-taʿlim yataʿarraḍ maʿa al-dustur wa-l-ittifaqiyyat al-duwaliyya (In a Seminar Organized by the Kuwaiti Democratic Forum about the *Katatib* of the Bidun: Depriving Students of Education Contradicts the Constitution and International Conventions)'. 12 November. *Majjalat al-Ṭaliʿa*. [online]. [accessed December 2014]. Available from: http://altaleea.com/?p=9819.

Abdullah, Muḥammad H. [No date]. *Diwan al-Shiʿr al-Kuwaiti* (The Diwan of Kuwaiti Poetry). Kuwait: Wikalat al-Maṭbuʿat.

Abdullah, Muḥammad H. 1973. *Al-Ḥaraka al-Adabiyya wa-l-Fikriyya fi al-Kuwait* (The Literary and Intellectual Movement in Kuwait). Kuwait: The Writers' Association in Kuwait.

Abdullah, Muḥammad H. 1987. *Al-Shiʿr wa-l-Shuʿaraʾ fi al-Kuwait* (Poetry and Poets in Kuwait). Kuwait: Dhat al-Salasil li-l-Nashr wa-l-Tawziʿ.

Abdulmuḥsin, Aḥmad. 2013. Ismail Fahad: al-Ṣahd wajba dasima yuqaddimuha al-Ẓafiri (Ismail Fahad: al-Ṣahd is a dense meal presented by al-Ẓafiri). 28 November. *Al-Jarida newspaper*. [online]. [accessed November 2013]. Available from: http://www.aljarida.com/news/index/2012634682/.

Abdulrahman, Suʿad. 1994. '*Al-Ightirab fi al-Shiʿr al-Kuwaiti* (Alienation in Kuwaiti Poetry)'. Annals of the Faculty of Arts. 14(94), pp. 55–157.

Abu-Deeb, Kamal. 1986. *Al-Ruʾa al-Muqannaʿa* (Veiled Insights). Cairo: al-Hayʾa al-Miṣriyya al-ʿAmma li-l-Kitab.

Al-ʿAbwini, Khalil. 1982. *Nafitha ila Ruʾya Naqdiyya* (A Window into Critical Insight). [no publisher].

Al-ʿAjmi, Mirsil F. 2013. *Al-Baḥth ʿan Ufuq Arḥab: mukhtarat min al-qiṣaṣ al-Kuwaitiyya al-muʿaṣira* (A Search for Broader Horizons: A Selection of Kuwaiti Contemporary Short Stories). Kuwait: Afaq li-l-Nashr.

ʿAli, Ahmad A. 2000. *Muʿjam al-Shuʿaraʾ al-Kuwaitiyyin* (A Glossary of Kuwaiti Poets). Kuwait: Dhat al-Salasil li-l-Nashr wa-l-Tawziʿ.

Ali, Uruk. 2010. 'A Reading of Female Voices'. 9 June. *Kikah*. [online].[accessed July 2011]. Available from: http://www.kikah.com/indexarabic.asp?fname=kikaharabic\archive\2010\2010-06-09\80.txt&storytitle=.

'Allam, Midḥat. 2010. 'Ta'bin- 'Udaba' fi Dhikra Ṣadiqihim Ali al-Ṣafi: al-ḥaḍir raghma ghiyabihi (A Commemoration- Writers in the Memory of Their Friend Ali al-Ṣafi Who Is Present Despite of His Absence)'. 1 January. *Al-Rai Newspaper*. [online]. [accessed February 2012]. Available from: http://www.alraimedia.com/alrai/ArticlePrint.aspx?id=177577 (alternatively: http://bidunliterature.blogspot.co.uk/2013/04/blog-post_8786.html).

Alshammiry, Areej. 2020. 'Writing in Exile: Bidoon Resistance and Speaking Truth to Power'. *Cultural and Pedagogical Inquiry*. 12(1), pp. 149–64.

Anderson, Benedict. 2006. *Imagined Communities*. London: Verso.

Al-Anezi, Rashid. H. 1989. *A Study of the Role of Nationality in International Law with Special Reference to the Law and Practice of Kuwait*. PhD thesis, University of Cambridge: Cambridge, UK.

Al-Anezi, Rashid. H. 1994. *Al-Bidun fi al-Kuwait* (The Bidun in Kuwait). Kuwait: Dar Qirṭas.

Anhar. 2012. 'Musabaqa Adabiyya Judhoor bi Ri'ayat Dr. Fatma al-Mattar (Judhour a Literary Contest Sponsored by Fatma al-Mattar)'. *Anhar*. 24 July. [online]. [accessed September 2012]. Available from: http://www.anhaar.com/arabic/index.php/permalink/14882.html (alternatively: http://bidunliterature.blogspot.co.uk/2013/12/blog-post.html?zx=373b2f45d001443e).

Al-Ansari, Abdullah Z. 1997 [1977]. *Fahad al-'Askar: ḥayatuhu wa shi'ruhu* (Fahad al-Askar's Life and Poetry). Kuwait: al-Rubay'an li-l-Nashr wa-l-Tawzi'.

Al-Ansari, Muhammad J. 1970. *Lamaḥat min al-Khalij al-'Arabi* (Glimpses from the Arabian Gulf). Bahrain: al-Sharika al-'Arabiya li-l-Wakalat wa-l–Tawzi'.

Apter, Emily. 2006. *The Translation Zone: A New Comparative Literature*. New Jersey: Princeton University Press.

Apter, Emily. 2008. 'Untranslatables: A World System'. *New Literary History*. 39(3), pp. 581–98.

Apter, Emily. 2013. *Against World Literature: On the Politics of Untranslatability*. London: Verso.

Al-Aradi, Wafa, A. 2008. *The Dilemma of Nationality a Comparative Case Study: The Case of the Bedoon in Kuwait and the Case of the Bihari in Bangladesh*. PhD thesis, University of South Carolina.

Arendt, Hannah. 1962. *The Origins of Totalitarianism*. Cleveland and New York: Meridian Books.

Arendt, Hannah. 1994. 'We Refugees'. In: Robinson, Marc. ed. *Altogether Elsewhere: Writers on Exile*. Winchester, MA: Faber and Faber, pp. 110–19.

Arendt, Hannah. 1998. *The Human Condition*. Chicago: University of Chicago Press.

Asfour, John. 1988. *When the Words Burn: An Anthology of Modern Arabic Poetry 1945–1987*. Dunvegan, Ontario: Cormorant Books.

Ashcroft, B., Griffiths, G., and Tiffin, H. 2013. *Post-Colonial Studies: The Key Concepts*. London: Routledge.

ʿAziz, Fawwaz. 2012. 'Saʿdiyya Mufarriḥ: La ʿilaqa li-l-Awraq bi-Ḥaqiqat Jinsiyyati (Saʿdiyya Mufarriḥ: papers are unrelated to my real citizenship)'. 11 September. *Al-Watan Online*. [online]. [accessed December 2012]. Available from: http://www.alwatan.com.sa/Culture/News_Detail.aspx?ArticleID=113074&CategoryID=7.

Al-Babtain Foundation. 1995a. *Muʿjam al-Babtain li-l-Shuʿaraʾ al-Muʿaṣirin al-Juzʾ al-ʾAwwal* (The al-Babtain Glossary of Contemporary Arab Poets Volume I). Kuwait: The Foundation of Abdulaziz Saud al-Babtain's Prize for Poetic Creativity.

Al-Babtain Foundation. 1995b. *Muʿjam al-Babtain li-l-Shuʿaraʾ al-Muʿaṣirin al-Juzʾ al-thani* (The al-Babtain Glossary of Contemporary Arab Poets Volume II). Kuwait: The Foundation of Abdulaziz Saud al-Babtain's Prize for Poetic Creativity.

Al-Babtain Foundation. 1995c. *Muʿjam al-Babtain li-l-Shuʿaraʾ al-Muʿaṣirin al-Juzʾ al-Thalith* (The al-Babtain Glossary of Contemporary Arab Poets Volume III). Kuwait: The Foundation of Abdulaziz Saud al-Babtain's Prize for Poetic Creativity.

Al-Babtain Foundation. 1995d. *Muʿjam al-Babtain li-l-Shuʿaraʾ al-Muʾaṣirṣn al-Juzʾ al-Rabiʿ* (The al-Babtain Glossary of Contemporary Arab Poets Volume IV). Kuwait: The Foundation of Abdulaziz Saud al-Babtain's Prize for Poetic Creativity.

Al-Babtain Foundation. 1995e. *Muʿjam al-Babtain li-l-Shuʿaraʾ al-Muʿaṣirin al-Juzʾal-Khamis* (The al-Babtain Glossary of Contemporary Arab Poets Volume V). Kuwait: The Foundation of Abdulaziz Saud al-Babtain's Prize for Poetic Creativity.

Al-Babtain Foundation. 1995f. *Muʿjam al-Babtain li-l-Shuʾaraʾ al-Muʿaṣirin al-Juzʾal-Sadis* (The al-Babtain Glossary of Contemporary Arab Poets Volume VI). Kuwait: The Foundation of Abdulaziz Saud al-Babtain's Prize for Poetic Creativity.

Al-Babtain Foundation. 1996. *Mukhtatrat min al-Shiʿr al-ʿArabi al-Ḥadith fi al-Khalij wa-l-Jazira al-ʿArabiyya* (Selections of Modern Arabic Poetry in the Gulf and the Arabian Peninsula). Kuwait: The Foundation of Abdulaziz Saud Al-Babtain's Prize for Poetic Creativity.

Al-Babtain Foundation. 2001. *Mukhtatrat min al-Shiʿr al-ʿArabi fi al-Qarn al-ʿIshrin* (Selections of Arabic Poetry in the 20th Century). Kuwait: The Foundation of Abdulaziz Saud al–Babtain's Prize for Poetic Creativity.

Bakhtin, Mikhail. M. 1981. *The Dialogic Imagination: Four Essays*. Translated by Caryl Emerson and Michael Holquist. Austin: University of Texas Press.

Balibar, Etienne. 2007. '(De)Constructing the Human as Human Institution: A Reflection on the Coherence of Hannah Arendt's Practical Philosophy'. *Social Research*. 74(3), pp. 727–38.

Al-Başir, Abdulrazzaq. 1986. *Al-Khalij al-ʿArabi wa-l-Ḥaḍara al-Muʿaṣira* (The Arabian Gulf and Modern Civilization). Kuwait: Maṭbaʿat Ḥukumat al-Kuwait.

Bassnett, Susan. 1993. *Comparative Literature: A Critical Introduction*. Oxford: Blackwell.

Al-Bazei, Saad. 1991. *Thaqafat al-Ṣahraʾ: Dirasat fi adab al-Jazira al-ʿArabiyya al-Muʿaṣir* (Desert Culture: Studies in contemporary literature of the Arabian Peninsula). Al-Riyadh: al-ʿUbaykan.

Al-Bazei, Saad. 2001. 'Tension in the House: The Contemporary Poetry of Arabia'. *World Literature Today*. 75(2), pp. 267–74.

Al-Bazei, Saad. 2012. *New Voices of Arabia, the Poetry: An Anthology from Saudi Arabia*. London: I.B. Tauris.

Al-Bazei, Saad. 2013. 'Desert Modernity: Myths and Paradoxes'. *Alif: Journal of Comparative Poetics*. 33, pp. 9–32.

Beaugrand, Claire. M. 2010. *Statelessness and Transnationalism in Northern Arabia: Biduns and State Building in Kuwait, 1959–2009*. PhD thesis, London, UK: The London School of Economics and Political Science.

Beaugrand, Claire. M. 2011. 'Statelessness & Administrative Violence: Biduns' Survival Strategies in Kuwait'. *The Muslim World*. 101(2), pp. 228–50.

Beaugrand, Claire. M. 2017. *Stateless in the Gulf Migration, Nationality and Society in Kuwait*. London: I.B. Tauris.

Bencomo, Clarisa. 2000. 'Kuwait, Promises Betrayed: Denial of Rights of Bidun, Women, and Freedom of Expression'. [online]. [accessed March 2012]. Available from: http://www.hrw.org/reports/2000/kuwait/kuwait-04.htm#P168_23590.

Bendix, Regina. 1997. *In Search of Authenticity: The Formation of Folklore Studies*. Madison, WI: University of Wisconsin Press.

Blanco, María del Pilar. 2012. *Ghost-watching American Modernity: Haunting, Landscape, and the Hemispheric Imagination*. New York: Fordham University Press.

Blitz, Brad and Lynch, Maureen. 2011. 'Statelessness and the Deprivation of Nationality'. In: Blitz, K and Lynch, M., eds. *Statelessness and Citizenship*. Cheltenham, UK: Edward Elgar Publishing Limited, pp. 1–22.

Braidotti, Rosi. 1994. *Nomadic Subjects: Embodiment and Sexual Difference in Contemporary Feminist Theory*. New York: Columbia University Press.

Buchanan, Ian. 2010. *Oxford Dictionary of Critical Theory*. Oxford: Oxford University Press.

Buṭi, Laṭifa. 1999. 'Bayat Shitwi' (Hibernation). *Majallat al-Bayan*. July–August 348, pp. 97–8.

Buṭi, Laṭifa. 2000. 'Al-ʿAdhab Waraqa' (Torture is a Paper). *Majallat al-Bayan*. October 363, pp. 84–95.

Buṭi, Laṭifa. 2001. *Baladi Iniyaku* (Inikayu: My Country). Dar ʿAlaʾ al-Din.

Childs, Peter. 1999. *The Twentieth Century in Poetry: A Critical Survey*. London: Routledge.

Childs, Peter. 2000. *Modernism*. London: Routledge.

Cooke, Miriam. 2014. *Tribal Modern: Branding New Nations in the Arab Gulf*. Berkeley, CA: The University of California Press.

Crystal, Jill. 2005. 'Public Order and Authority: Policing Kuwait'. In: Dresch, P and Piscatori, J., eds. *Monarchies and Nations: Globalisation and Identity in the Arab States of the Gulf*. London: I.B. Tauris, pp. 158–81.

Currie, Mark. 2004. *Difference: The New Critical Idiom*. London and New York: Routledge.

Damrosch, David. 2003. *What Is World Literature?* Princeton, NJ: Princeton University Press.

Demaghtech. 2012a. 'Qaḍaya al-ʾIbdaʿ al-ʿArabi al-Muʿaṣir 1 (Issues in Contemporary Arab Creativity 1)'. [online]. [accessed May 2012]. Available from: https://www.youtube.com/watch?v=7b1aDtahZjY.

Demaghtech. 2012b. 'Hal Yujad ʾIbdaʿ fi al-Khalij? (Is Their Creativity in the Gulf?)' [online]. [accessed May 2012]. Available from: https://www.youtube.com/watch?v=VW43ToTsviY.

Dominguez, Cesar. 2012. "World Literature and Cosmopolitan Studies."In: Haen,

Theo d', David Damrosch, and Djelal Kadir, eds. *The Routledge Companion to World Literature*. Milton Park, Abingdon, Oxon: Routledge, pp. 242–52.

Domínguez, César, Saussy, Haun, and Villanueva, Darío. 2015. *Introducing Comparative Literature: New Trends and Applications*. New York: Routledge.

Duḥan, Fahad. 1996. *ʾAzmat al-Shiʿr al-Nabaṭi wa Muḥawalat al-Ḥadatha* (The Crisis of Nabaṭi Poetry and Modernisation Attempts). [no publisher].

Eagleton, Terry. 1996. *Literary Theory: An Introduction*. Minneapolis, MN: University of Minnesota Press.

The Editors of Encyclopædia Britannica. [no date]. Sir John Bagot Glubb. In *Encyclopædia Britannica*. [online]. [accessed June 2015]. Available from: https://www.britannica.com/biography/John-Bagot–Glubb.

Al-Eisa, Bader. 1985. *A Qualitative Study: The Low and Middle-Income Housing Problem in the State of Kuwait*. Ph.D. thesis, University of Minneapolis. Minneapolis, MN.

Fabian, Johannes. 1983. *Time and the Other: How Anthropology Makes Its Object*. New York: Columbia University Press.

Al-Fahad, Mohammed. 1989. *An Historical Analysis of Police in Kuwait: Prospects for the Future*. PhD thesis, Exeter, UK: The Univesity of Exeter.

Fahad, Ismail. 2013. *Fi Ḥaḍrat al-ʿAnqaʾ wa-l-Khil al-Wafi* (In the Presence of the Pheonix and the Loyal Friend). Beirut: al-Dar al-Arabiyya li-l-ʿUlum Nashirun.

Al-Faysal, Mashaʿil. 2011. 'Ana Saḥiḥ Bidun Jinsiyya, Lakinni Lastu Bidun Waṭan (It is true that I am Without Citizenship, but I am Not Without a Homeland)'. 3 June. *Sabr*. [online]. [accessed December 2011]. Available from: http://www.sabr.cc/inner.aspx?id=3897 (alternatively: http://bidunliterature.blogspot.co.uk/2016/08/blog-post.html).

Fajr, Tahani. 2011. ʾAbnaʾ Fahad al-ʿAskar (The Sons of Fahad al-Askar). February. *Al–Ghawun*. 36, pp. 28–9.

Fajr, Tahani. 2014. 'al-Kuwaiti Nasir al-Ẓafiri: al-ʾighraq fi al-ʿamiyya la yaṣnaʿ Riwaya Waqiʿiyya ' (The Kuwaiti Nasir al-Ẓafiri: An immersion in dialect does not produce a realist novel). *Al-Quds al-Arabi*. July 15. [online]. [accessed November 2015]. Available from: http://www.alquds.co.uk/?p=193013.

Al-Faraj, Khalid M. 2002. *Diwan Abdullah al-Faraj*. Kuwait: The Foundation of Abdulaziz Saud al-Babtainʾs Prize for Poetic Creativity.

Farrin, Raymond. 2010. *Abundance from the Desert: Classical Arabic Poetry*. New York: Syracuse University Press.

Al-Farsi, Saʿida bint Khaṭir. 2004. *Intiḥar al-ʾAwtad fi Ightirab Saʿdiyya Mufarriḥ* (A Suicide of Moorings in the Estrangement of Saʿdiyya Mufarriḥ). The Center for Arab Civilization. Cairo: Egypt.

Al-Fayiz, Muhammad. [no date]. *Mudhakkarat Baḥḥar* (Memoirs of a Seafarer). Kuwait: [no publisher].

Al-Flayyiḥ, Sulayman. 1979. *Diwan al-Ghinaʾ fi Ṣaḥraʾ al-ʾAlam* (Singing in the Desert of Agony). [no publisher].

Al-Flayyiḥ, Sulayman. 1981. *Diwan Aḥzan al-Badu al-Ruḥḥal* (The Sorrows of Journeying Bedouins). [no publisher].

Al-Flayyiḥ, Sulayman. 1993. *Diwan Thiʾab al-Layali* (Night Wolves). [no publisher].

Al-Flayyiḥ, Sulayman. 1996a. *Diwan Ruʿat ʿala Masharif al-Fajr* (Grazers Approaching Dawn). [no publisher].

Al-Flayyiḥ, Sulayman. 1996b. *Rusum Mutaḥarrika* (Moving Sketches). Kuwait: Dar Qurtas Publishing.

Al-Flayyiḥ, Sulayman. 2007. 'Waṭanan Li (I Have Two Homelands)'. 10 October. *Al-Jarida Newspaper*. [online]. [accessed February 2012]. Available from: http://www.aljarida.com/news/index/192364/(alternatively: http://bidunliterature.blogspot.com/2016/07/blog-post.html).

Al-Flayyiḥ, Sulayman. 2008a. 'Thiʾabi al-Wadiʿa wa-l-Kasira (My Tame and Voracious Wolves)'. 3 February. *Al-Jarida Newspaper*. [online]. [accessed February 2012]. Available from: http://www.aljarida.com/news/print_news/221343/(alternatively: http://bidunliterature.blogspot.com/2016/07/2.html).

Al-Flayyiḥ, Sulayman. 2008b. 'Mujarrad ʿItab (A Reproach)'. 8 June. *Al-Jarida Newspaper*. [online]. [accessed February 2012]. Available from: http://www.

aljarida.com/news/word/254484 (alternatively: http://bidunliterature.blogspot.com/2016/05/blog-post_25.html).

Al-Flayyiḥ, Sulayman. 2008c. 'al-Hackers Saʿalik al-ʿAsr (Hackers are the Saʾalik of the Era)'. 25 May. *Al-Jarida Newspaper. [online]. [accessed* May 2018]. *Available from* https://www.aljarida.com/articles/1461697859788293400/*(alternatively:* https://bidunliterature.blogspot.com/2020/07/blog-post.html).

Al-Flayyiḥ, Sulayman. 2009a. 'Naji al-ʿAli ʿAmman (Naji al-ʿAli as an Uncle)'. 13 September. *Al Jazirah Newspaper*. [online]. [accessed February 2012]. Available from: http://www.al-jazirah.com/2009/20090913/ln18.htm (alternatively: http://bidunliterature.blogspot.co.uk/2016/09/blog-post_8.html).

Al-Flayyiḥ, Sulayman. 2009b. *Al-Barq Fawq al-Bardawil* (Lightning over Bardawil). [no publisher].

Al-Flayyiḥ, Sulayman. 2013. *Al-ʾAʿmal al-Kamila* (The Complete Works). Kuwait: Dar Suʿad al-Ṣabaḥ li-l-Nashr wa-l-Tawziʿ.

Fouad, Jehan F. and Saeed, Alwakeel. 2013. 'Representations of the Desert in Silko's Ceremony and Al-Koni's the Bleeding of the Stone'. *Alif: Journal of Comparative Poetics*. 33, pp. 36–62.

Freeth, Zahra Dickson. 1972. *A New Look at Kuwait*. London: Allen and Unwin.

Freud, Sigmund. 1975. "Mourning and Melancholia", *The Standard Edition of the Complete Psychological Works of Sigmund Freud Vol. 14*. London: The Hogarth Press, pp. 239–60.

Front Line Defenders. 2016. *Case History: Abdulhakim al-Fadhli*. Dublin: Front Line Defenders. [online]. [accessed May 2016]. Available from: https://www.frontlinedefenders.org/en/case/case-history-abdulhakim-al-fadhli.

Frydman, Jason. 2012. "World Literature and Diaspora Studies." In: Haen, Theo d', David Damrosch, and Djelal Kadir, eds. *The Routledge Companion to World Literature*. Milton Park, Abingdon, Oxon: Routledge, pp. 232–41.

Al-Ghabra, Shafiq. 2011. *Al-Kuwait: dirasa fi aliyyat al-dawla wa-l- ṣulṭa wa-l-mujtamaʿ*. Kuwait: A Study of State Mechanisms, Government, and Society. Kuwait City: Afaq Publishing.

Al-Ghadeer, Moneera. 2009. *Desert Voices: Bedouin Women's Poetry in Saudi Arabia*. London: I.B. Tauris.

Al-Ghaythi, Ṣhtaiwī. 2017. Hadathat al-Bawadi: Qalaq al-Hawiyya fi al-Khitab al-Shiʾri Sulayman al-Flayyiḥ Namojan (The Modernity of the Bedouin: Anxious identity in the poetic discourse – The case of Sulayman al-Flayyiḥ). Beirut: Muʾsassat al-intishar al-Arabi.

Ghulum, Ibrahim A. 1981. *Al-Qiṣṣa al-Qaṣira fi al-Khalij al-ʿArabi* (The Short Story in the Arabian Gulf). Basra: Centre of Arabian Gulf Studies.

Ḥadath al-Yawm. 2011. 'Russia Today TV'. 2 December. [online]. [accessed December 2011]. Available from: https://arabic.rt.com/media/vids/2011.12/2b66aef1494ef3ea784171407bf07557.mp4.

Al-Ḥaddad, Abbas Y. 2002. *Iṭlalah 'Ala Sayf Kaẓima* (An Insight into Sword of Kaẓima). [no publisher].

Al-Ḥaddad, Abbas Y. 2012. *Khalid al-Faraj Sha'ir al-Khalij* (Khalid al-Faraj the Poet of the Gulf). Kuwait: The National Council for Culture, Arts and Letters.

Al-Ḥaddad, Abbas Y. 2018. *Arabic Poetry in the Gulf and the Arabian Peninsula* (al-Shi'r al-Arabi fi al-Khalij wa-l Jazira al-Arabiyya). Kuwait: Abdulaziz Saud Al-Babtain Cultural Foundation.

Ḥaddad, Lutfi. 2004. *An Anthology of Contemporary Arabic Migrant Literature, Vol. I.* Beirut: Dar Sadir.

Al-Ḥaddad, Mohammad S. 1981. *The Effect of Detribalization and Sedentarization on the Socio-economic Structure of the Tribes of the Arabian Peninsula: The Ajman Tribe as a Case Study*. PhD thesis, University of Kansas. Ann Arbor, Mich: UMI dissertation services.

Ḥaddad, Qasim. 2005. 'Al-Shi'r Fi Makanihi (Poetry in Its Place)'. *Jehat.com*. [online]. [accessed April 2016]. Available from: http://www.jehat.com/ar/JehatAlkalb/2005/Pages/qhaddad1.html.

Ḥaddad, Qasim. 2006. *The Direction of Poetry Jehat.com: Testimonials of Ten Years of the Direction of Poetry* (Jehat al-Shi'r Jehat.com: 'Ashr Sanawat min Jehat al-Shi'r, Shahadat). Beirut: The Arab Foundation for Studies and Publishing.

Ḥaddad, Qasim. 2018. 'Words Following the Closure of Jehat.com (Kalimat 'an Jehat al-Shi'r Ba'd Tawaqufiha)'. *Jehat.com*. [online]. [accessed April 2016]. Available from: http://www.jehat.com/ar/AljehaAhkhamesa/Pages/lastWords.html.

Haen, Theo d', Domínguez, César, and Thomsen, Mads Rosendahl. 2013. *World Literature: A Reader*. London: Routledge.

Al-Hajeri, Abdullah M. 2004. *Citizenship and Political Participation in the State of Kuwait: The Case of National Assembly* (1963–1996). PhD thesis, Durham University. [online]. [accessed June 2014]. Available from: http://etheses.dur.ac.uk/1261/.

Al-Hajeri, Abdullah M. 2014. ''The Bedoun': Kuwaitis without an Identity'. *Middle Eastern Studies*. 51(1), pp. 17–27.

Ḥalibi, Khalid. 2003. *Al-Shi'r al-Ḥadith fi al-Aḥsa'* (Modern Poetry in al-Iḥsa'). Nadi al-Manṭaqa al-Sharqiyya al-'Adabi.

Al-Ḥarbi, Miz'il. 2009. 'Adab al-Bidun (Bidun Literature)'. 23 November. *Al Rai Newspaper*. [online]. [accessed March 2012]. Available from: http://www.alraimedia.com/Alrai/Article.aspx?id=169003&searchText=%C8%CF%E6%E4

(alternatively: http://bidunliterature.blogspot.co.uk/2013/04/blog-post_3167.html).

Al-Hashimi, ʿAlawi. 1981. *Ma Qalathu al-Nakhla li-l-Baḥr: dirasa fi al-shiʿr al-Bahraini al-Ḥadith* (What the Palm Tree Told the Sea: A study of modern Bahraini poetry). Dar al–Ḥuriyya.

Hassan, Wail. S. and Saunders, Rebecca. 2003. 'Introduction'. *Comparative Studies of South Asia, Africa and the Middle East*. 23(1), pp. 18–31.

Al-Hazzaʿ, Karim. 1995. 'Al-Khuruj fi Ṣabaḥ Maṭir'. (Going Out on a Rainy Morning). *Majallat al-Bayan*. July–August 300–1, pp. 175–6.

Al-Hazzaʿ, Karim. 1996. 'Qiṣas Qaṣira' (Short Stories). *Majallat al-Bayan*. August–July 312–13, pp. 68–70.

Al-Hazzaʿ, Karim. 1999. 'Jaḥim al-Sayyid Thamir'. (Mister Thamer's Hell). *Majallat al–Bayan*. 351 October, pp. 92–3.

Al-Hazzaʿ, Karim. 2011. *Ṣunduq Zujaji* (Glass Box). Kuwait: Platinum Books.

Al-Hazzaʿ, Karim. 2012. 'Email to Tareq al-Rabei'. 9 February.

Ḥifni, Abdulhalim. 1979. *Shiʿr al-Ṣaʿalik: manhajuhu wa khaṣaʾiṣuhu* (The Poetry of Ṣaʿalik: methods and characteristics). Cairo: al-Hayʾa al-Miṣriyya al-ʿAmma li-l-Kitab.

Al-Ḥijji, Yaʿqub Y. 1993. *Al-Shaikh Abdulaziz al-Rushaid* (Sheikh Abdulaziz al-Rushaid). Kuwait: Centre for Research and Studies on Kuwait.

Al-Ḥijji, Yaʿqub Y. 2010. *Kuwait and the Sea: A Brief Social and Economic History*. Translated by Fahad Bishara. London: Arabian Publishing.

Al-Hindal, Afraḥ. 2009. 'Ishkalat al-Thulathaʾ.min Ḥawalli Ḥatta al-Ḍajij Aham Multaqayat al-Muthaqqafin fi al-Kuwait. ila ʾAyn?' (The Problems of the Tuesday Gathering from Ḥawalli to al-Ḍajij – Where Are the Most Important Gatherings of Intellectuals Headed?). 21 June. *Awan Newspaper*. [online] [accessed September 2011]. Available from: http://www.awan.com/pages/culture/206890 (alternatively: http://bidunliterature.blogspot.co.uk/2016/04/blog-post_2.html).

The Home Office. 2014. '*Country Information and Guidance Kuwaiti Bidoon*'. 3 February. The Home Office. [online]. [accessed June 2014]. Available from:https://www.gov.uk/government/uploads/system/uploads/attachment_data/file/311943/Kuwait_country_information_guidance_2014.pdf.

Human Rights Watch. 1992. *Human Rights World Report: Kuwait*. New York: Human Rights Watch. [online]. [accessed June 2013]. Available from: https://www.hrw.org/reports/1992/WR92/MEW2.htm#P8_0.

Human Rights Watch. 1995. *The Bedoons of Kuwait: Citizens without Citizenship*. New York: Human Rights Watch.

Human Rights Watch. 2011a. *Prisoners of the Past: Kuwaiti Bidun and the Burden of Statelessness*. New York: Human Rights Watch. [online]. [accessed June 2013].

Available from: https://www.hrw.org/report/2011/06/13/prisoners-past/kuwaiti-bidun-and-burden-statelessness.

Human Rights Watch. 2011b. *Kuwait: Dozens Injured, Arrested in Bidun Crackdown*. New York: Human Rights Watch. [online]. [accessed June 2013]. Available from: https://www.hrw.org/news/2011/02/19/kuwait-dozens-injured-arrested-bidun-crackdown.

Human Rights Watch. 2014. *Kuwait: 5 Critics Stripped of Citizenship*. New York: Human Rights Watch. [online]. [accessed August 2014]. Available from: https://www.hrw.org/news/2014/08/10/kuwait-5-critics-stripped-citizenship.

Human Rights Watch. [no date]. *Report on the Human Rights Watch Report Response to Its Questions and Inquiries*. [online]. [accessed 10 August 2015]. Available from: https://www.hrw.org/sites/default/files/reports/Response%20of%20the%20Kuwaiti%20Government%20to%20HRW_0.pdf.

Hussayn, Haytham. 2014. 'Ismail Fahad: al-Qari' Awsa' Ufuq Min al-Katib' (Ismail Fahad: The Reader's Horizon is wider than the Writer's). 8 February. *AlJazeera.net* [online]. [accessed June 2014]. Available from: http://www.aljazeera.net/news/cultureandart/2014/2/8/.

Idris, Abdulla bin. 1960. *Shu'ara' Najd al-Mu'aṣirun* (Contemporary Najdi Poets). Dar al-Kitab.

Idris, Najma. 1998. *Al-'Ajniḥa wa-l-Shams* (The Wings and the Sun). Kuwait: The Kuwaiti Writers' Association.

Idris, Najma. 2012. 'Udaba' al-Bidun 1-2 (Bidun *Litterateurs 1-2)*. 24 January. *Al-Jarida Newspaper*. [online]. [accessed February 2012]. Available from: http://www.aljarida.com/2012/01/24/12427691/(alternatively: http://bidunliterature.blogspot.co.uk/2013/04/1-2.html).

Al-'Inizi, Falah. 2010–2011. *Inkisar al-'Aḥlam fi Shi'r Sa'diyya Mufarriḥ* (Broken Dreams in the Poetry of Sa'diyya Mufarriḥ). MA thesis, Middle East University: Jordan. [online]. [accessed June 2014]. Available from: http://www.meu.edu.jo/ar/index.php?option=com_content&view=article&id=1165:2012-11-14-01-49-32&catid=158:2012-11-12-17-58-26&Itemid=863.

Al-'Inizi, Su'ad. 2013. 'Ṣurat al-Manfi al-Bidun fi al-Fikr wa-l-'Adab wa-l-Fann (The Representations of the Exiled Bidun in Thought, Literature and Art)'. 19 March. *Al Rai Newspaper*. [online]. [accessed March 2013]. Available from: http://www.alraimedia.com/ar/article/culture/2013/03/19/397013/nr/nc. (alternatively: http://bidunliterature.blogspot.co.uk/2013/12/blog-post_4.html).

Al-'Isa, Buthayna. 2004. *Irtiṭam Lam Yusma' Lahu Dawiyy* (An Unheard Collision). Damascus: Dar al-Mada.

Al-'Isa, Buthayna. 2011. 'Salalim al-Nahar (Staircases of Day)'. 16 December. *Goodreads Reviews*. [online]. [accessed May 2014]. Available from: https://www.goodreads.com/review/show/247381647?book_show_action=true&from_review_page=1.

Ismail, Fahad I. 1980. *Al-Qiṣṣa al-ʿArabiyya fi al-Kuwait* (The Arab Story in Kuwait). Beirut: Dar al-ʿAwda.

Jabbur, Jibra'il Sulayman. 1996. *The Bedouins and the Desert: Aspects of Nomadic Life in the Arab East*. Albany: State University of New York Press.

Al-Jaffal, Husayn. 2011. 'Al-Shaʿir Dikhil Khalifa: al-Bidun Yaqudun al-Mashhad al-Shiʿri fi al-Kuwait (The Poet Dikhil Khalifa: The bidun lead the poetic scene in Kuwait)'. 18 August. *Al-Quds al-Arabi*. [online]. [accessed September 2011]. Available from: http://www.alquds.co.uk/pdfarchives/2011/08/08-18/qad.pdf.

Al-Jaffal, Husayn. 2012. 'Muhammad al-Nabhan: al-Waṭan kidhba aw raṣaṣa ṭaʾisha (Muhammad al-Nabhan: The homeland is a lie or a stray bullet)'. 31 May. *Jehat al-Shiʿr*. [online] [accessed September 2012]. Available from: http://www.jehat.com/Jehaat/ar/Ghareeb/4-6-12u.htm (alternatively: http://bidunliterature.blogspot.co.uk/2016/04/blog-post_8.html).

Jameson, Fredric. 1986. 'Third-World Literature in the Era of Multinational Capitalism'. *Social Text*. 15 (Autumn), pp. 65–88.

Jelloun, Tahar Ben. 2000. *Nuzl al-Masakin* (The Hotel of the Poor). Damascus: Dar Ward.

Jones, Alan. 2011. *Early Arabic Poetry*. Reading: Ithaca Press.

Al-Juwayyir, Saʿad. 2006. *Bawṣalat al-Jihat al-ʿAshr, al-Mashhad al-Shiʿri fi al-Kuwait: al-tisʿinat namudhajan* (A Compass of the Ten Directions, the Poetic Scene in Kuwait: The case of the 90s). Kuwait: The Writers' Association in Kuwait.

Kanafani, Ghassan. 2013. *Rijal fi-l-Shams* (Men in the Sun). Cyprus: Rimal Publications.

Kareem, Mona. 2002. *Naharat Maghsula bi Maʾ al-ʿaṭash* (Mornings Washed by Waters of Thirst). Kuwait: Dar Qirṭas.

Kareem, Mona. 2014a. 'Salalim al-Nahar (Staircases of Day)'. 17 April. *Goodreads Reviews*. [online]. [accessed May 2014]. Available from: https://www.goodreads.com/review/show/912872478?book_show_action=true&from_review_page=1.

Kareem, Mona. 2014b. 'Interview with Mona Kareem'. 3 December, Skype call.

Al-Khaldi, Ibrahim. 2013. *Dhikra Ṭaʾir al-Shamal* (Tributes to the Northern Bird). [no publisher].

Khaled Mansur. 2016. 'Khaled Mansur Maʿa al-Katiba al-Kuwaitiyya Fawziyya Shwaish al-Salim Ḥawl Salalim al-Nahar Fi Layal 10 2 2016 (Khaled Mansur with the Kuwaiti Writer Fawziyya Salim al-Shwaish on Salalim al-Nahar)'. [online]. [accessed February 2016]. Available from: https://www.youtube.com/watch?v=u-w93JIPsTU.

Khalidi, Rashid. 2010. *Palestinian Identity: The Construction of Modern National Consciousness*. New York: Columbia University Press.

Khalifa, Dikhil. 1993. *ʿUyun ʿala Bawwabat al-Manfa* (Eyes on the Gate of Exile). [no publisher].

Khalifa, Dikhil. 1999. *Baḥr Yajlis Al-Qurfusa'* (A Squatting Sea). Damascus: Dar Al-Mada.

Khalifa, Dikhil. 2003. 'Malaf al-Qaṣida al-Kuwaitiyya al-Ḥaditha (A Portfolio of the New Kuwaiti Poem)'. 10 July. *Jasad al-Thaqaafa*. [online]. [accessed January 2011]. Available from: aljsad.org/showthread.php?t=20746(alternatively: http://bidunliterature.blogspot.co.uk/2016/03/blog-post_7.html).

Khalifa, Dikhil. 2007. *Ṣahra' Takhruju Min Faḍa' al-Qamiṣ* (A Desert Emerging Out of a Shirt). Damascus: Dar al-Mada.

Khalifa, Dikhil. 2012. *Yadun Maqtu'a Taṭriqu al-Bab* (A Severed Arm Knocking the Door). Saudi Arabia: Dar Athar.

Khalifa, Dikhil. 2013. 'Interview with Dikhil Khalifa'. 18 August, Kuwait.

Khalifa, Dikhil. 2014. *Ṣa'idan 'Asfal al-Bi'r* (Ascending to the Pit of the Well). Bahrain: Dar Mas'a.

Al-Khaṭib, Rasha. 2011. 'Multaqa al-Thulatha' Ya'ish Ṣira'an Ḥawl Asbaqiyyat al-Ta'sis' (The Tuesday Gathering Witnesses a Struggle over Its Establishment). 25 June. *Poetry News Agency*. [online]. [accessed September 2011]. Available from: http://www.alapn.com/ar/news.php?cat=2&id=7397 (alternatively: http://bidunliterature.blogspot.co.uk/2016/04/blog-post_29.html).

Khulayf, Yusif. 1978. *Al-Shu'ara' al-Ṣa'alik fi-l-'Aṣr al-Jahili* (The Ṣu'luk Poets of the Jahiliyya). Cairo: Dar al-Ma'arif.

Al-Khuwayldi, Mirza. 2010. 'Sa'diyya Mufarriḥ: al-mad al-uṣuli fi al-Kuwait aham asbab al-taraju'' (Sa'diyya Mufarriḥ: The spread of fundamentalism is a main reason behind the fall back of Kuwait). 25 April. *Al-Sharq al-Awsat*. [online]. [accessed July 2010]. Available from: http://www.aawsat.com/details.asp?section=19&article=566771&issueno=11471 (alternatively: http://bidunliterature.blogspot.co.uk/2015/08/blog-post_92.html).

Al-Khuwayldi, Mirza. 2012. 'al-Sha'ir al-Kuwaiti Dikhil Khalifa: al-musabaqat al-shi'riyya ḍaḥikun 'ala al-dhuqun (The Kuwaiti Poet Dikhil Khalifa: Literary Competitions are a Joke)'. 13 May. *Al-Sharq al-Awsat*. [online]. [accessed July 2012]. Available from: http://archive.aawsat.com/details.asp?section=19&article=676945&issueno=12220#.VwhGgnr9miw (alternatively: http://bidunliterature.blogspot.co.uk/2016/04/blog-post_52.html).

Kurpershoek, Marcel. P. 1994. *Oral Poetry and Narrative from Central Arabia*. Leiden: Brill.

Kurpershoek, Marcel. P. 1995. *The Story of a Desert Knight: The Legend of Shlaiwiḥ al- 'Aṭawi and Other 'Utaybah Heroes*. Leiden: Brill.

Lane, Edward William and Stanley, Lane-Poole. 1863. *Arabic-English Lexicon*. London: Williams and Norgate. Retrieved from: http://www.tyndalearchive.com/TABS/Lane/.

Layali Programme. 2016. 'Nile Culture TV'. 19 February, 22.00.

Layne, Linda L. 1994. *Home and Homeland: The Dialogics of Tribal and National Identities in Jordan*. Princeton: Princeton University Press.

Lentricchia, Frank and McLaughlin, Thomas. 1995. *Critical Terms for Literary Study* (2nd ed.). Chicago; London: University of Chicago Press.

Lewis, Bernard. 1985. 'The Crows of the Arabs'. *Critical Inquiry*. 12(1)Race, Writing, and Difference, pp. 88–97.

Longva, Anh Nga. 1997. *Walls Built on Sand: Migration, Exclusion, and Society in Kuwait*. Boulder, CO: Westview Press.

Longva, Anh Nga. 2000. 'Citizenship in the Gulf States'. In: Butenschøn, Nils, Davis, Uri, and Hassassian, Manuel S., eds. *Citizenship and the State in the Middle East: Approaches and Applications*. Syracuse, New York: Syracuse University Press, pp. 179–200.

Longva, Anh Nga. 2005. 'Neither Autocracy Nor Democracy but Ethnocracy: Citizens, Expatriates and the Social Political System in Kuwait'. In: Piscatori,

James and Dresch, Paul, eds. *Monarchies and Nations: Globalization and Identity in the Arab States of the Gulf*. London: I.B. Tauris, pp. 114–35.

Longva, Anh Nga. 2006. 'Nationalism in Pre–modern Guise: The Discourse of Haḍhar and Badu in Kuwait'. *International Journal of Middle East Studies*. 38, pp. 171–87.

Loomba, Ania. 1998. *Colonialism/Postcolonialism*. London and New York: Routledge.

Lowe, Lisa. 1993. "Literary Nomadics in Francophone Allegories of Postcolonialism: Pham Van Ky and Tahar Ben Jelloun." *Yale French Studies*. 82, pp. 43–61.

El-Lozy, Mahmoud. 1998. 'Rebel with a Cause'. 22–28 October. *Al-Ahram Weekly Online*. [online]. [accessed August 2013]. Available from: http://weekly.ahram.org.eg/Archive/1998/400/cu5.htm.

Majallat al-Bayan. 1976. 'Mahrajan Shiʿri li-l-Shiʿr wa-l-Shuʿara'' (A Poetry Festival for Poetry and Poets). *Majallat al–Bayan*. 123 June, pp. 4–10.

Majallat al-Bayan. 1978. 'Mahrajan Shiʿri Ḥashid' (A Crowded Poetry Festival for). *Majallat al-Bayan*. 147 June, p. 40.

Majallat al-Bayan. 1981. 'Mahrajan al-Shiʿr fi Rabiṭat al-Udaba'' (A Poetry Festival in the Writers' Association). *Majallat al-Bayan*. 183 June, p. 40.

Majallat al-Bayan. 1982. 'Mahrajan al-Shiʿr' (A Poetry Festival). *Majallat al–Bayan*. 196 July, pp. 17–24.

Majjalat al-Ṭaliʿa. 2016. 'Naṣir al-Ẓafiri: Nobel Mu'assasat al-Mutaʿaṭifin maʿa al-Yahud (Nasser al-Ẓafiri: Nobel is an institution of Jew Sympathisers)'. *Majjalat al-Ṭali'a*. 24 February. [online]. [accessed February 2016]. Available from: http://altaleea.com/?p=16392.

Maktabat Iqla'. 2012. 'Al-Katiba Buthayna al-'Isa Tujib 'Alaykum (The Writer Buthayna al-'Isa Answers your Questions)'. *Shabakat Iqla'*. [online]. [accessed June 2014]. Available from: http://www.vb.eqla3.com/showthread.php?t=1165386. (alternatively: http://bidunliterature.blogspot.co.uk/2016/05/blog-post.html).

Malkki, Liisa H. 1995. 'Refugees and Exile: From 'Refugee Studies' to the National Order of Things'. *Annual Review of Anthropology*. 24, pp. 495–523.

Al-Maqaliḥ, Abdulaziz. 2011. *Maraya al-Nakhil wa-l-Ṣaḥra'* (Mirrors of Palms and the Dessert). Dar al-Ṣada.

Al-Mas'udi, 'Ali. 1992. *Mamlakat Al-Shams* (The Kingdom of the Sun). Kuwait: Dar Su'ad al-Sabaḥ.

Al-Mas'udi, 'Ali. 1998. *Taqaṭi'* (Pieces). Kuwait: Dar al-Ḥadath.

Al-Mattar, Fatma. 2012. *Judhour* (Roots). [no publisher].

Maxim, Ana-Maria. 2009. 'Ploiestiul a devenit 'Mecca poeziei romanesti' (Ploiesti became the 'Mecca of Romanian poetry'). April 1. *Prahova*. [online].[accessed January 2016]. Available from: http://www.ziarulprahova.ro/stiri/cultura/50401/memoria-zidurilor (alternatively: http://bidunliterature.blogspot.co.uk/2016/09/ploiestiul-devenit-mecca-poeziei.html).

Minutes of the Constituent Assembly: Session 23. 16 October 1962.

Mitchell, Timothy. 1988. *Colonizing Egypt*. Berkeley: University of California Press.

Al-Moosa, Abdulrasoul, A. 1976. *Bedouin Shanty Settlements in Kuwait: A Study in Social Geography*. PhD thesis, The School of Oriental and African Studies: London, UK.

Mufarriḥ, Sa'diyya. 1992. *Akhir al-Ḥalimin Kan* (He Was the Last of the Dreamers). Kuwait: Dar Su'ad al-Ṣabaḥ li-l-Nashr wa-l-Tawzi'.

Mufarriḥ, Sa'diyya. 1994. *Taghib fa Usriju Khayl Ẓununi* (When You Are Absent, I Saddle the Horse of My Doubts). Beirut: Dar al-Jadid.

Mufarriḥ, Sa'diyya. 1997a. 'Rabiṭat al-Udaba' (The Writers' Association)'. In: Najm, M. Y. ed. *Al-Thaqafa fi al-Kuwait* (Culture in Kuwait). Kuwait: Dar Su'ad Al-Ṣabaḥ li-l-Nashr wa-l–Tawzi', pp. 895–900.

Mufarriḥ, Sa'diyya. 1997b. *Kitab Al-Atham* (The Book of Sins). Cairo: al-Hay'a al-Miṣriyya al-'Amma li-l-Kitab.

Mufarriḥ, Sa'diyya. 1999. *Mujarrad Mir'a Mustalqiya* (Merely a Mirror Laying). Beirut: Arab Scientific Publishers, Inc.

Mufarriḥ, Sa'diyya. 2000. *Al-Nakhl wa-l-Buyut: shi'r li-l-aṭfal* (Palms and Homes: Poetry for Children). Kuwait: al-Arabi Magazine.

Mufarriḥ, Sa'diyya. 2006. *Tawaḍa'at Aḥlami Kathiran* (My Dreams Often Humble Themselves). Beirut and Amman: al-Mu'assasa al-'Arabiyya li-l-Dirasat wa-l-Nashr.

Mufarriḥ, Sa'diyya. 2007. *Ḥudat al-Ghaym wa-l-Wiḥsha* (The Cameleers of Clouds and Estrangement). Algeria: Manshurat al-Bayt.

Mufarriḥ, Sa'diyya. 2008. *Layl Mashghul bi-l-Fitna* (A Night Busy with Temptation). Beirut: Arab Scientific Publishers, Inc.

Mufarriḥ, Sa'diyya. 2009. *Hawamish 'Ala Shahwat al-Sard* (Comments on the Lust of Narration). Beirut: Arab Scientific Publishers, Inc.

Mufarriḥ, Sa'diyya. 2010a. *Mashiat al-Iwizza* (The Stride of the Swan). Beirut: Arab Scientific Publishers, Inc.

Mufarriḥ, Sa'diyya. 2010b. *Waja' al-Dhakira* (Memory's Pain). Kuwait: al-Arabi Magazine.

Mufarriḥ, Sa'diyya. 2011. *Sin: naḥwa sira dhatiyya naqiṣa* (Q: An Incomplete Autobiography). Beirut: Arab Scientific Publishers, Inc.

Mufarriḥ, Sa'diyya. 2014. *Riwayat al-Tahmish* (The Novel of Marginalisation). The 2nd Symposium of Prose in the Gulf, 6–8 May, Kuwait City.

Muffariḥ, Sa'diyya, and Al-'Ajmi, Ahmad. 2008. *Diwan al-Shi'r al-Arabi fi al-Rub' al-Akhir min al-Qarn al-'Ishrin: al-Khalij al-Arabi- al-Kuwait wa-l-Bahrain* (Arabic Poetry in the Last Quarter of the 20th Century: The Arabian Gulf-Kuwait and Bahrain). UNESCO and MBI al-Jaber Foundation.

Al–Musawi, Muhsin. J. 2002. 'Engaging Tradition in Modern Arab Poetics'. *Journal of Arabic Literature*. 33(2), pp. 172–210.

Al-Nahban, Ahmad. 1999. *Al-'Ab: muftataḥ sira thatiyya li-l-walad* (The Father: An introduction to an autobiography of the son). Kuwait: Al-Majmu'a al-I'lamiyya al-Kuwaitiyya.

Al-Nahban, Muhammad J. 2001. 'Al-Muthaqaf al-Arabi wa- 'alam al-Internet' (The Arab Intellectual and the Internet). *Ufouq.com*. 1 September. [online]. [accessed June 2014]. Available from: http://www.ofouq.com/today/modules.php?name=News&file=article&sid=255. Alternatively: https://bidunliterature.blogspot.com/2014/06/2.html.

Al-Nahban, Muhammad J. 2002. 'Ufouq Jadid' (A New Horizon). *Ufouq.com*. 1 September. [online]. [accessed June 2014]. Available from: http://www.ofouq.com/today/modules.php?name=News&file=article&sid=503 (alternatively: http://bidunliterature.blogspot.co.uk/2014/06/blog-post_930.html).

Al-Nahban, Muhammad J. 2004. *Ghurba Ukhra* (Another Estrangement). Damascus: Dar al-Mada.

Al-Nahban, Muhammad J. 2005. *Dami Ḥajarun 'Ala Ṣamt Babik* (My Heart Is Stone by Your Silent Door). Indiana, USA: Jozoor Cultural Foundation.

Al-Nahban, Muhammad J. 2011. *Imra'a min Aqsa al-Madina* (A Women from the Limits of City). Bahrain: Dar Mas'a.

Al-Nahban, Muhammad J. 2013a. 'Interview with Muhammad Jaber al-Nabhan'. 4 September, Bahrain.

Al-Nahban, Muhammad J. 2013b. *Ḥikayat al-Rajul al-ʿAjuz* (The Old Man's Tale). Bahrain: Dar Masʿa.

Al-Nahban, Muhammad J. 2013c. *Bayna Madinatayn Ṣaghiratayn* (Between Two Small Cities). Cairo: Al-Hay'a al-ʿAmma li Qusur al-Thaqafa al-Miṣriyya.

Al-Nabhan, Saliḥ. 2001. 'Ufouq wa-l-Mustaḥil (Ufouq and the Impossible)'. 1 September. *Ufouq.com*. [online]. [accessed June 2014]. Available from: http://www.ofouq.com/today/modules.php?name=News&file=article&sid=249 (alternatively: http://bidunliterature.blogspot.co.uk/2014/06/blog-post_9540.html).

Al-Najjar, Ghanim. 2001. 'Human Rights in a Crisis Situation: The Case of Kuwait after Occupation'. *Human Rights Quarterly*. 23(1), pp. 188–209.

Al-Najjar, Ghanim. 2003. 'Dirasa Tafṣiliyya ʿan al-Bidun' (A Detailed Study on the Bidun)'. [online]. [accessed June 2011]. Available from: http://www.kuwbedmov.org/index.php?option=com_content&view=article&id=175%3A2010-05-28-11-27-05&catid=52%3A2010-04-11-11-16-07&Itemid=78&lang=ar.

Al-Nakib, Farah. 2010. 'The Bidoon and the City: An Historical Account of the Politics of Exclusion in Kuwait'. *Volume*. September 23, pp. 384–7.

Al-Nakib, Farah. 2014. 'Revisiting *Hadar* and *Badu* in Kuwait: Citizenship, Housing, and the Construction of a Dichotomy'. *International Journal of Middle East Studies*. 46(1), pp. 5–30.

Al-Naqeeb, Khaldoun. 1990. *State and Society in the Gulf and Arab Peninsula: A Different Perspective* (trans. L. M. Kenny and amended Ibrahim Hayani). London, New York, and the Centre for Arab Unity Studies: Routledge.

Naṣr, Muhab. 2010. 'Maraya Ali al-Safi: Muttaka' li-l-Bawḥ 'Am Qina' li-l-Idana? (Mirrors of Ali al-Safi: A Cushion for Whispers or a Mask of Condemnation?)'. 8 January. *Al-Qabas Newspaper*. [online]. [accessed September 2011]. Available from: http://www.alqabas.com.kw/node/579959 (alternatively: http://bidunliterature.blogspot.co.uk/2014/01/blog-post.html).

Nixon, Rob. 2011. *Slow Violence and the Environmentalism of the Poor*. Cambridge, MA: Harvard University Press.

Noyes, John K. 2004. 'Nomadism, Nomadology, Postcolonialism: By Way of Introduction'. *Interventions*. 6, pp. 159–68.

Nuriddin, Hassan J. 2007a. *Mawsuʿat al-Saʿalik: min al-Jahiliyya ila al-ʿasr al-ḥadith I* (The Encyclopaedia of Saʿalik from the Jahiliyya to the Modern Age I). Beirut: Rashad Press.

Nuriddin, Hassan J. 2007b. *Mawsuʿat al-Saʿalik: min al-Jahiliyya ila al-ʿasr al-ḥadith II* (The Encyclopaedia of Saʿalik from the Jahiliyya to the Modern Age II). Beirut: Rashad Press.

Ouyang, Wen-chin. 2012. *Poetics of Love in the Arabic Novel: Nation-State, Modernity and Tradition*. Edinburgh: Edinburgh University Press.

Perkins, David. 1993. *Is Literary History Possible?* Baltimore, MD: Johns Hopkins University Press.

Pollock, Sheldon. 2000. 'Cosmopolitan and Vernacular in History'. *Public Culture*. 12(3), pp. 591–625.

Potter, Lawrence G, ed. 2009. *Persian Gulf in History*. New York: Palgrave Macmillan US.

Potter, Lawrence G, ed. 2014. *The Persian Gulf in Modern Times: People, Ports, and History*. New York: Palgrave Macmillan US.

Pratt, Mary Louise. 1995. 'Comparative Literature and Global Citizenship'. In: Bernheimer, Charles, ed. *Comparative Literature in the Age of Multiculturalism*. Baltimore, MD: Johns Hopkins University Press, pp. 58–65.

Al-Rabei, Tareq. 2014. *Translating the Seafaring Tradition from the Vernacular to Arabic Fuṣḥa: Memoirs of a Seafarer (1964) by Muhammad al-Fayiz*. In: 2014 Exeter-Georgetown Gulf Conference- The Heritage Boom in the Gulf: critical and interdisciplinary perspectives. 2 September 2014. Exeter, UK.

Refugees International. 2007. 'About Being Without: Stories of Statelessness in Kuwait'. October. [online] [accessed May 2011], available from: http://www.refworld.org/docid/47a6eb910.html.

Al-Rubayi', Nawaf. 2018. 'Fi Nadi Fasih al-Adabi Qasa'id min Daftar al-Sha'ir Muhammad al-Nabhan (Poems from the Notebook of Muhammad al-Nabhan in Fasih Literary Club)'. 17 April. *Al-Qabas Newspaper*. [online]. [accessed September 2018]. Available from: https://alqabas.com/article/525264.

Al-Rumi, Nuriya. 1978. *Shi'r Fahad al-'Askar: dirasa naqdiyya wa taḥliliya* (The Poetry of Fahad al-Askar: A Critical and Analytical Study). [no publisher].

Al-Ruwayli, Mijan, and Al-Bazei, Saad. 2002. *Dalil al-Naqid al-Adabi* (A Literary Critic's Guide). Beirut: al-Markaz al-Thaqafi al-Arabi.

Al-Sa'ad, Faysal. 1987. 'Muqaddimat Diwan al-Shi'ir al-Kuwaiti' (An Introduction to Kuwaiti Poetry)'. *Majallat al-Bayan*. 254 May, pp. 124–9.

Al-Ṣabaḥ, 'Awaṭif. 1973. *Al-Shi'r al-Kuwaiti al-Ḥadith* (Modern Kuwaiti Poetry). Kuwait: Kuwait University Press.

Al-Saddah, Hoda. 2012. *Gender, Nation, and the Arabic Novel*. New York: Syracuse University Press.

Saliḥ, Salaḥ. 2003. 'Al-Makan fi al-Qiṣṣa al-Kuwaitiyya'. In: Al-barraj, Ilyas, and Hajjawi, Ghada, eds. *Al-Adab al-Kuwaiti Khilal Niṣf Qarn* (Half a Century of Kuwaiti Literature). Kuwait: The National Council for Culture, Arts and Letters, pp. 320–55.

Al-Ṣafi, Ali. 1998. *Khadija la Tuḥarrik Sakinan* (Khadija Doesn't Move). [no publisher].

Said, Edward W. 1978. *Orientalism*. New York: Pantheon Books.

Said, Edward. 1983. *The World, the Text, and the Critic*. Cambridge, MA: Harvard University Press.

Said, Edward. 2001. *Reflections on Exile and Other Literary and Cultural Essays*. London: Granta Books.

Said, Edward. 2003. *Orientalism*. London: Penguin Books.

Salam Ya Kuwait. 2011. 'Al–Kut TV'. 13 August 2011.

Al-Sanousi, Haifa. 2001. *The Echo of Kuwaiti Creativity: A Collection of Translated Kuwaiti Poetry*. Kuwait: Centre for Research and Studies on Kuwait.

Al-San'usi, Saud. 2012. Saq al-Bambu (The Bamboo Stalk). Beirut: al-Dar al-Arabiyya li al-'Ulum Nashirun.

Saussy, Haun. 2006. *Comparative Literature in an Age of Globalization*. Baltimore, MD: Johns Hopkins University Press.

Shankar, Subramanian. 2012. *Flesh and Fish Blood: Postcolonialism, Translation, and the Vernacular*. Berkeley: University of California Press.

Al-Shaṭṭi, Sulayman. 1993. *Madkhal ila al-Qiṣṣa al-Qaṣira fi al-Kuwait* (An Introduction to the Short Story in Kuwait). Kuwait: Dar al-'Uruba.

Al-Shaṭṭi, Sulayman. 2007. *Al-Shi'r fi al-Kuwait* (Poetry in Kuwait). Kuwait: Dar al–'Uruba.

Al-Shehabi, Omar. 2016. 'Contested Modernity: Divided Rule and the Birth of Sectarianism, Nationalism, and Absolutism in Bahrain'. *British Journal of Middle Eastern Studies*. 44(3), pp. 333–55.

Shiblak, Abbas. 2011. 'Arabia's Bidoon'. In: Blitz, K. and Lynch, M., eds. *Statelessness and Citizenship*. Cheltenham, UK: Edward Elgar Publishing Limited, pp. 172–93.

Al-Shimmiri, Hanadi. 2017. 'Al-Maṣtar'. 2 December. *Goodreads Reviews*. [online]. [accessed May 2018]. Available from: https://www.goodreads.com/book/show/36702219?from_search=true&from_srp=true&qid=A4sOWBuPe4&rank=4.

Al-Shimmiri, Jasim M. 1992. *Ummi, 'Aynan wa Bariq* (The Sparkling Eyes of My Mother). Kuwait: Dar Su'ad al-Ṣabaḥ li-l-Nashr wa-l-Tawzi'.

Al-Shimmiri, Jasim M. 1998. *Badawiyyan Ja'a Badawiyyan Raḥal* (A Bedouin He Came, A Bedouin He Left). [no publisher].

Al-Shimmiri, Jasim M. 2014. 'Personal Interview with Jasim al-Shimmiri'. 4 August, Kuwait.

Al-Shimmiri, Jasim M. 2015. *Yatasallaqun Ajlisu Munzawiyyan li Aghfu* (They Climb, I Sit Quietly to Sleep). Kuwait: Dar Masarat.

Shimon, Samuel. 2003. 'Limatha Jaridat Kika al-Electroniyya (Why Kikah as an Online Newspaper?)'. Available at: www.kikah.com (alternatively: https://bidunliterature.blogspot.com/2020/07/kikah.html). [accessed February 2018].

Shimon, Samuel. 2013. 'Majalat Kikah lil-Adab Al-Alami (Kikah World Literature Magazine)'. *Kikah lil-Adab al-ʿAlami*. 1 Summer, pp. 4–5.

Somekh, Sasson. 1995. 'Biblical Echoes in Modern Arabic Literature'. *Journal of Arabic Literature*. 26(1/2), pp. 186–200.

Al-Sowayan, Saad Abdullah. 1985. *Nabati Poetry: The Oral Poetry of Arabia*. Berkeley: University of California Press.

Al-Sowayan, Saad Abdullah. 2008. *Al-Shiʿr al-Nabaṭī: dhaʾiqat al-shaʿb wa ṣulṭat al-naṣ* (Nabati Poetry: Public Taste and the Authority of the Text). Riyadh: al-Ansaq.

Spivak, Gayatri. C. 1987. *In Other Worlds: Essays in Cultural Politics*. New York and London: Routledge.

Spivak, Gayatri. C. 2005. *Death of a Discipline*. New York: Columbia University Press.

Stetkevych, Suzanne P. 1983. 'Structuralist Interpretations of Pre-Islamic Poetry: Critique and New Directions'. *Journal of Near Eastern Studies*. 42(2), pp. 85–107.

Stetkevych, Suzanne P. 1984. 'The Ṣuʿluk and His Poem: A Paradigm of Passage Manqué'. *Journal of the American Oriental Society*. 104(4), pp. 661–78.

Stetkevych, Suzanne P. 1986. 'Archetype and Attribution in Early Arabic Poetry: al-Shanfara and the Lamiyyat al-Arab'. *International Journal of Middle East Studies*. 18(3), pp. 361–390.

Suwaydan, Lilas. 2018. 'Takrim al-Adib Nasir al-Zafiri (A Tribute to Nasir al-Thafiri)'. 18 April. *Al-Qabas Newspaper*. [online]. [accessed September 2018]. Available from: https://alqabas.com/article/525730-525730 alternatively: https://bidunliterature.blogspot.com/2018/05/blog-post.html.

Tally Jr, Robert T. 2013. *Spatiality: The New Critical Idiom*. London: Routledge.

al-Tariq al-Mufdhi ila al-Yunbuʾ (The Path That Leads to the Fountain). 2000. Ufouq.com, Vol. 2. [online]. [accessed June 2015]. Available from: http://www.ofouq.com/today/modules.php?name=News&file=article&sid=41 alternatively: https://bidunliterature.blogspot.com/2014/06/blog-post_3834.html.

Treadgold, Warren T. 'A Verse Translation of the Lamīya of Shanfara'. *Journal of Arabic Literature*. 6(1), pp. 30–4.

Al-Turki, Fahad. 2012. 'Ṣarf Biṭaqat al-Bidun al-Jadida al-Shahr al-Muqbil. (The Bidun's New ID Cards Issued Next Month)'. 19 April. *Al-Jarida Newspaper*. [online]. [accessed April 2012]. Available from: http://aljarida.com/2012/04/19/2012475242/.

UN Educational, Scientific and Cultural Organisation (UNESCO). 2003. Charter on the Preservation of Digital Heritage, 15 October, [accessed July 2018] Available from: http://portal.unesco.org/en/ev.php-URL_ID=17721&URL_DO=DO_TOPIC&URL_SECTION=201.html.

Union of Emirati Writers. 1986. *Kulluna Nuḥib al-Baḥr: qiṣṣas qaṣira min al-Imarat* (We All Love the Sea: Short Stories from the Emirates). The United Arab Emirates: The Union of Emirati Writers.

Al-ʿUtaybi, Munir, Al-maghribi, Muhammad, and Malallah, Jassim. 2012. *Dalil al-Udabaʾ al-Muʿaṣirin fi al-Kuwait: al-shiʿr w-al-nathr* (The Guide to Contemporary Writers in Kuwait: Poetry-Prose). Kuwait: National Council for Culture, Arts and Letters.

Wazin, Abdu. 2001. 'Qassim Ḥaddad: Nahnu Kaʾinat Lughawiyya wa al-Shiʿr Yubarrir al-Hayat (Qassim Ḥaddad: We Are Linguistic Beings and Poetry Justifies Our Existence)'. 12 September. *Al-Hayat Newspaper*. [online]. [accessed April 2016]. Available from: http://www.qhaddad.com/ar/dialogue/dia51.asp.

Williams, Raymond. 1975. *The Country and the City*. New York: Oxford University Press.

World Intellectual Property Organisation (WIPO). Kuwaiti Constitution 1962. [online]. [accessed July 2015]. Available from: http://www.wipo.int/wipolex/en/text.jsp?file_id=181003.

Al-Wuqayyan, Faris. 2006. 'Al-Bidun wa-l-Mujtamaʿ al-Madani'. (The Bidun in a Civil Society). [online]. [accessed June 2011]. Available from: http://www.kuwbedmov.org/index.php?option=com_content&view=article&id=184%3A2010-06-02-08-39-47&catid=52%3A2010-04-11-11-16-07&Itemid=78&lang=ar.

Al-Wuqayyan, Faris. 2009. 'ʿAdimu al-Jinsiyya fi al-Kuwait: al-ʾazma wa-l-tadaʿiyat' (The Stateless in Kuwait: The Crisis and Its Consequences). [online]. [accessed June 2011]. Available from: http://www.kuwbedmov.org/index.php?option=com_content&view=article&id=174%3A2010-05-28-11-07-25&catid=52%3A2010-04-11-11-16-07&Itemid=78&lang=ar>.

Al-Wuqayyan, Khalifa. 1977. *Al-Qaḍiyya al-ʿArabiyya fi al-Shiʿr al-Kuwaiti* (The Arab Cause in Kuwaiti Poetry). [no publisher].

Al-Wuqayyan, Khalifa. 2011 [2006]. *Al-Thaqafa fi al-Kuwait: bawakir-ittijahat-riyadat* (Culture in Kuwait: Beginnings-Currents-Pioneers). [no publisher].

Al-Wuqayyan, Khalifa. 2012 [1977]. *Al-Qaḍiyya al-ʿArabiyya fi al-Shiʿr al-Kuwaiti* (The Arab Cause in Kuwaiti Poetry). [no publisher].

Al-Wushayḥi, Muhammad. 2011. 'Mu Minni Kil al- Ṣuch (It is not all my fault)'. 28 June. *Al-Jarida Newspaper*. [online]. [accessed September 2011]. Available from: http://aljaridaonline.com/2011/06/28/113098/(alternatively: http://bidunliterature.blogspot.co.uk/2013/04/blog-post.html).

Young, Robert. 2012. "World Literature and Postcolonialism." In: Haen,

Theo d', David Damrosch, and Djelal Kadir, eds. *The Routledge Companion to World Literature*. Milton Park, Abingdon, Oxon: Routledge, pp. 213–22.

Yusuf, Adam. 2009. *Qaṣidat al-Tafaṣil al-Yawmiyya fi al-Shi'r al-Khaliji al-Mu'aṣir* (The Poem of Everyday Detail in Contemporary Gulf Poetry). Bahrain: Dar Mas'a.

Yusuf, Adam. 2010. 'Al-Raḥil wa Badirat al-Aṣdiqa' (Departure and the Initiative of Friends)'. 10 January. *Al-Jarida Newspaper*. [online]. [accessed January 2011]. Available from: http://www.aljareeda.com/aljarida/article.aspx?id=142926 (alternatively: http://bidunliterature.blogspot.co.uk/2014/11/blog-post_17.html).

Al-Ẓafiri, Nasir. 1990. *Walima li-l-Qamar* (A Feast for the Moon). Nicosia: al-Ghadir Publications.

Al-Ẓafiri, Nasir. 1992. *'Ashiqat al-Thalj* (Snow Lover). Kuwait: [no publisher].

Al-Ẓafiri, Nasir. 1993. *Awwal al-Dam* (First Blood). [no publisher].

Al-Ẓafiri, Nasir. 1995. *Sama' Maqluba* (An Upturned Sky). Kuwait: Dar al-Siyasa.

Al-Ẓafiri, Nasir. 2008. *Aghrar*. Beirut: Arab Scientific Publishers, Inc and Dar Mas'a.

Al-Ẓafiri, Nasir. 2013. *Al-Ṣahd* (Scorched Heat). Bahrain: Dar Mas'a.

Al-Ẓafiri, Nasir. 2014. '*Ṣurat al-Bidun fi al-Riwaya al-Kuwaitiyya* (The Representations of the *Bidun* in the Kuwaiti Novel)'. In: The Tuesday Gathering. 2 February 2014.

Al-Ẓafiri, Nasir. 2015. *Kaliska*. Bahrain: Dar Mas'a.

Al-Zaid, Khalid S. 1967. *Udaba' al-Kuwait fi Qarnayn* (Kuwaiti Writers in Two Centuries). Kuwait: al-Maktaba al-'Aṣriyya.

Al-Zaid, Khalid S. 1981. *Udaba' al-Kuwait fi Qarnayn al-Juz' al-Thani* (Kuwaiti Writers in Two Centuries Part 2). Kuwait: al-Rubay'an li-l-Nashr wa-l-Tawzi'.

Al-Zaid, Khalid S. 1982. *Udaba' al-Kuwait fi Qarnayn al-Juz' al-Thalith*. (Kuwaiti Writers in Two Centuries Part 3). Safat-Kuwait: [no publisher].

Al-Zanati, al-'Adl. 2003. 'Ḥiwar Ma'a al-Sha'ira Sa'diyya Mufarriḥ 'Abr al-Internet. (An Online Dialogue with Sa'diyya Mufarriḥ)'. 20 January. *Jasad al-Thaqafa*. [online]. [accessed January 2012]. Available from: http://aljsad.org/showthread.php?t=16036 (alternatively: http://bidunliterature.blogspot.co.uk/2016/06/blog-post.html).

Al-Zuhairi, Qays. 2007. 'An Interview with the Émigré Poet Muhammad al-Nabhan'. 14 June. Kuwaiti Bidun Forum (Muntadayat al-Kuwaitiyyin al-Bidun). [online]. [accessed June 2012]. Available from: http://bedoon.net/vb/showthread.php?t=477(alternatively: http://bidunliterature.blogspot.co.uk/2016/05/blog-post_99.html).

Index

Abd Al-Ṣabur, Salah 101
Abdullah, Muhammad Hasan 65
Abu-Deeb, Kamal 104
Adonis 101
al-Adsani, Khalid 66
Al-Ali, Naji 9, 131
Appiah, Anthony 63
Appadurai, Arjun 30
Arab digital publishing 149–152
Arab literary modernism 74
Arab Spring 14, 133, 156
Al-Askar, Fahad 43, 66, 69, 73–4
al-Babtain Central Library for Arabic Poetry 12
Al-Badir, Abd al-Muhsin 66, 70

Bahrain 48, 64–5, 68, 72, 77–8, 150, 155
Basra 64, 67, 136
al-Baṣir, Abd al-Razzaq 78
Bakhtin, Mikhail 19
al-Bazei, Saʿad 90, 100, 106, 110
Bidun
- Anthropological approaches to 21–4
- Historical development of 24–8
- Legal denomination 17–18
- Protests 4, 14, 26, 133
- Studies on 1–2

Bidun literature
- Approaches to 2–6
- Debates on 37–9
- Digital 40, 43, 48, 149
- Publishing 41–4, 155
- Placement 44–5, 71–9
- Scope 11–12

Bin Sanad, ʿUthman 67, 69
Ben Jalloun, Taher 11
Bendix, Regina 91

Canada 11, 132–3, 138–41, 145, 148, 150, 152–4
Central Committee for Illegal Residents 17, 26
Columbia 145
Cosmopolitan literature (Al-Adab al-Kawni) 151

Desert life
- Apocalypse of 95–101
- Authenticity of 91
- Demise of 88
- Representations of 84–6

Eagleton, Terry 63
Eliot, T.S. 99
Fabian, Johannes 33.
al-Faḍala, Salih 17.
al-Faḍli, Abdulhakim 18
al-Faḍli, Shahad 43, 59

Fahad, Ismail 48, 129–32.
Failaka 67
al-Faraj, Abdullah 66
al-Faraj, Khalid 65, 68
Al-Fayiz, Muhammad 74–5, 101
Al-Flayyiḥ, Sulayman 1, 9, 37, 41, 69, 71, 81–2, 86–111, 115
Folk studies 91

Gates, Bill. 149
Glubb, Sir John Bagot 86
Gulf societies 33–5

Ḥaddad, Qassim 150–2
Haḍhar/Badu 31–4, 93
al-Hasa 65, 68
Al-Hazzaʾ, Karim 6, 39–40, 46, 49, 52, 54, 149, 150, 152
Human Rights Watch 2, 17, 20–1, 28, 113
al-ʿInizi Muhammad Wali 26.

International Prize for Arabic Fiction 118, 142
Iraq 25, 27, 32, 71, 83, 88, 135–7, 115
al-'Isa, Buthayna 49, 122–5
Jehat.com 48, 150–4.

Jordan 83, 86, 88, 148
Juzoor Cultural Foundation 149, 154

Kanafani, Ghassan 85
Khalidi, Walid 156
Khalifa, Dikhil 6, 12–13, 38, 41–2, 44, 46–8, 50, 54–6, 71, 115, 129
Kikah 48, 150–1, 153
Al-Kuni, Ibrahim 85
Kuwaiti literary history 63–9

Lorimer, J.G. 34

Majallat al-Bayan 12, 46
Malkki, Lisa 3, 6
Mufarriḥ, Sa'diyya 7, 10, 13, 37–8, 41–4, 54–5, 71–9, 118–20, 125, 129–30, 132, 145–6, 149
Munif, Abdulrahman 98
al-Musawi, Muhsin 107
Al-Nabhan, Mohammad 10, 37, 41–2, 46–7, 57, 145–9, 152–7.

Najd 32, 65, 67, 72
Al-Nakib, Farah 23
Al-Naqib, Khaldun 33
Nationality Committees 83
Nationality Law 1959 82–3
Nixon, Rob 98
Nomadology 103
Palestinian 9–10, 21, 65, 85, 130–1, 135, 137–8, 140–1, 156, 161
Pan-Arabism 65, 66, 68, 90–1

Qatar, 65–8

Romania 145
Al-Rushaid, Abdulaziz 64

Sa'alik 90, 103–11, 149
Al-Sabti, Ali 74
Al-Ṣafi, Ali 39, 43, 49–60.
Said, Edward 89, 156
Saudi 11, 42, 67–8, 77, 83, 87–8, 106, 137
al-Sayyab Badir Shakir 75, 101
Shantytowns
  History of 114–15
  In Kuwaiti literature 117
  Literary representations of 120
al-Shaṭṭi, Sulayman 44, 69
al-Shimmiri, Hanadi 43, 157
al-Shimmiri, Jassim 42–3
Shimon, Samuel 150–1
Stetkevych, Suzanne 105
al-Ṭabṭaba'i, Abduljalil 63–5, 67–8, 69

Tammuzi movement 101
The Tuesday Gathering *Multaqa al-Thulatha'* 47–8, 56, 129, 145.

Ufouq.com 152–4
UN, 1954 Convention Relating to the Status of Stateless Persons and the 1961 Convention on the Reduction of Statelessness 18
UNESCO 55, 153–4

Williams, Raymond 90–1
World literature 146
Writers Association (*Rabita*) 46–7, 71, 81
al-Wuqayyan, Khalifa **66–7**
Al-Ẓafiri, Nasir 5, 11, 13, 38–9, 41–2, 47, 116–21, 125, 132–4, 142, 157
Al-Zaid, Khaled, S. 61, 63, 75, 81

www.ingramcontent.com/pod-product-compliance
Lightning Source LLC
Chambersburg PA
CBHW061832300426
44115CB00013B/2354
9780755644889